The most promising Open Source Tool for Data Analysis

DATA ANALYSIS FOR SOCIAL SCIENCE & MARKETING RESEARCH USING PYTHON
A Non – Programmer's Guide

Manoj Morais | Sreekumar Radhakrishna Pillai, PhD

Data Analysis for Social Science & Marketing Research using Python; A Non-Programmer's Guide

By Manoj Morais & Sreekumar Radhakrishna Pillai, PhD

Published by

ASPIRE ANALYTIC SOLUTIONS

Transforming data into solutions

Aspire Analytic Solutions, 19 West, Suite 1018
New York, NY, 10001

Contact details:

Web: www.aspireanalyticsolutions.com * Email: info@aspireanalyticsolutions.com

Editor: Manju Sreekumar MSW, RSW

Proof Reader: Stephy

Cover Designer: Thomas George

You could download the data by visiting our blog http://blog.pythonresearch2016.com/. Once you are on the page, click on Data to access the datasets. If you have any queries or difficulties or for further guidance, please contact us at info@aspireanalyticsolutions.com

ISBN-13: 978-0692860823

ISBN-10: 0692860827

Table of Contents

Acknowledgement

First of all, we thank God Almighty for helping us and making this book a reality. We express our heartfelt thanks for the constant support from our friends and colleagues who gave their valuable suggestions on a book that they expect to read. Indeed, we are jubilant to make their dreams a reality.

We would like to express our sincere gratitude to Python and its various module developers for developing this extremely useful open source platform for the variety of users all across the world. Here we would like to mention Scipy, Pandas, Numpy, Matplotlib for their valuable contribution to the data analysts community. We express our sincere thanks to all of them in this context. We also sincerely thank Enthought Canopy for the interactive data analysis environment.

Python for Data Analysis is the Core text we referred to while preparing our work. Our special thanks to Wes McKinney, the author of Python for Data Analysis. We would also express our special thanks to those who gave their valuable comments throughout the work and also those who participated in the try-out of this book. Their valuable suggestions and comments helped to make this work more user-friendly and simple to follow.

We also thank our family members for their encouragement in all our endeavours.

Preface

The book is written for researchers in social science and marketing field, especially for those with little or no knowledge in computer programming. Data analytics has become part and parcel in the contemporary technologically fast paced world. We have amazing tools and software that allow us to analyse data available in various formats. However, most of the popular paid software and packages for data analysis is not affordable or not even accessible for the students, researchers. This is true in the case of many NGOs and agencies who are involved in community based research in developing countries.

We have popular open source platforms and tools such as R and Python for data analysis. This book makes use of Python because of its simplicity, adaptability, broader scope and greater potential in advanced data mining and text mining contexts. We found it as a need to educate and train the researchers from social science and marketing research background, so that they could make use of Python, a promising tool to meet simple to extremely complex data analyses needs free of cost. The learnings from this book will not only help them in doing their conventional data analyses but also enable them to pursue advanced knowledge in machine learning algorithms, text analytics and other new generation techniques with the support of freely accessible open source platforms.

Since the objective of the book is to educate the researchers with no programming background, we have made every effort to give hands-on experience in learning some basic coding in Python, which is sufficient for the readers to follow the book. The step-by-step procedure to do various data processing and analysis described in this book will make it easy for the users. Apart from that, we have tried our level best to give explanations on specific codes and how they perform to get us the desired output. We also request you to give your valuable comments and suggestions on the book, via our blog, so that we could improve the same in the upcoming volumes. We commit ourselves to providing explanations to the readers' questions related to the codes and analysis provided in this book.

The book specifically deals with data sets of row and column format, as the general format commonly used in social science research, which most of the researchers are familiar with. So we do not work with arrays and dictionaries, except in one or two occasions (only to make you familiar with that) instead prefer to make use of Excel data and pandas data frame.

The book consists of thirteen chapters. The first chapter gives an introduction to Python and its relevance and scope in contemporary data analysis contexts. Ch. 2 teaches the basics and Python coding, Ch. 3-7, provide a step-by-step narration of how to enter data, process it, preliminary analysis and data cleaning with the help of Python, Ch.8-9, present data visualizations and narration techniques using Python; Ch.10.demonstrate how Python can use for statistical analysis. The remaining chapters are focusing on giving more real life situations in data analysis and the practical solutions to handle them.

The exercises provided in the book are similar to real analysis situations, and that will help the reader for an easy transition to the data analyst jobs. The authors have taken utmost care identifying and providing solutions to all practical difficulties the readers may face while using Python for data analysis purpose. The authors have developed a series of codes and have incorporated them to make data processing and analysis convenient and easy for the researchers. The self-learning materials given in this book will help social science and marketing researchers to deepen their understanding of various steps in data processing and analyses and to gain advanced skills in using Python for this purpose.

You could download the data from blog.pythonresearch2016.com. You could also contact us via blog if you need further help or if you have any queries.

CHAPTER 1
An Introduction

1.1

About the book

This book is for the students and researchers in social sciences, marketing research, and other relevant fields and also for anyone who wants to get familiar with data analysis using open source programs, specifically Python-a most promising and easy to use open source platform for the purpose of data cleaning, management and analysis. Data analysis is often found to be one of the most difficult tasks for research scholars in all academic disciplines. However, in modern era, open source data analysis tools are getting popular among them because of its free accessibility, convenience to use, adaptability, and easy to learn nature. But researchers with a little or no background in computer programming often find it difficult to work on these platforms. Many of the books available in the market are written in a sophisticated way from a programmer's perspective to present the concepts and methods. In many cases, they use data sets that are either generated from random numbers or in formats that are not familiar for social science researchers and often not even visible to the readers. For a non-programmer, it is not easy to understand these data sets and the codes given to work with. This book is relevant and especially important in this context because it is specifically written for the researchers with little or no programming background. Moreover, all the steps of data management, cleaning, and analysis have been presented in a lucid manner with the support of screen shots of the codes and outputs obtained while doing analysis for this book. We have also made every effort to explain the logic behind each code. So it is easy to follow without any external help and will equip the readers to work with various data sets they want to analyse. Another advantage is that the authors have attempted to explain most of the available python tools for data cleaning, data visualization and the most commonly used data analysis techniques to explore the data.

It seems to be important here to mention that explaining different data analysis tools and its appropriateness to various contexts is not the focus of this book; and we, the authors, hope that the readers are already familiar with or have learnt various statistical tools and their applications in their research methodology and statistics classes. Here, the purpose is to teach them how they can apply Python, an open source program, to meet researchers' needs such as data cleaning, management and analyses. Moreover, once they get familiar with these tools, they can easily update their skills, adapt and tailor them to explore highly complex and challenging data sets and data analysis demands. This book helps non-programmers to incorporate popular python based tools for data analysis in their data analysis tool kit and makes their transition to advanced analytics world easy and flexible. Getting in to the world of python opens new avenues for researchers to better sell their skills in the job market. In addition, Python is especially useful for data mining/text mining, and that provides greater possibility for the researchers to excel in their future career. This book will give fundamental knowledge and essential skills for using Python in today's research settings, and the reader can continue and extend their learning further with the support of other available resources in this field. The Scenarios and exercises given in this book are specifically designed to enhance the confidence of the readers to work in the current competitive data analytics field.

This book provides hands-on training on Data Preparation & Cleaning, Data management, Analysis, and basic coding in Python. These sections will be helpful for the students, teachers, and researchers from both academic and applied research fields in all relevant disciplines. Though it focuses on Social Science/Marketing research, it is equally useful for other disciplines as well and can be useful for NGOs and other agencies involved in various research projects. . We have incorporated both basic and advanced level analyses including parametric and non-parametric techniques. The Advanced statistical tools discussed in this book are beyond the scope of other related tools.

1.2

Advantages of the book

Many of the books available on Python programming for data analysis are written in programmer's language. For a researcher with no programming background often finds it difficult to understand and follow the steps presented in them to get the analysis done. Even if the researcher using those books could run the codes successfully, in many cases, he/she may not be familiar with the scenarios presented because of their familiarity only with conventional data sets in social science research. Moreover, insufficient knowledge in programming may create difficulty in understanding the codes presented in such books. But, this book is written from a non-programmer's perspective and we have made every effort to make things simple, with possible explanations, wherever and whenever necessary, which will in turn be helpful for non-programmers to understand, practice, and to adapt them to meet their needs. Apart from explanations, we have given examples and scenarios that will be helpful for anyone to master Python when it comes to data analysis.

Another unique nature of this book is its detailed explanations of codes and how to apply them in a variety of data analysis contexts. Since we make use of conventional data sets and data types, it is easy for researchers to import or export Excel and CSV files to and from python platform, to do necessary operations and to save files back to Excel. So data is visible in row and column format (table format). We also talk about how Python and Excel read data in table format and also give descriptions of a few things that need to be taken care of, while opening Excel data in Python and saving it back to Excel. The program codes for exercises, practice questions and illustrations used throughout this book are screenshots of the work done by the authors while making this book and it ensures the codes will work perfectly with similar situations.

1.3

About Python

It is an open source programming language and therefore we can modify and adapt it according to our needs and conveniences. There are numerous uses for Python in the contemporary world. Some of the major ones are given below:

- ➢ Data Analysis
- ➢ Predictive Modelling/Techniques
- ➢ Text Mining and Analytics
- ➢ Fraud detection – Customer based detection of online fraud
- ➢ Face recognition
- ➢ Medical science
- ➢ Psychometric functions
- ➢ Morse Code Translator

Python could be widely used in different environments. As a highly adaptable programming language, it allows easy developments and maintenance of projects at various levels (www.quintagroup.com). It is important to mention here that it is recognized as an official language at Google, along with C++ and Java. Python has been an important part of Google since the beginning and remains so as the system grows and evolves and today dozens of Google engineers uses Python (Peter Norvig, Director of search quality at Google, Inc).

Most of the popular packages available for social science researchers are often not accessible or not even affordable to the students, researchers and agencies especially in the developing countries. Here, Python can be a solution to them by providing freely accessible, open source programming platform. Python is more flexible and time-saving for data preparation and has advanced data visualization and analytics tools. Though we could do basic statistical analysis in Excel, Python has taken the analysis to the next level. For example, Python has single codes for replacing row value and column values. Alternatively, with a single code, we could fill in a missing value or remove duplicated rows or columns.

Python is becoming more popular day-by-day due to increasing availability of new codes and solutions to newly emerging demands of the analytics professionals at various levels; and it is expected to become the backbone of Data science in the coming decades. Once you master Python codes, you could easily manipulate codes to cater your specific analytic needs. Learning Python at the earliest and timely up-gradation of relevant knowledge and skills will make you a high caliber and highly demanding professional in the current competitive job market.

1.4

Installing Python on Windows

To begin with, we have to install Python program. Here we have given step-by-step procedure to install Python for windows and also provide steps to install various libraries and supporting modules to do various analyses at different stages. The installation step for Python is taken from the book, Python for Data Analysis by Wes McKinney.

First of all, you visit the following link:

https://www.enthought.com/products/epd/free/

You will see Download options for both 64-bit Windows and 32-bit Windows. You have to check your computer specifications and make sure whether it is 64 bit or 32 bit before beginning the installation process. Depending on your requirements, you can click the option and download the same. It is totally free of cost.

1.5

Installing Python Modules on Windows

Now it is time to install the Python modules and for that go to the following links:

1. lxml-2.3.win32-py2.7
    https://pypi.Python.org/pypi/lxml/2.3#downloads

2. patsy-0.2.1-1_py27
    http://code.google.com/p/Pythonxy/downloads/detail?name=patsy-0.2.1-1_py27.exe&can=2&q
    OR
    https://sourceforge.net/projects/Python-xy/

3. scikit-learn-0.14.1.win32-py2.7
    https://pypi.Python.org/pypi/scikit-learn/0.14.1

4. statsmodels-0.5.0.win32-py2.7
    https://pypi.Python.org/simple/statsmodels/

5. xlrd0.7.1.exe
    https://pypi.python.org/pypi/xlrd/0.7.1

Once you copy and paste the above links in your web browser, such as Google chrome, or firefox or internet explorer, or any browser, you will be directed to the specific page. There you will be able to find **file name.exe. (**An exe is file is the set up /installation file for a module) In some scenarios, there will be a list of .exe files, and you may need to scroll down or up the page, to find the exact .exe file as mentioned in the book. Once you identify the correct file name, you need to click on that, and it will be downloaded. Once it is downloaded, you need to open the downloaded file from your download folder, and double-click on the downloaded .exe file and the program will guide you automatically and finish the installation. Mostly you need to keep clicking 'Yes'/'Agree' and in some cases you will be asked to verify the location such as 'C' drive or other drives in your system. Once it is done, the installation is completed. Please make sure to keep all the modules in the same drive, where Python is installed. Python will automatically load necessary modules while we run and execute the codes.

1.6

Coding in Python; an easy process

If you don't like programming, you need not worry. Here you do not have so much of complex coding. Instead, you just need to follow the book, and you can get your job done. Therefore, we thought, it would be better to give a short introduction and explanations about basic coding used in this book.

In programming, it is always better to store certain functions, data, and even results, number or text in a variable (a variable is a single letter or words) so as to use the same with much ease throughout the codes. These variables, we would call as Temporary containers as it would be alive only till the Python window is closed. Once you open Python again, you need to re-define variables if you want to use. However, if you happen to save these codes, and re-open again, you could use it again. In this book, we have not saved any codes as such. For example in real life, when you buy a Chocolate, you open it, take the chocolate and throw away the packet. Similarly, here once the program executes or you close the Python window, those variables are done with it.

Following are some examples of temporary variables. To do these exercises, please refer the section on 'Opening Python in windows' in Chapter 3. Simultaneously you could open Python by clicking the Enthought Canopy icon on your desktop. Once you click the icon you will get the Canopy window, and click on the 'Editor' with in the Canopy window, as shown in the Exhibit 1.1

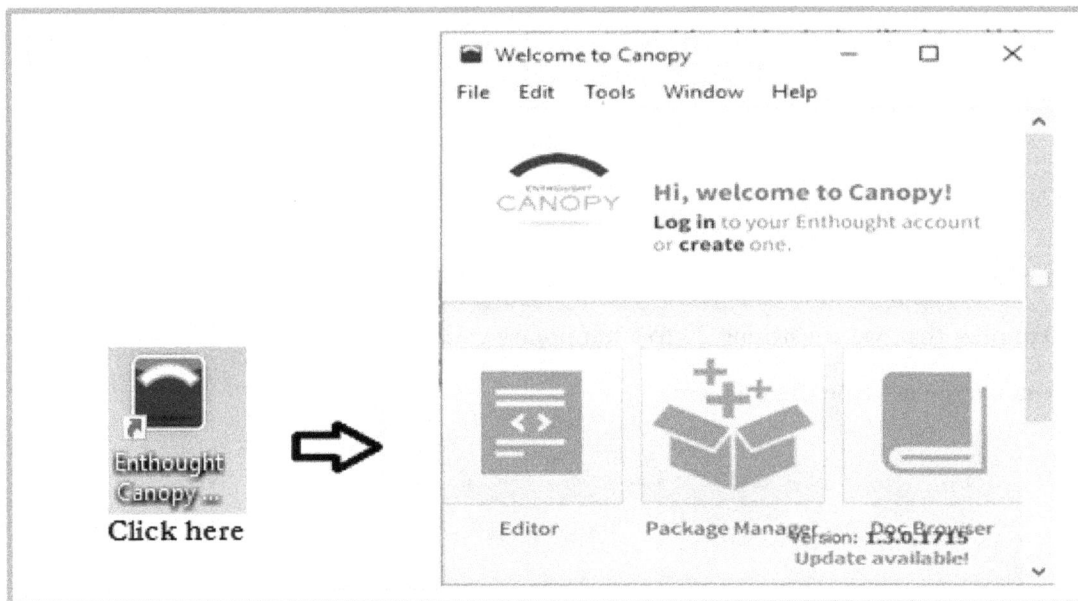

Exhibit 1.1 opening Python window

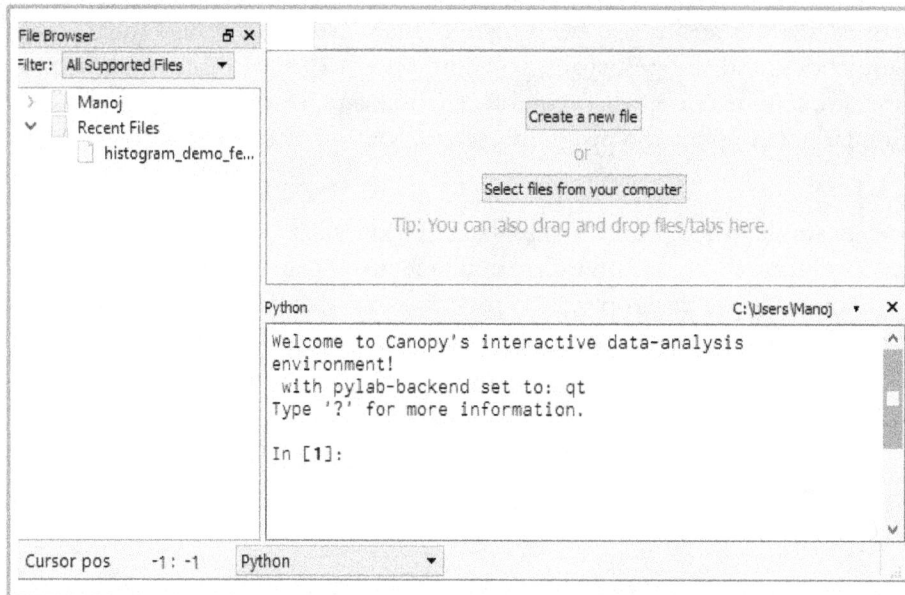

Exhibit 1.2 Maximised view of the Python Window

Here, you are assigning 20 to a variable named 'a'.

Assigning 20 implies that, we are storing 20 to a temporary variable, named 'a'.

In Python window, please type the following:

```
In [2]: a = 20

In [3]: a
Out[3]: 20
```

Suppose if you want to do an addition

```
In [4]: a+10
Out[4]: 30
```

Here, it is 20+10 which equals 30

Suppose if(at this stage) you close the Python window and re-open it and type 'a':

```
In [1]: a
```

```
-------------------------------------------------------------------
NameError                              Traceback (most recent call last)
<ipython-input-1-60b725f10c9c> in <module>()
----> 1 a

NameError: name 'a' is not defined
```

Here 'a' is a temporary variable that stores any given input until the Python window is closed. However, in case you want every time 'a=20', you need to save the program as **name.py**, with which, each time open and run the code, you have 'a' as 20. In this book, we are not saving anything as **.py**, and it is not necessary for our use.

The following code will further explain more about assigning number or text or even results in a temporary container.

```
In [2]: x = 10,20, 30, 40

In [3]: mean(x)
Out[3]: 25.0
```

Here you have the mean value of 'x' as 25. Suppose you want to re-use the result; then you need to type in mean(x) or use the value 25. Sometimes it could add further complexity as you write complex codes. Instead, you just need to store this result in some variable so that the results could be re used with ease.

```
In [4]: mean = mean(x)

In [5]: mean
Out[5]: 25.0
```

Therefore, anytime you require the result of mean(x), you need to type mean. This will make the codes simpler and easy to manage and at the same time you can also re-use the results with much ease.

Moreover, it is possible to have multiple temporary containers in one code; each container will have its values.

1.6.1

Logical tests:

In programming, you have the 'IF' statements, which is used to do logical operations. In this book, we have made use of 'IF' statement which you will learn in upcoming chapters. Just to give an idea of IF statements, we are providing you with a scenario. For example, if 'a = true', then b is 1, else, b is 2. 'Else' implies, if 'a' is false, then 'b' is 2.

Well, you may or may not understand the example above. To make it further clear we are giving you yet another example on how to decide whether a student passed or failed in the exam. To pass the exam, say, one needs to get minimum 40 out of 100 marks. In this scenario, we say, 'if marks = 40, then student passed else student failed.' We will also have multiple conditions, and are made use in only one section of this book.

1.6.2

Loop statements/Iteration:

Here we give a particular number or condition, and the program runs until it meets the condition.

For example, someone has to get five tables from block A to block B of a building. The first time, he takes one table and put it in block B. He goes back to block A and collects one more and put it in B, and this repeats until he finishes transferring all five tables from block A to block B. Here the condition is to transfer five tables only.

In a programming language, we specify a condition, and in this book, we made use of **'while'** statement. To do this exercise, please open Python window and type the following:

```
In [8]: j = 0

In [9]: while j<5:
   ...:     print j
   ...:     j=j+1
   ...:


    0
    1
    2
    3
    4
```

Here 'j' is a temporary container, and we assign 'j' as 0. We also give a 'while' statement, which says j is less than 5. The following code says, print j and new j value will be j+1.

The above code implies that, when the program runs for the first time, it checks, if j is less than 5. In this case, j is 0, and it is less than 5 and therefore, 'print j' command will print j value as 0. Then new j value will be j+1 (0+1) which is equal to '1'. Again, the program iterates until new j value is 4. Once the new j value becomes 5, the program terminates. In case, you want to see the new 'j' value once the program ends, just do the following:

```
In [10]: j
Out[10]: 5
```

In short, the program repeated, until the given condition is being met which is 'j<5.'

Similar logic is used in handling the data too. In most of the cases, we assign a particular column in a temporary container, which, we give the name of the column itself. Then we do the manipulations and are appended back to the table.

While using Python, in most cases, one single command is enough to make changes in the entire data. For e.g: filling missing values. If you execute 'data.fillna(0)', the entire missing values in the data will be Zero.

```
In [3]: data
```
Out[3]:

	Category	Year	Sales	City	Salcat	Gender	Cat
0	Non	2000	50000	ohio	1	M	NaN
1	Non	2001	100000	ohio	1	M	NaN
2	Non	2002	110000	albama	1	F	NaN
3	Non	2003	115000	montreal	1	M	NaN
4	Non	2004	125000	ohio	1	M	NaN
5	Non	2005	NaN	NaN	1	F	NaN
6	Non	NaN	160000	montreal	1	M	NaN

Table 1.1 Sales data with NaN values

```
In [6]: data.fillna(0)
```

```
Out[6]:
```

	Category	Year	Sales	City	Salcat	Gender	Cat
0	Non	2000	50000	ohio	1	M	0
1	Non	2001	100000	ohio	1	M	0
2	Non	2002	110000	albama	1	F	0
3	Non	2003	115000	montreal	1	M	0
4	Non	2004	125000	ohio	1	M	0
5	Non	2005	0	0	1	F	0
6	Non	0	160000	montreal	1	M	0

Table 1.2 Sales data after filling NaN with Zero

But, if you want to fill in different values in different columns, then it is better to assign the column to any variable, and then do the operation and append back to the original data. More on this will be explained in the coming chapters.

Similarly, we also use a 'temporary container' to open and assign the entire data. This part should be done at the time of loading the data itself. Here you can modify, edit or do any manipulation you want with this stored data, and you could easily save the same; however, the original data is retained as it is.

In this book, we use the term 'data', to load and store the excel data (**.csv and .xls, .xlsx**). However, you are most welcome to give any name of your choice, especially while dealing with your own data and operations. Here, we introduce you to manage Excel data because Excel is the most popular and widely used one among students and researchers particularly for data entry. In order to make the learning process simple and easy, we advise you to follow the book as it is; so when you try the examples in the book, you will get the same results given in the text book and then you can use these codes for any other data sets in your project.

There are codes such as 'import pandas as pd,' 'import numpy as np', *and similar codes on importing.* **Pandas, numpy, scipy and matplotlib are Python libraries**

Importing **pandas** will load pandas, but to use it in different occasions, you need to type 'pandas' whenever it is necessary. To avoid it we load pandas using an alias 'pd'. You are free to give any name of your choice. In this book, we follow as 'pd.' Therefore, "import pandas as pd" means, instead of typing pandas, we could type pd and get the job done and that will ease our task. Similarly, all other libraries are being imported using an alias of single or two letters. In this book, we use two letters.

CHAPTER 2
Basic Coding in Python

The purpose of this section is to make you familiar with basic coding in Python using very simple steps and basic codes. We took special attention while preparing this session to make this learning material interesting and easy to follow for a non-programmer. As you go through this lesson, you will acquire a good amount of insight on coding and its logic, which will help you to move easily to the other chapters. Here we are not trying to teach coding in general, but want to equip you with what is required to follow the book quite comfortably Before you begin with exercises, please refer Chapter 1: 1.6 Coding in python; an easy process, section on coding.

This chapter will specifically talk about Temporary containers, Loop statement such as 'While' and IF statement with illustrations. Please refer chapter one or three to open Python in windows.

Exercise 2.1

Input & Output in Python editor window

When you open Python, in the editor window, you will always see the following on the left side:

```
In [1]: |
```

If you simply press enter, you will get the following:

```
In [0]:

In [1]:
```

The above screenshot is for the input. The following code will explain this in detail:

```
In [1]: a = 2          →  Input

In [2]: a
Out[2]: 2              →  Output

In [3]:
```

In order to get the output, type 'a', then press enter. Input and output can be at any '**in[number]**'. You need not have input at 'in[1] and output at 'Out[2]' OR 'in[20] and 'Out[21]'.You can have it anywhere.

The following code will illustrate the same. Here we purposefully mistyped as 'A' which is not defined.When we say 'A' is not defined, it means we have not assigned any number or text to 'A', but we have assigned 'a=2.' Since Python is case sensitive when you give 'A', without defining, it will give you an error.

```
In [5]: a=2

In [6]: A
---------------------------
NameError
<ipython-input-6-bf072e91190
----> 1 A

NameError: name 'A' is not d

In [7]: a
Out[7]: 2
```

So here we have the input at 'in [5]' and output at 'in [7]'. Therefore, while you follow the codes written in this book, please note that the **input number and output number in the text and on your Python window, could be different, which has nothing to do with the output/answers.**

Exercise 2.2

1. Assign 50 to 'L' and display the value of L

    ```
    In [1]: L=50

    In [2]: print L
    50
    ```

2. Assign 'Green' to 'L' and display L

    ```
    In [3]: L='green'

    In [4]: L
    Out[4]: 'green'
    ```

Exercise 2.3

1. Assign 50 to x and 40 to y
2. Add x and y and assign the answer to another variable called z
    We add x and y and assign the answer to z in two ways

    Scenario 1:
    ```
    In [7]: x+y
    Out[7]: 90

    In [8]: z=90
    ```

Scenario 2 (preferred):

```
In [9]: z=x+y

In [10]: z
Out[10]: 90
```

In scenario 1, we first added x and y then assigned the number to z. However, the scenario 2 is most preferred because we have assigned entire calculation in 'z' itself. By doing so it will make it more convenient while dealing with complex codings.

3. Use the result, and divide the result by 2 and save the result in a new variable named M

```
In [15]: M=z/2

In [16]: M
Out[16]: 45
```

4. Multiply M with x and then by y

```
In [21]: (M*x)*y
Out[21]: 90000
```

Exercise 2.4

Solve the equation $(a + b)^2$

$$= a^2 + 2ab + b^2$$

Where a = 5 and b = 8

Here we assign 5 to a and 8 to b and use these temporary variables in the equation

```
In [1]: a=5

In [2]: b=8
```

Now substituting these temporary containers in the equation and storing the result in another variable named answer.

```
In [5]: answer = [(a*a)+2*(a*b)+(b*b)]
```

To view the solution, type the temporary container 'answer' and press enter

```
In [6]: answer
Out[6]: [169]
```

2.5

Indentation

Before you begin with working on **loop** and **IF** statements, it is imperative to learn about Indentation. Being said that you will not have complex coding here or anywhere in the book; this is to make you more familiar with '**While**' and '**IF** statements,' which you need in the coming chapters.

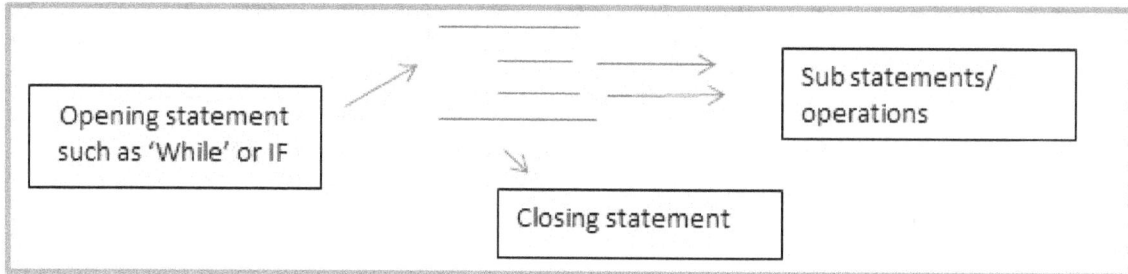

Exhibit 2.1 representation of indentation

The exhibit 2.1 is an example of indentation in coding. Whether in IF or While, we will have an opening statement, such as 'While n<=20', or in case of IF, 'If a=b'. The rest of the codes are connected to the opening statement; rest of the codes mean the sub-statements or the operations. For e.g.: If a=b, then what? The answer of 'then what' is the sub-statements or operations. Moreover, at the end, we will have a closing statement which might be to print the job is done or 'the end', or it could be anything. If indentation is not proper, even by a small space, you will get an error. There could be multiple numbers of opening and closing statements, and same applies to the sub-statements. You should be cautious here that the opening statement and the closing statement should be in line with each other. In other words, if you connect opening and closing statements with a line, then you get a straight line. In certain cases, you may have an opening statement, followed by a substatement, which is yet another opening statement, followed by a few operations, then the closing statement. We do have a similar style of coding in this book, and we have explained the same in the specific section.

Exercise 2.6

Loop statements

a. Print multiples of 2 or Even number up to 20

```
In [15]: e =2

In [16]: while e<=20:
    ...:     print e
    ...:     e=e+2
    ...: print "Even Numbers"
    ...:
```

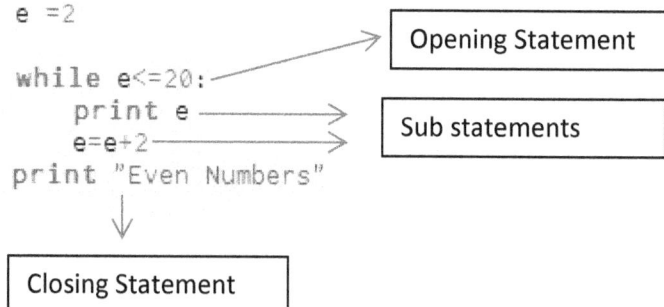

The Same thing applies to IF statements too. However, when we have both While and IF together, While becomes an opening statement, IF becomes substatement of 'While'. However, IF is another opening statement, because IF will also have substatement and its closing statement. As you progress further, you will learn about it more. To execute the code above, after typing **print "Even Numbers,"** you have to press 'enter' twice. First time when you press enter, you will get the dotted lines below the 'Print Even Numbers'. When you press enter for the second time, you will get the following output:

```
2
4
6
8
10
12
14
16
18
20
Even Numbers
```

The above code has three parts
  ➢ Assigning even number 2 to a temporary container called 'e.'
  ➢ We have made use of a loop statement called 'While' and ask the program to run till 'e' become 20 (e<=20)
  ➢ Finally, we specify that, e =e+2, which means, for the first time 'e' will be 2 and the program will print it as 2. Now e = 2. Therefore, e=e+2 will be 4, and it will print 4. Next time 'e' will become six until 'e' becomes 20, the program will run, and it will exit once it is 20.

  b. Print multiples of 2 up to 40
     Similar logic is being used here, except the fact that here e<=40

```
In [17]: e=2

In [18]: while e<=40:
    ...:     print e
    ...:     e=e+2
    ...: print "Even Numbers"
    ...:
```

```
2
4
6
8
10
12
14
16
18
20
22
24
26
28
30
32
34
36
38
40
Even Numbers
```

Hope now you can try yourself to print multiples of two up to any numbers, say up to 60 or 80 and so on. We urge you to try out the same.

c. Print first 5 odd numbers.

```
In [19]: on = 1

In [21]: while on<=10:
   ...:     print on
   ...:     on= on+2
   ...: print 'job done'
   ...:
1
3
5
7
9
job done
```

Here the logic used is a little different from that of printing even numbers, rest of the things are same; except that here we made on = on+2, which means, first time on is 1, and it will print as 1. Next time on will be 3 (on=on+2 implies 1+2) and then 5 and so on.

d. Print odd numbers up to 19

```
In [22]: on = 1

In [23]: while on<=20:
   ...:         print on
   ...:         on= on+2
   ...: print 'job done'
   ...:
1
3
5
7
9
11
13
15
17
19
job done
```

Similarly, you can change the condition on<=20 to any number of your choice.

While making loop statements, please remember that you must follow indentation. If not you will get an error. For example

```
In [24]: while on<=20:
   ...: print on
   ...:         on= on+2
   ...: print 'job done'
  File "<ipython-input-24-da976b4cf732>", line 2
    print on
           ^
IndentationError: expected an indented block
```

'Print on' is causing the error, because it is not indented properly.

Indentation is crucial to While and IF statements. Because the execution of such codings is step-by-step and since it iterates, it is connected to the beginning of the coding. In this example, it is connected to 'While on<=20.'

Example 2.7

Leap year

```
In [20]: p=1

In [21]: y=2016
```

```
In [22]: while p<=5:
    ...:        print str(y) + ',is a leap year'
    ...:        y=y+4
    ...:        p=p+1
    ...: print 'job done'

2016,is a leap year
2020,is a leap year
2024,is a leap year
2028,is a leap year
2032,is a leap year
job done
```

In the above code, we assigned 'p' as 1, and we have applied that along with 'While'. As you know, each time program executes, it will be 'p+1', and program terminates when 'p' equals five. Each time program runs, the value of 'y' also changed. For example, in the first case, 'y' is 2016. When program runs again, y will be 2020 because y+4 in turn imply 2016 + 4. The program iterates until value of P is 5 and it terminates once P is 5.

Here in the code, we have used **str(y)**, which means we have converted integer y to string so as to print both number and text together.

Exercise 2.8 IF Statement

Assign a as 6 and b as 3

Calculate a*b and store the result in Cal

And write If statement to display if it is even number or odd number

```
In [25]: a=6

In [26]: b=3

In [27]: cal = a*b

In [28]: cal
Out[28]: 18


In [44]: if (cal%2)==0:
    ...:        print str(cal) +'is an Even number'
    ...: else:
    ...:        print str(cal)+'is an Odd number'
    ...:
18is an Even number
```

Here cal%2 implies cal divisible by 2, which in turn means if 18 is divisible by 2 then it is an even number

Scenario 2:

Now make Cal as 19

```
In [45]: cal=19

In [46]: if (cal%2)==0:
    ...:     print str(cal) +'is an Even number'
    ...: else:
    ...:     print str(cal)+'is an Odd number'
    ...:
19is an Odd number
```

Exercise 2.9 on Leap year using IF statements

We have done leap year using 'While'. Now we will check if an year is a leap year or not using IF statements

```
In [47]: year = 2016

In [48]: if year%4==0:
    ...:     print str(year) + ' is a Leap year'
    ...: else:
    ...:     print str(year) + 'is not a Leap year'
    ...:
2016 is a Leap Year
```

One of the conditions for a year to be leap year is that it should be divisible by 4, and in this case it is divisible by 4 and therefore, year 2016 is a leap year.

Here, just to give some practise on coding, we are going to make a program, that will ask the user to enter a specific year, and the program will tell, if it is a leap year or not.

However, float and raw input that you see in the following code is made use only in this exercise. The main aim of this coding is to show you how to use a loop ('While') and IF statement together, with proper indentation.

```
In [54]: j=1

In [53]: while j<=2:
    ...:     year = float(raw_input('Enter a Year:'))
    ...:     if (year%400)==0:
    ...:         print str(year) + ', is a Leap year'
    ...:     elif (year%4)==0:
    ...:         print str(year)+ ', is a Leap year'
    ...:     else:
    ...:         print str(year) + ', is not a Leap year'
    ...:     j=j+1
    ...: print 'End'
    ...:
```

When you execute the code, the following will be displayed:

```
Enter a Year:
```

Here you have to type the year. In this example, we gave it as 2020 in the first case. Again the program repeats for one more time, and now we gave it as 2019, you could try and give any year and press enter. You will get the following:

```
Enter a Year:2020
2020.0, is a Leap year

Enter a Year:2019
2019.0, is not a Leap year
End
```

In the above code, we have made use of a few conditions that need to be satisfied to decide if a particular year is leap year or not. Either a year should be divisible by 400 or 4 but not by 100 then it is a leap year. Simultaneously every 4 years is a leap year. So we have made use of these conditions in the IF statement. When we enter a year, the IF condition will check if it is divisible by 400, if yes, then it will print the year as leap year, if not, it will check if it is divisible by 4, if yes, then it will print us leap year. If both these conditions are false, then straight away it will print it as not a leap year.

When we talk about Indentation in the aforementioned code, 'While' is an opening statement, followed by a sub statement. IF is another opening statement followed by a sub statement, and a closing statement (Else: print str(year) is not a leap year is closing statement of IF), followed by sub statement and closing statement of 'While'.

Exercise 2.10

Write a code to find out if the number entered by the user is divisible by 3 or not

```
In [2]: j=0

In [3]: j = 1

In [4]: while j<=1:
   ...:     number = float(raw_input('Enter any number:'))
   ...:     if (number%3) == 0:
   ...:         print str(number) + 'is divisible by 3'
   ...:     else:
   ...:         print str(number) + 'is not divisible by 3'
   ...:     j = j+1
   ...: print 'Program ended'
   ...:

Enter any number:18
18.0is divisible by 3
Program ended
```

So when you first execute the program, you will get the following screen:

Enter any number, here you have to enter any number and the program will run and you will get aforementioned output

Let us try another example to check if a given number is divisible by 3.

```
In [5]: j=0

In [6]: while j<=1:
   ...:     number = float(raw_input('Enter any number:'))
   ...:     if (number%3) == 0:
   ...:         print str(number) + 'is divisible by 3'
   ...:     else:
   ...:         print str(number) + 'is not divisible by 3'
   ...:     j = j+1
   ...: print 'Program ended'
   ...:


Enter any number:27
```

Here we have entered a number 27 and then pressed enter

```
Enter any number:27
27.0is divisible by 3
```

In the above code, we gave 'While j<=1'. This is because we want the program to terminate after it runs for the first time (j=1) so that it won't repeat again and again for 'n' number of times. In this case the program terminates when 'j' becomes one (j=j+1 implies 0+1 which is 1). However, you could change the 'j' value less than or equal to any number.

Download data from http://blog.pythonresearch2016.com/p/data.html

Exercise 2.11

While loading Data, we store it in the temporary container. Perhaps we straight away load the data in to a temporary container.

```
In [56]: import pandas as pd
```

This code will import/load pandas in a temporary container pd.

```
In [58]: d = pd.read_csv('D:/stud_clean.csv')

In [59]: d.head(3)
Out[59]:
```

	Stud_id	Gender	Dept	Attendance	Sem_marks	Name
0	M197	Female	Science	63	475	Ritu
1	M181	Male	Commerce	86	303	Victor
2	S137	Female	Commerce	79	587	Daven

Table 2.1 importing and displaying data stud_clean.csv

We have directly loaded data in to a temporary container 'd'.

Throughout the book, similar coding is used to load data and perform the necessary analysis. Similarly, we import necessary modules into some temporary containers and make use of them in our coding.

Before you proceed further, we recommend you to go through Appendix I – A Few things to know.

CHAPTER 3
Data Loading & Preparation

3.1

Introducing Excel data in Python.

The third chapter introduces you to the data set for analysis in the column and row format (generally used in social science research). The column represents variable names and row represents the values for each subject. In academic research, we use this format for data entry, and it is a generally acceptable format for most of the popular data analysis packages; and almost all social science and marketing researchers are familiar with this format, and they feel convenient and comfortable to do data analysis with this; therefore we also use the same format in our book.

The following is the screen shot of an excel data imported in Python. We have explained the procedures for importing data in the upcoming chapters.

The excel data is shown below:

	Studnt ID	Gender	Dept	Attendanc	Sem Marks	Name
1						
2	M197	Female	Science	63	475	Ritu
3	M181	Male	Commerce	86	303	Victor
4	S137	Female	Commerce	79	587	Daven
5	M193	Male	Commerce	47	403	Fernado

Table 3.1 Preview of Excel data

We can see the same data in Python as shown below:

	Studnt ID	Gender	Dept	Attendance	Sem Marks	Name
0	M197	Female	Science	63	475	Ritu
1	M181	Male	Commerce	86	303	Victor
2	S137	Female	Commerce	79	587	Daven
3	M193	Male	Commerce	47	403	Fernado
4	C166	Female	Science	59	461	Rose

Table 3.2 Preview of Excel data in Python

However, there is a noted difference on how Python reads data when compared to Excel. The following explains how Python reads data:

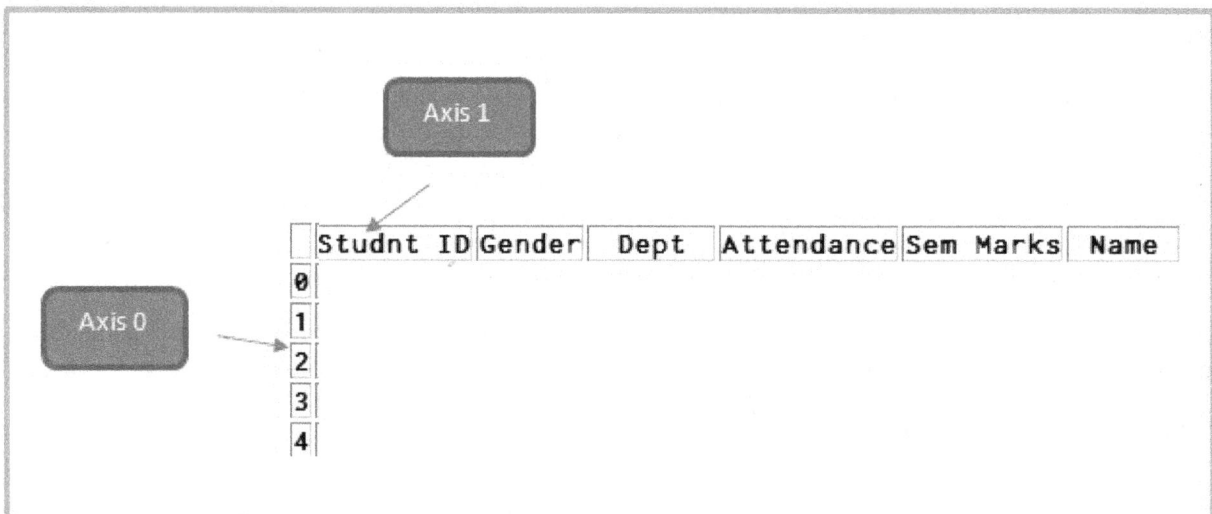

Exhibit 3.1 Pictorial representation on how Python treats data of table format

Python reads the table on two Axes namely Axis 0 and Axis 1. Please remember that Python indexing starts from zero. For example, the data above, first five cases are given and Python counts it from 0 to 4 (5 in total). The same rule is applicable for axis 1which represents the Column. In this example, 0 represents Student ID, 1 represents Gender and so on. The following is the pictorial representation of the same:

	0	1	2	3	4	5
	Studnt ID	Gender	Dept	Attendance	Sem Marks	Name
0						
1						
2						
3						
4						

Exhibit 3.2 Pictorial representation of Axis/column location

In Python, Missing values will be represented as **NaN.** There will be no empty/blank cell for missing values for imported files. We have given detailed explanation in the section on handling missing values (Ch.7: 7:4 Handling Missing values-Data Imputation)

On the other hand, it is entirely different in Excel. Excel treats data from one, not from zero, as you already know.

.3.2

Opening Python in Windows

This section talks about another way of opening Python in Windows. Please follow the steps:

> go to 'all programs' and find **Enthought Canopy** and click on Code editor 32/64 bit as show in the following figure:

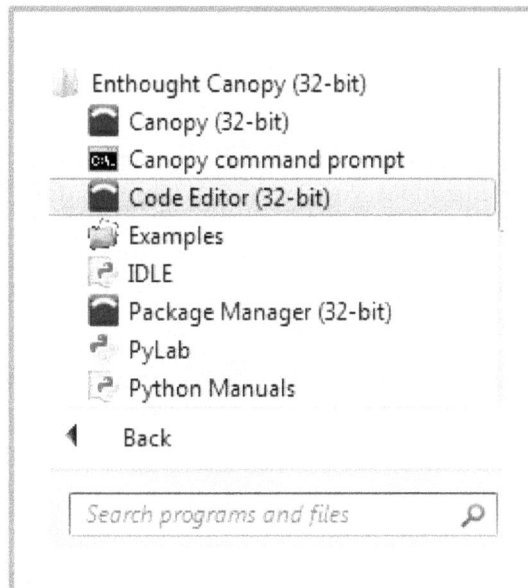

Exhibit 3.3 opening code editor

Once you click on Code editor, you will get the following Screen:

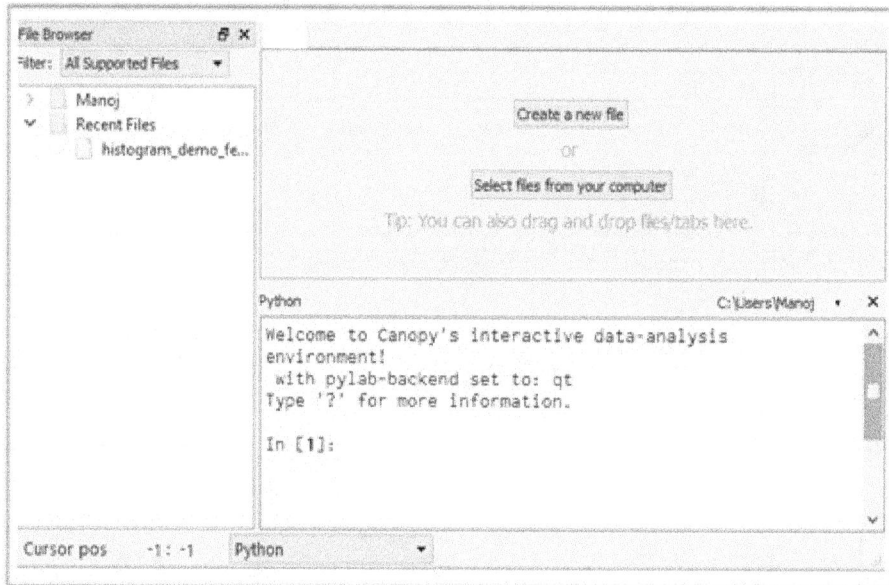

Exhibit 3.4 Screen shot of Python window

In Python Window, **In [1]:** implies Code or input. **Out [1]:** implies the output.

3.3

Loading Data in Python

In most cases, researchers prefer to enter data in Excel spreadsheet because of easy accessibility and convenience. So in this book we introduce you on how to import data from Excel to Python. For doing this, you have to import Pandas first.

Our Excel data is **stud_data.xlsx** and the file is in F drive in our example. (You can choose from any drive, provided that the file exists within that drive).

Python code to import any data involves: the path, file name with extension and the sheet name.

You can see this in Exhibit 3.5 given below:

```
Welcome to Canopy's interactive data-analysis environment!
 with pylab-backend set to: qt
Type '?' for more information.

In [1]: import pandas as pd        [ Path name ]

In [2]: data = pd.read_excel('F:\Stud_data.xlsx', 'Sheet1')

In [3]:
```

| Temporary container | Using pandas to open excel | File name with extension | Excel Sheet Name |

Exhibit 3.5 Importing Excel data in Python

To import data, first and foremost, you have to import **pandas** using an alias. In this case, it is '**pd**'. You can use any name or letters, such as 'p' or 'ps' or anything you choose.   For example, if you say, import pandas as 'p', then you have use 'p_excel'. However, using pd as alias for importing pandas is most preferred.

 The above step will import pandas. Python codes for loading data involve attributes and arguments. The attribute is 'read_excel' because it is an excel file. The path name and Excel Sheet name is the Arguments. So we have two arguments here. Moreover, we are performing the process of importing data in a temporary variable called 'data'. You could give any name to the temporary variable. Suppose, if Excel sheet has any name, you have to type the name instead of Sheet1. You will see similar examples in coming chapters.

So if you want to to load an external data, first you import pandas using an alias pd, then write the code in another temporary container which could be named data, or table or anything of your choice. Now you have loaded the data, and it is time to view the same.

Since the data **stud_data.xlsx** has been loaded into a temporary container named '**data**', you have to type the temporary container's name 'data' and then press enter. In doing so, you can view the Excel data in Python. The following codes illustrate the same:

```
In [3]: data
Out[3]:
<class 'pandas.core.frame.DataFrame'>
Int64Index: 107 entries, 0 to 106
Data columns (total 6 columns):
Studnt _ID    107   non-null values
Gender        104   non-null values
Dept          105   non-null values
Attendance    105   non-null values
Sem Marks     106   non-null values
Name          51    non-null values
dtypes: float64(2), object(4)
```

In case of big data, you will get the output as shown above; It indicates the summary of the entire data set. Since it is very hard to see the large data set in a single file in table format in Python, the above output will help you to get an overall summary of the data set.

In this example, the data is about student details in a college; here we have Student id no., which is studnt_ID, Gender, Department (Dept.), Attendance, Semester Marks (Sem_Marks) and Name.

In order to view a part of the data, you need to specify the number of records/items that you want to see; for example, if you want to see first five records, then type the following and press enter:

```
In [4]: data.head(5)
Out[4]:
```

	Studnt _ID	Gender	Dept	Attendance	Sem Marks	Name
0	M197	Female	Science	63	475	Ritu
1	M181	Male	Commerce	86	303	Victor
2	S137	Female	Commerce	79	587	Daven
3	M193	Male	Commerce	47	403	Fernado
4	C166	Female	Science	59	461	Rose

Table 3.3 displaying first five records of Stud_data.xlsx

```
In [13]: data[:5]
Out[13]:
```

	Studnt _ID	Gender	Dept	Attendance	Sem Marks	Name
0	M197	Female	Science	63	475	Ritu
1	M181	Male	Commerce	86	303	Victor
2	S137	Female	Commerce	79	587	Daven
3	M193	Male	Commerce	47	403	Fernado
4	C166	Female	Science	59	461	Rose

Table 3.4 Alternative way of displaying first five records of a data

[Here we are temporarily storing the loaded file in a variable, named 'data' in this particular example. You can give any name instead of **data** in the Python code as you prefer.

In case of small data, you could view the entire data set in table format on Python itself using the previous code as it is. You can play with the variable 'data', and at the same time, the original data will not be affected. In other words, you can make any make changes in the data without altering the original data. The reason is quite simple; you are dealing with the data that is being loaded in a temporary container and any modification you make will be on that data; and the original is still not affected. If you want, you can save the data with a different name, or you can replace the original data with the new modified one

It is advisable to view the large data sets in Excel itself while processing with Python.

3.4

How to Retrieve a Particular Column

Once you open the data, you have to see or inspect the variables in detail, at least the ones which you would want to analyse. In our example, 'Attendance' is one of the variables that could be very important at the time of analysis. This section will guide you to view specific columns based on your needs and interest.

It can be done in two ways, and the following codes illustrate the same:

```
In [3]: attendance = data.Attendance
```

OR

```
In [4]: attendance= data['Attendance']
```

Variable   Column name

```
In [5]: attendance
Out[5]:
0      63
1      86
2      79
3      47
4      59
5      88
```

In the above code, we have 'attendance = data.Attendance' in one scenario and the other, we have 'attendance= data['Attendance']'. Well, **data.Attendance** and **data[Attendance]** refers to the column in the data set named Attendance. We are storing the details of the column attendance to a temporary variable named '**attendance**'. In case you are getting confused, we will explain the same in a different way.

We shall explain it using the following code:

```
In [9]: hey = data.Attendance
```

Here, we are assigning/storing the column Attendance in a temporary container called 'hey.' To view the details of the column Attendance, now you should type 'hey' and press enter and you can view the first few parts of the data.

```
In [10]: hey.head(3)
Out[10]:
0    63
1    86
2    79
```

However, we suggest you to give any names for temporary containers which are closely related or similar to that of column names. This will be helpful to recognise and remember respective temporary variables when you have to manage multiple temporary containers.

Here you have yet another example of retrieving a column. In this example, we will retrieve column 'Gender.'

Here we will assign column Gender to a temporary variable 'gen' and display a few parts of the column.

```
In [11]: gen = data['Gender']
```

Now we will view first 5 records of column Gender.

```
In [12]: gen.head(5)
Out[12]:
0    Female
1      Male
2    Female
3      Male
4    Female
```

3.5

How to Retrieve a Particular Row:

This section specifically demonstrates on retrieving a specific row of your choice. The following code explains the same:

```
In [6]: data.ix[25]
Out[6]:
Studnt _ID     A118
Gender         Male
Dept           Arts
Attendance       89
Sem_ Marks      443
Name          Anuja
Name: 25, dtype: object
```

In the code, **.ix[row number]** refers to the row of a particular data.

Here, you have another example on the same

```
In [13]: data.ix[55]
Out[13]:
Stud_id          A120
Gender         Female
Dept         Commerce
Attendance         47
Sem_ Marks        487
Name              NaN
Name: 55, dtype: object
```

Here, we are viewing the details of row 55.

> It is always good to assign temporary containers for the data set including for selecting individuals columns. It would retain the original data, and at the same time will make us easy to process further.

Example 3.1

1. Load and view first 5 records of stud_clean1.xlsx data.
   In order to load data, you have to import pandas. If you have already imported, you need not import it again. We assume that you have imported pandas. The following code will help you to load and view the data.

```
In [15]: prac = pd.read_excel('D:/Stud_clean1.xlsx', 'stud_clean')
```

Excel Sheet Name

Now we are loading the excel data in a temporary container called prac. To view first 5 records, we run the following code:

```
In [16]: prac.head(5)
Out[16]:
```

	Stud_id	Gender	Dept	Attendance	Sem_marks	Name
0	M197	Female	Science	63	475	Ritu
1	M181	Male	Commerce	86	303	Victor
2	S137	Female	Commerce	79	587	Daven
3	M193	Male	Commerce	47	403	Fernado
4	C166	Female	Science	59	461	Rose

1. Retrieve Column Sem_marks.

```
In [17]: smark = prac.Sem_marks
```

The above- mentioned code will assign column Sem_marks to 'smark' and to view this, you type smark, and press enter. Here we display a part of the data.

```
In [18]: smark.head(4)
Out[18]:
0    475
1    303
2    587
3    403
```

If you want to view entire column, type smark and press enter.

2. Retrieving specific row details:

```
In [19]: prac.ix[30]
Out[19]:
Stud_id           C172
Gender          Female
Dept              Arts
Attendance          60
Sem_marks          332
Name               Ann
Name: 30, dtype: object
```

Well, now you have learned how to retrieve specific column and row from a given data. In the coming chapters you will learn how to retrieve information/data based on specific conditions.

3.6

Saving Data/Exporting Data from Python

You can easily save data sets in other formats from Python, for that either you can use the same file name, which will replace the existing file or you can give a new file name using the following code:

```
In [15]: data.to_csv('F:\sample.csv')
```

You can go to the respective folder to access the newly saved data file.

At this point, we give you the procedure to save the file in **Microsoft Excel Comma Separated Values format (CSV).**

3.6.1

Saving data in to a particular folder

```
In [138]: data.to_csv('D:/Mydata/newd.csv')
```

We have saved the data as **newd.csv** into a folder Mydata, which is in D drive. To access it directly, you just open the respective folder and double click on the file.

CHAPTER 4
Data Entry & Processing in Python

This chapter covers the basics of data entry and data processing using Python and our intention is to give you an exposure on how to do data entry and processing using Python. The basics given here could be used for external data, such as Excel, CSV or other types of data sets that you want to be loaded in Python.

Example 4.1

In this example, we create a sample data set for practice in which we have different cities and their corresponding temperatures.

Entering City and its temperature as columns:

```
In [9]: from pandas import DataFrame

In [7]: newdata = DataFrame({'City':['Dubai', 'Muscat', 'Kuwait'],
   ...:                      'Temp':[35, 32, 36]})

In [155]: newdata
Out[155]:
```

	City	Temp
0	Dubai	35
1	Muscat	32
2	Kuwait	36

'Data Frame' is an amazing tool in Python, as it helps to make data in table and row format as you see above. You can give multiple columns and its values as you like.

Saving data to Excel format:

```
In [156]: newdata.to_csv('F:\city.csv')
```

So the data is about a few Cities in the Middle East and its temperature. 'Temp' in the data implies temperature.

4.2

Sorting

In most cases, we sort data on various criteria to perform various analysis. Following are the types of sorting we use:

4.2.1

Sorting String: Ascending Order

When we deal with text data, we often need to sort them alphabetically. To explain this, we take a variable, City for example and apply the code to sort the city names in ascending order. Here is the code:

```
In [158]: newdata.sort_index(by='City')
Out[158]:
```

	City	Temp
0	Dubai	35
2	Kuwait	36
1	Muscat	32

In this example, we sorted our data based on City; to be more precise, it sorted the data on ascending alphabetic order. Therefore, we have Dubai first, as D comes ahead of K and M, followed by K for Kuwait and M for Muscat.

Sorting String: Descending Order

In previous example, we have sorted string on ascending order, but here we will teach you how to sort on descending order; the following codes will explain you how to do it:

```
In [33]: newdata.sort_index(by='City', ascending=False)
Out[33]:
```

	City	Temp
1	Muscat	32
2	Kuwait	36
0	Dubai	35

In this case, we have made 'ascending' as false, which implies that sorting is based on descending order, as you could see in the data displayed. Here, M for Muscat comes first, followed by Kuwait and then Dubai in descending order of alphabets.

> **Note: In Python, sorting is done in ascending order by default; if you want sorting in descending order, give ascending as false in the code as shown above.**

4.2.2

Sorting Numerical Data: Ascending Order

Now we want to sort numerical data instead of String and here is the solution:

In this example, we take Temperature across four cities as our variable and the code for sorting follows:

```
In [11]: newdata.sort_index(by='Temp')
Out[11]:
```

	City	Temp
1	Muscat	32
0	Dubai	35
2	Kuwait	36

In the above example we have sorted data by the criterion temperature which in turn implies that, we have sorted numbers and in ascending order.

Sorting Numerical Data: Descending Order

Here we shall sort the data based on temperature; descending order.

```
In [38]: newdata.sort_index(by='Temp', ascending=False)
Out[38]:
```

	City	Temp
2	Kuwait	36
0	Dubai	35
1	Muscat	32

You can see that temperature, a purely numeric data, is sorted in descending order.

4.3.

Deleting Rows/Dropping

This section explains on how to delete specific Row of a data set

We will first view data before deleting the rows

Before dropping:

```
In [12]: newdata
```

```
Out[12]:
```

	City	Temp
0	Dubai	35
1	Muscat	32
2	Kuwait	36

Now we will delete or drop row 0 and 2 by using the following code.

```
In [161]: newdata.drop([0,2], axis = 0)
Out[161]:
```

	City	Temp
1	Muscat	32

In the code, we have specified row numbers and axis number.

However, if you want to drop only row 1, the code is slightly different.

Before dropping:

```
In [12]: newdata
```

```
Out[12]:
```

	City	Temp
0	Dubai	35
1	Muscat	32
2	Kuwait	36

After dropping row 1:

```
In [163]: newdata.drop(1, axis=0)
Out[163]:
```

	City	Temp
0	Dubai	35
2	Kuwait	36

4.4

Deleting a Column

Displaying the data before deleting a column

```
In [42]: newdata
Out[42]:
```

	City	Temp
0	Dubai	35
1	Muscat	32
2	Kuwait	36

Now we will delete column 'Temp'

The following code illustrates the same

```
In [44]: del newdata['Temp']
```

Now we will view the data

```
In [45]: newdata
Out[45]:
```

	City
0	Dubai
1	Muscat
2	Kuwait

You will learn how to delete single column and multiple columns in coming chapters.

4.5

Create Empty Column in Python

This section talks about how to add/create an empty column to an existing data in Python. Please use the following steps to insert a new column in our data set:

Download **citytemp.csv** from our blog: http://blog.pythonresearch2016.com/

```
In [1]: import pandas as pd

In [2]: data = pd.read_csv('F:\citytemp.csv')

In [3]: data
```

```
Out[3]:
```

	City	Temp
0	Ohio	20
1	Calgary	24
2	Ontario	25
3	Toronto	26

Create an Empty column

```
In [30]: data['new'] = ' '
```

```
In [54]: data.head(3)
```

```
Out[54]:
```

	City	Temp	new
0	Ohio	20	
1	Calgary	24	
2	Ontario	25	
3	Toronto	26	

Please note that, when you create an empty column in Python, it will show blank. But if you load data into Python and the existing data has already an empty column or row, Python will treat as **Nan**.

Here, you have executed the code to append an empty column. By default, Python will append a column to the end of the table as evident from above. However, it might not be ideal to append a column to the end of a table depending on our needs and the data type. Therefore, the following section will teach you on how to add an empty column to a specific location.

Adding an empty column on a particular location

```
In [4]: data.insert(1, 'Province', ' ' , allow_duplicates=False)
```

```
In [5]: data
Out[5]:
```

	City	Province	Temp
0	Ohio		20
1	Calgary		24
2	Ontario		25
3	Toronto		26

In this example, suppose we add the province column to the end of the table that is after column 'Temp'; then we will have 'City', 'Temperature', and 'Province'. So it will be confusing that if the temperature belongs to the City or the Province. Things will be clear if we have 'City', 'Province' and then 'Temperature'

Example 4.2

Let us see another example on data entry (in Python) of students belonging to three different streams, namely, Arts, Science, and Commerce.

In order to do data entry in Python, please follow the steps as shown below:

Step 1:

```
In [57]: import pandas as pd

In [58]: from pandas import DataFrame
```

Data frame is very much needed to have the data in row and column format.

Step 2:

Data Entry

```
In [63]: record =DataFrame({'Dept':['Arts', 'Arts', 'Science', 'Arts', 'Science', 'science', 'Arts', 'Arts'
   ...: 'Arts', 'Arts', 'Arts', 'Arts', 'Science', 'Science', 'Arts', 'Arts', 'Arts',
   ...: 'Arts', 'Arts', 'Arts', 'Arts', 'Arts', 'Arts', 'Arts', 'Arts', 'Arts', 'Arts',
   ...: 'Arts', 'Arts', 'Science', 'Science', 'Comm', 'Comm', 'Commerce', 'Science',
   ...: 'Science', 'Arts', 'Comm', 'Comm', 'Comm', 'Scence', 'Science', 'Comm', 'Comm', 'comm',
   ...: 'Comm', 'Science', 'Science', 'Comm', 'Comm', 'Comm', 'Science', 'comm', 'Comm', 'Science',
   ...: 'Science', 'Comm', 'Comm', 'Comm', 'science', 'Science', 'Comm', 'Comm','Science', 'Science'],
   ...:  'Grade':['A', 'B', 'A+', 'C', 'D', 'C+', 'B+', 'A', 'C', 'D', 'D', 'D+', 'B', 'C', 'D', 'D',
   ...: 'A', 'A+', 'C', 'B', 'B+', 'C', 'D','C', 'A+', 'D', 'D','D','A+', 'A+', 'D', 'C', 'A', 'D',
   ...: 'C', 'D', 'A', 'A', 'B', 'C', 'D', 'A', 'C', 'D', 'A', 'A', 'B', 'A', 'D', 'A+', 'D', 'A', 'C', 'C',
   ...: 'C+', 'C+', 'B+', 'D+', 'A+', 'C+', 'B', 'A', 'A+', 'C+'], 'Studno':['A1001', 'A1002', 'S1002', 'A1003',
   ...: 'S1001', 'S1003', 'A1004', 'A1005', 'A1004', 'A1006', 'A1007', 'A1008', 'S1007', 'S1006', 'A1009',
   ...: 'A1010', 'A1011', 'A1012', 'A1013', 'A1014', 'A1015', 'A1016', 'A1017','A1001', 'A1018', 'A1019',
   ...: 'A1020', 'A1002', 'S1007', 'S1008','C1001', 'C1002', 'C1003', 'S1009', 'S1010', 'A1020', 'C10010', 'C1005',
   ...:  'C1006', 'S1011', 'S1012','C1007', 'C1008', 'C1009', 'C1010', 'S1013', 'S1014', 'C1011', 'C1012', 'C1013',
   ...:  'S1015', 'C1014', 'C1015', 'S1015', 'S1016', 'C1016', 'C1017', 'C1018', 'S1017', 'S1018', 'C1019', 'C1020',
   ...: 'S1019', 'S1020']})
```

Here the format is DataFrame ({'Dept':['Values'] , 'Grade': ['Values'] and so on. In order to enter numerical data, you could do it without punctuation mark. For example Marks:[100, 200] and so on. Simultaneously you could download **studrec.csv** from our blog

Once you have entered the data, the next process is to view the data, for that use the following code:

```
In [90]: record
Out[90]:
<class 'pandas.core.frame.DataFrame'>
Int64Index: 64 entries, 0 to 63
Data columns (total 3 columns):
Dept       64   non-null values
Grade      64   non-null values
Studno     64   non-null values
dtypes: object(3)
```

Let us view a part of the data.

```
In [93]: record.head(5)
Out[93]:
```

	Dept	Grade	Studno
0	Arts	A	A1001
1	Arts	B	A1002
2	Science	A+	S1002
3	Arts	C	A1003
4	Science	D	S1001

At this stage, you could save the data in **.csv** format. However, you could continue working without opening the CSV data unless you close Python window now and want to work later.

```
In [138]: record.to_csv('D:\studrec.csv')
```

Now let's have some fun, playing around with this data. You could download **studrec.csv** from our blog (blog.pythonresearch2016.com) and proceed further.

Here we have Grade A+, A, B+, B, C+, C and D+, D

D is failed and D+ is just passing the exam.

1. Display those Students who failed in the exam?

   Here we group data based on Column Grade, with 'D'

```
In [99]: rec = record[record['Grade'] == 'D']
```

```
In [100]: rec
Out[100]:
```

	Dept	Grade	Studno
4	Science	D	S1001
9	Arts	D	A1006
10	Arts	D	A1007
14	Arts	D	A1009
15	Arts	D	A1010
22	Arts	D	A1017
25	Arts	D	A1019
26	Arts	D	A1020
27	Arts	D	A1002
30	Comm	D	C1001
33	Science	D	S1009
35	Arts	D	A1020
40	Science	D	S1012
43	comm	D	C1009
48	Comm	D	C1012
50	Science	D	S1015

Here we are retrieving information/details based on a condition. To be more precise, we would like to view the list of those students who failed in the exam.

In the code you might have noticed that record [record ['Grade'] = = 'D']

What does this imply?

As you already know, record ['Grade'] implies the Column Grade. Therefore, the code record [record['Grade]=='D'] will check for 'D' in Column Grade and will display all the students who have grade D. Now we say record ['Grade'], because, we have stored the data in a temporary variable named 'record.'

1. Display those students who are just passed?

    This can be done in two ways:

    ```
    In [127]: rec = record[record['Grade'] == 'D+']

    In [128]: rec
    Out[128]:
    ```

	Dept	Grade	Studno
11	Science	D+	A1008
57	Comm	D+	C1018

    Or

    ```
    In [129]: rec = record[record['Grade'] > 'D']

    In [130]: rec
    Out[130]:
    ```

	Dept	Grade	Studno
11	Science	D+	A1008
57	Comm	D+	C1018

    Similar logic has been used here as well.

2. Display those who got A+ and A grades.

    ```
    In [131]: rec = record[record['Grade'] < 'B']
    ```

    A part of the result is being shown below:

```
In [132]: rec
Out[132]:
```

	Dept	Grade	Studno
0	Arts	A	A1001
2	Science	A+	S1002
7	ArtsArts	A	A1005
16	Arts	A	A1011
17	Arts	A+	A1012
24	Arts	A+	A1018
28	Science	A+	S1007
29	Science	A+	S1008
32	Commerce	A	C1003
36	Comm	A	C10010
37	Comm	A	C1005
41	Comm	A	C1007

2. How many students are failed in the exam?

In order to compute this first we have to get those with D grade and we can get it using the following code

```
In [133]: result = record[record['Grade'] =='D']
```

```
In [134]: result
Out[134]:
```

	Dept	Grade	Studno
4	Science	D	S1001
9	Arts	D	A1006
10	Arts	D	A1007
14	Arts	D	A1009
15	Arts	D	A1010
22	Arts	D	A1017
25	Arts	D	A1019
26	Arts	D	A1020
27	Arts	D	A1002
30	Comm	D	C1001
33	Science	D	S1009
35	Arts	D	A1020
40	Science	D	S1012
43	comm	D	C1009
48	Comm	D	C1012
50	Science	D	S1015

Now we will compute the number of students with D grade.

```
In [135]: len (result)
Out[135]: 16
```

So we have 16 students who have failed in the examination. Please note that we used 'len' function to count the number of records in a particular data, irrespective of its type. I.e., even if the data is of text, 'len' function will return the total number of records in that data.

3. A Company named XYZ Ltd. has come to the campus for recruiting purposes. You are asked to help the company in terms of organising the interview and also to provide the academic details/ records of a particular batch of students. The company would like to recruit only from those students who got A and A+ grades. In order to conduct the interviews, the company wants you to do the following:

    a. Display/print, the details of students with A and A+.
    b. Compute the total number of students with A and A+ so that they could plan the duration of interview per student.

    a)

```
In [142]: ans = record[record['Grade'] <'B']
 In [143]: ans
Out[143]:
```

	Dept	Grade	Studno
0	Arts	A	A1001
2	Science	A+	S1002
7	ArtsArts	A	A1005
16	Arts	A	A1011
17	Arts	A+	A1012

A part of the data has been shown above.

b)

```
In [144]: len(ans)
Out[144]: 20
```

Therefore, we have 20 students with A and A+ grades respectively. Though, in reality grade B is less than grade A, Python has nothing as such. Since the alphabet starts from A, B and so on, it will treat B as greater than A. Similarly C is greater than B and so on. Therefore, <B implies A+ and A.

Display the students with C grade in Commerce department, so that these students could be given special attention, so as to improve their grades?

To do this, first you have to get the students in Commerce department by the following code:

```
In [161]: comm = record[record['Dept'] == 'Comm']
```

If you want to view the result, you could perform the following:

```
In [162]: comm
Out[162]:
```

	Dept	Grade	Studno
30	Comm	D	C1001
31	Comm	C	C1002
36	Comm	A	C10010
37	Comm	A	C1005
38	Comm	B	C1006
41	Comm	A	C1007

A part of data has been show above.

Now you have the students only from Commerce stream. From here we need to get those with C grades.

```
In [163]: ans = comm[comm['Grade'] == 'C']

In [165]: len(ans)
Out[165]: 3
```

So we have three students with C grade in Commerce. If you want to view the result of ans = comm[comm[[Grade'] == 'C'], then you need to simply type **ans**.

```
In [164]: ans
Out[164]:
```

	Dept	Grade	Studno
31	Comm	C	C1002
42	Comm	C	C1008
52	Comm	C	C1015

Help the Dean of academics

College has decided to see which department is doing well in terms of number of students who got good grades (not just passed) in the exam and will be rewarded the head of the departments and teachers accordingly. Being an expert in Python, you are asked by the dean to help him in getting the calculations done for him.

In order to do this, first you need to make a data of those who are passed. In other words, you need to get those students with exception of D and D+ Grade in all departments.

```
In [189]: ans = record[record['Grade'] <'D']

In [191]: len(ans)
Out[191]: 46
```

From the output, we can see 46 students have grades higher than D.

Now we have the result of students with higher grades than D and D+. The result is stored in a temporary container '**ans**', and we will make use of this to compute further. The reason is, ans has only those students who have higher grades than D, D+.

a). Computing for Arts Stream

In order to compute department wise, we need to do the following:

```
In [195]: arts = ans[ans['Dept'] == 'Arts']
```

This displays the arts department students those who are passed the exam with higher grades.

```
In [196]: arts
Out[196]:
```

	Dept	Grade	Studno
0	Arts	A	A1001
1	Arts	B	A1002
3	Arts	C	A1003
6	Arts	B+	A1004
8	Arts	C	A1004
13	Arts	C	S1006
16	Arts	A	A1011
17	Arts	A+	A1012
18	Arts	C	A1013

Now we shall compute how many passed in Arts

```
In [197]: len(arts)
Out[197]: 14
```

14 Arts students passed with higher grades than D, D+

b). Computing for Science Stream

```
In [230]: sc = ans[ans['Dept'] == 'Science']

In [232]: len(sc)
Out[232]: 12
```

We have 12 students from science with higher grades than D and D+. If you would like to view the result of 'sc', please type 'sc' and press enter

Computing for Commerce stream

```
In [225]: com = ans[ans['Dept'] == 'Comm']
```

The aforementioned code will first group department based on Commerce.

Viewing data, which is optional

```
In [226]: com
Out[226]:
```

	Dept	Grade	Studno
31	Comm	C	C1002
32	Comm	A	C1003
36	Comm	A	C10010

A part of data has been shown above

```
In [227]: len(com)
Out[227]: 16
```

We have16 students in Commerce with higher grades than D and D+

However, you might have noticed that 46 students have higher grades, from the answer A., and if we add up the answers for individual departments, it is only 42. This is because we have performed these calculations on data which is not cleaned and processed and when there is an error such as spelling mistakes; software will not take that into consideration, when we specify a condition. From such situations, we could learn that, prior to do any computation or other grouping or any such things on a given data, it is better to do data cleaning and preparation unless it is done already. This will be discussed in the coming chapters.

Example 4.3

Another example on Data entry in Python

```
In [1]: import pandas as pd

In [2]: from pandas import DataFrame

In [5]: data = DataFrame({'Month':['Jan','Feb', 'Mar', 'Apr', 'May',
   ...:  'June', 'July', 'Aug', 'Sep', 'Oct','Nov', 'Dec'],
   ...: 'Sales':[1000, 1200, 900, 950, 1120, 1250, 1300, 1000,
   ...: 1000, 1400, 1399, 1400]})
```

Viewing data

```
In [6]: data
```

```
Out[6]:
```

	Month	Sales
0	Jan	1000
1	Feb	1200
2	Mar	900
3	Apr	950
4	May	1120
5	June	1250
6	July	1300

A part of data has been shown above. The following code will save the data:

```
In [10]: data.to_csv('D:\Sales.csv')
```

CHAPTER 5
Playing with Python

Here we have some fun-filled exercises that will make you more comfortable, and familiarize with Python and coding that is required to proceed further.

Get ready, set, GOOO.......

Exercise: 5.1.

Load a data in to Python:

Open wxyz_ca.xlsx data in Python

5.1.1

Step 1: import pandas

```
In [83]: import pandas as pd
```

Importing Pandas has to be the first thing you do before loading any external data. However, if you are creating data using Python, then you have to import Data Frame from pandas to get spreadsheet format.

5.1.2

Step 2: load the data in to a temporary variable. The temporary variable can have any name as you wish.

```
In [86]: as_i_wish = pd.read_excel('F:\wxyz_ca.xlsx', 'Sheet1')
```

View part of the data

```
In [96]: as_i_wish.head(4)
Out[96]:
```

	Year	Sales	City	Mkt_exp
0	2000	50000	Dryden	10000
1	2001	60000	Mississauga	12000
2	2002	75000	Toronto	13500
3	2003	100000	Kingston	16000

If you want to view full data, then:

```
In [97]: as_i_wish
```

Out[97]:

	Year	Sales	City	Mkt_exp
0	2000	50000	Dryden	10000
1	2001	60000	Mississauga	12000
2	2002	75000	Toronto	13500
3	2003	100000	Kingston	16000
4	2004	125000	North Bay	17000
5	2005	150000	Pickering	19000
6	2006	165000	Markham	19500
7	2007	200000	Kitchener	20000
8	2008	250000	Brantford	21200
9	2009	249000	Ottawa	21000
10	2010	251000	Oshawa	21100

So from here on, any manipulation needs to be done in the data, you can do that by using the temporary container 'as_i_wish'. However, try not to give longer names for the temporary container. You can even give a single letter or anything that is easy to type repeatedly.

5.1.3

a. Add an empty column to the data.

The following will add the column at the end of the table:

```
In [2]: as_i_wish = pd.read_excel('F:\wxyz_ca.xlsx', 'Sheet1')
In [3]: as_i_wish['Empty'] = ' '
```

```
In [4]: as_i_wish.head(3)
```
Out[4]:

	Year	Sales	City	Mkt_exp	Empty
0	2000	50000	Dryden	10000	
1	2001	60000	Mississauga	12000	
2	2002	75000	Toronto	13500	

But our empty column is not happy being at the end of the table. It wants to be in between other columns. What to do now??

We have to specify the location; as simple as that!

The following will display the same:

```
In [5]: as_i_wish.insert(3, 'Empt', ' ' , allow_duplicates=False)
```

Here we are adding the column on 3rd location. As you already know, Python tables starts from 0.

```
In [6]: as_i_wish.head(2)
Out[6]:
```

	Year	Sales	City	Empt	Mkt_exp	Empty
0	2000	50000	Dryden		10000	
1	2001	60000	Mississauga		12000	

Empty column is happy now!!!

5.1.4

Now we have a new problem??

The new empty column 'Empt' is not happy, because, the name is missing a 'y'. So it wants to leave the table.

The following codes will help doing the same:

```
In [7]: del as_i_wish['Empt']
```

```
In [9]: as_i_wish.head(3)
Out[9]:
```

	Year	Sales	City	Mkt_exp	Empty
0	2000	50000	Dryden	10000	
1	2001	60000	Mississauga	12000	
2	2002	75000	Toronto	13500	

Now 'Empty' wants to be renamed as beauty; Here it goes. You could do it in two ways

```
In [16]: as_i_wish.columns = ['Year', 'Sales', 'City', 'Mkt_exp', 'Beauty']
```

OR

```
In [26]: as_i_wish.rename(columns = {'Empty': 'Beauty'}, inplace=True)
```

```
In [17]: as_i_wish.head(3)
Out[17]:
```

	Year	Sales	City	Mkt_exp	Beauty
0	2000	50000	Dryden	10000	
1	2001	60000	Mississauga	12000	
2	2002	75000	Toronto	13500	

Now to perform certain analysis, Mr. Jack has loaded **stud_clean.csv** data

The codes are as follows:

We assume that you have imported Pandas before loading data.

```
In [18]: data = pd.read_csv('F:\stud_clean.csv')
```

```
In [19]: data.head(3)
Out[19]:
```

	Stud_id	Gender	Dept	Attendance	Sem_marks	Name
0	M197	Female	Science	63	475	Ritu
1	M181	Male	Commerce	86	303	Victor
2	S137	Female	Commerce	79	587	Daven

5.1.5

After viewing the data, Jack felt, he did not need the entire table; instead, he wants only a few variables such as gender, sem_marks, and department and makes a new data for his studies.

You being a magician in Python will have to perform something that will help Jack to get his job done.

Here is the stepwise format:

Step 1: Select the columns Jack wants to use

```
In [20]: cols = ['Gender', 'Dept', 'Sem_marks']
```

Step 2: Assign data to selected columns

```
In [21]: newdata = data[cols]
```

Here is the magic

```
In [22]: newdata.head(3)
Out[22]:
```

	Gender	Dept	Sem_marks
0	Female	Science	475
1	Male	Commerce	303
2	Female	Commerce	587

5.1.6

Well, Jack is happy, but he has some specifications that need to be done in the outlook of the data. He wants the Dept. column first, followed by gender and marks.

Oops... Well, yes, you could repeat the same magic

```
In [23]: cols = ['Dept', 'Gender', 'Sem_marks']
```

```
In [24]: newdata = data[cols]
```

```
In [25]: newdata.head(3)
Out[25]:
```

	Dept	Gender	Sem_marks
0	Science	Female	475
1	Commerce	Male	303
2	Commerce	Female	587

Job is done…..

At this point you can save the data

```
In [26]: newdata.to_csv('F:\den.csv')
```

> Here, we saved the file as CSV. However, if you want to save it as Excel, it is advised to open this CSV file in Excel, and save it as excel file; for that, open the CSV file, go to save us option and select Excel

Exercise 5.2

Load **practise.xlsx** data and perform the following:

Step 1: Load data in to a temporary variable named 'd' and display first 5 records.

Step2: Fill the missing value in the year, with 2001 and City with North Bay.

Step3: Replace 'Dyden' with 'Dryden', 'Tronto' with 'Toronto', 'Makham' with 'Markham'.

Step4: Create a new empty column at the end of the table and name it as

rev percentage

Step5: Calculate revenue percentage and fill the column 'rev_percentage' with the calculated value.

Answers:

Step 1:

```
In [1]: import pandas as pd

In [2]: d = pd.read_excel('F:\practise.xlsx', 'Sheet1')

In [7]: d.head(5)
Out[7]:
```

	Year	Sales	City	Mkt_exp	Revenue
0	2000	50000	Dyden	10000	40000
1	NaN	60000	Mississauga	12000	48000
2	2002	75000	Tronto	13500	61500
3	203	100000	Kingston	16000	84000
4	2004	125000	NaN	17000	108000

> You must be wondering why it is displaying records till 4, because Python counts from 0 and therefore, when we choose first 5 records, it displays first five records that count from zero; here we have a missing value, which is treated as NaN

Step 2:

a. Assign column Year to a temporary variable named 'd1'.

```
In [8]: d1 = d.Year
```

b. Assign the operation of filling the missing value to another temporary container called 'result'.

```
In [13]: result = d1.fillna(2001)
```

c. Filling the Year column by equating temporary container 'result'.

```
In [14]: d.Year=result
```

d. Viewing the data:

```
In [15]: d.head(2)
Out[15]:
```

	Year	Sales	City	Mkt_exp	Revenue
0	2000	50000	Dyden	10000	40000
1	2001	60000	Mississauga	12000	48000

Similar steps are followed for filling in the missing values of 'City':

```
In [18]: c = d.City

In [48]: result = c.fillna('North Bay')

In [49]: d.City = result
```

4	2004	125000	North Bay	17000	108000
5	2005	150000	Pickering	19000	131000

Step 3:

Assigning column 'city' to a temporary container called 'city'

```
In [51]: city = d.City

In [53]: result =city.replace(['Dyden', 'Tronto', 'Makham'], ['Dryden', 'Toronto', 'Markham'])

In [55]: d
```

	Year	Sales	City	Mkt_exp	Revenue
0	2000	50000	Dryden	10000	40000
1	2001	60000	Mississauga	12000	48000
2	2002	75000	Toronto	13500	61500
3	203	100000	Kingston	16000	84000
4	2004	125000	North Bay	17000	108000
5	2005	150000	Pickering	19000	131000
6	2006	165000	Markham	19500	145500
7	2007	200000	Kitchener	20000	180000
8	2008	250000	Brantford	21200	228800
9	2009	249000	Ottawa	21000	228000
10	2010	251000	Oshawa	21100	229900

Similarly replacing 203 with 2003

```
In [56]: y= d.Year

In [57]: result = y.replace(203, 2003)

In [58]: d.Year = result
```

```
In [59]: d.head(5)
Out[59]:
```

	Year	Sales	City	Mkt_exp	Revenue
0	2000	50000	Dryden	10000	40000
1	2001	60000	Mississauga	12000	48000
2	2002	75000	Toronto	13500	61500
3	2003	100000	Kingston	16000	84000

Step 4:

```
In [60]: d['Rev_percentage']= ' '
```

```
In [61]: d.head(2)
Out[61]:
```

	Year	Sales	City	Mkt_exp	Revenue	Rev_percentage
0	2000	50000	Dryden	10000	40000	
1	2001	60000	Mississauga	12000	48000	

Step 5:

First assign the column to a variable:

```
In [62]: rev = d.Revenue
```

Find the total revenue

```
In [63]: sum(rev)
Out[63]: 1484700.0
```

Now, we are ready to compute the percentage.

```
In [64]: result = rev/1484700.0*100.0
```

Fill the empty column with the result.

```
In [65]: d.Rev_percentage = result
```

View the data:

```
In [66]: d.head(5)
Out[66]:
```

	Year	Sales	City	Mkt_exp	Revenue	Rev_percentage
0	2000	50000	Dryden	10000	40000	2.694147
1	2001	60000	Mississauga	12000	48000	3.232976
2	2002	75000	Toronto	13500	61500	4.142251
3	2003	100000	Kingston	16000	84000	5.657709
4	2004	125000	North Bay	17000	108000	7.274197

Exercise 5.3

To do this exercise, you are required to load the practise1.xlsx.

1. Fill in the missing values in the year with 2001 and 2006.

2. Fill in the missing text with British Columbia and Alberta.

3. Replace 'Kitchner' with 'Fort St.John' and 'Ottawa' with 'Calgary'

Answers:

```
In [83]: data = pd.read_excel('F:\practise1.xlsx', 'Sheet1')
```

```
In [84]: data.head(3)
Out[84]:
```

	Year	Sales	City	Mkt_exp	Revenue
0	2000	50000	Dyden	10000	40000
1	NaN	60000	Mississauga	12000	48000
2	2002	75000	Tronto	13500	61500

1. Select the column Year and fill the values.

```
In [95]: year = data.Year
```

```
In [102]: year.ix[1] = 2001
```

```
In [103]: year.ix[6] = 2006
```

```
In [104]:      data
Out[104]:
```

	Year	Sales	City	Mkt_exp	Revenue
0	2000	50000	Dyden	10000	40000
1	2001	60000	Mississauga	12000	48000
2	2002	75000	Tronto	13500	61500
3	203	100000	Kingston	16000	84000
4	2004	60000	NaN	17000	43000
5	2005	150000	Pickering	19000	131000
6	2006	165000	NaN	19500	145500
7	2007	60000	Kitchener	20000	40000
8	2008	250000	Brantford	21200	228800
9	2009	249000	Ottawa	21000	228000
10	2010	251000	Oshawa	21100	229900

2. Filling the missing text.

```
In [105]: city = data.City

In [106]: city.ix[4] = 'British Columbia'

In [107]: city.ix[6] = 'Alberta'
```

Viewing a part of the Column 'City':

```
In [108]: city.head(7)
Out[108]:
0                   Dyden
1              Mississauga
2                  Tronto
3                Kingston
4        British Columbia
5                Pickering
6                  Alberta
Name: City, dtype: object
```

```
In [109]: data.head(7)
Out[109]:
```

	Year	Sales	City	Mkt_exp	Revenue
0	2000	50000	Dyden	10000	40000
1	2001	60000	Mississauga	12000	48000
2	2002	75000	Tronto	13500	61500
3	203	100000	Kingston	16000	84000
4	2004	60000	British Columbia	17000	43000
5	2005	150000	Pickering	19000	131000
6	2006	165000	Alberta	19500	145500

3. Replacing 'Kitchener' with 'Fort St. John' and 'Ottawa' with 'Calgary'.

 Since column city is already assigned to a variable called city, you need not assign it again. Instead we could use the same.

Here we want to replace two words with new words at a time. We have to replace 'Kitchener' with 'Fort St.John' and Ottawa with Calgary in the same data.

```
In [118]: city.ix[7]= 'Fort St.John'

In [119]: city.ix[9] ='Calgary'
```

6	2006	165000	Alberta	19500	145500
7	2007	60000	Fort St.John	20000	40000
8	2008	250000	Brantford	21200	228800
9	2009	249000	Calgary	21000	228000
10	2010	251000	Oshawa	21100	229900

You could also use the following code to perform the aforementioned

```
In [8]: city = city.replace(['Kitchener', 'Ottawa'], ['Fort St.John', 'Calgary'])
```

Note: To select a row, your code should include the following.

Column.ix[number], where column is the column name or a temporary container where you have assigned a column and the [number] implies row number.

CHAPTER 6
Preliminary Analysis: Descriptive

Descriptive statistic is an important part of data analysis. To be very precise, descriptive statistics are the numbers that will help us to summarize and describe any given data. Using Python, we can find all relevant descriptive statistics of a given data. In this chapter, you will learn various functions of Python to describe the data.

Here, we can find the summary statistics of semester marks as an example.

Example 6.1

First of all, we have to open the cleaned data set that we saved in the last chapter (**stud_clean.csv**)

```
In [92]: data = pd.read_csv('F:\stud_clean.csv')
```

Now, we can run the following code to summary stat:

```
In [98]: marks = data.Sem_marks
```

We retrieve column **Sem_marks** and stored in a variable called marks.

The following code will run the summary stats:

```
In [99]: marks.describe()
```

The output is as show below:

```
Out[99]:
count     96.000000
mean     395.260417
std      110.107626
min      200.000000
25%      305.250000
50%      393.000000
75%      483.250000
max      594.000000
dtype: float64
```

The following section talks about Measures of Central Tendency such as Mean, Median, and Mode:

6.2

Measures of Central Tendency

> ➢ **Mean**
> ➢ **Median**
> ➢ **Mode**

6.2.1

Mean

```
In [102]: mean(marks)
Out[102]: 395.26041666666669
```

In case there are missing values in your data set, you can find the Mean value by suppressing the missing value by entering the following code:

```
In [133]: marks.mean(axis = 1, skipna=False)
Out[133]: 395.26041666666669
```

In this case, we have done Mean based on the data we have loaded from Excel. The following codes will demonstrate on doing Mean based on numbers you directly give to Python, rather than loading from an existing data.

Let us say, we have to find Mean of x.

```
In [1]: x = (10,30,50,20,35,23)

In [2]: mean(x)
Out[2]: 28.0
```

At this time we have given data directly, rather than extracting from an existing one.

Example 6.1

The monthly Sales of Health and beauty department of KLM, a Canadian retail store is given here (in dollars). You are asked to find the average Sales for the same.

Jan: $ 5000; Feb: $ 5500; March: $ 6000; April: $ 6250; May: $ 6500.

You can see above the sales of 5 months. First we will assign the Sales to a temporary variable.

```
In [4]: s = 5000, 5500, 6000, 6250, 6500
```

With the above code we have assigned sales to a temporary variable 's'.

Now we shall compute the Average Sales;

```
In [5]: mean(s)
Out[5]: 5850.0
```

Therefore, the mean or average sale is $5850.0.

6.2.2

Median

```
[103]: median(marks)
[103]: 393.0
```

Now, let us find the Median of x. We will be using the same numbers as we have used to find the mean of x.

```
In [4]: median(x)
Out[4]: 26.5
```

Example 6.2

Find the Median for the monthly Sales of KLM retail store.

To do this example, we shall use the same data as we have used to calculate average sales.

First and foremost, you have to assign the Sales to a temporary variable. However if you have already assigned, then need not assign it again and again. Now please follow the steps:

In this example, we have assigned sales to 'sm'

```
In [7]: sm = 5000, 5500, 6000, 6250, 6500

In [8]: median(sm)
Out[8]: 6000.0
```

Here we have assigned sales to 'sm'.

So we have the median sales as $ 6000.00.

Example 6.3

Inter Quartile Range

To proceed further, please import **stat.xlsx**.

First and foremost, we will import pandas.

The data contains 3 sets of numerical data and we shall find interquartile range for set 2.

```
In [74]: import pandas

In [75]: data = pd.read_excel('D:/stat.xlsx', 'Sheet1')

In [76]: data.head(2)
Out[76]:
```

	Set One	Set Two	Set 3
0	5	3	5
1	6	4	6

Now we shall assign column Set Two to a variable **n**.

```
In [80]: n=data['Set Two']

In [81]: n.head(3)
Out[81]:
0    3
1    4
2    5
```

Now we shall check for the descriptive statistics.

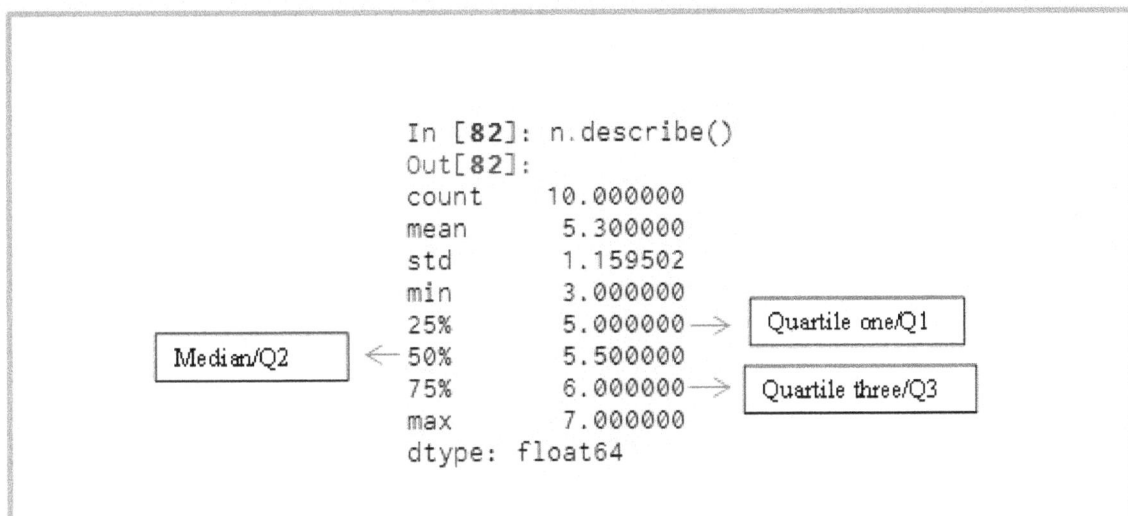

```
In [82]: n.describe()
Out[82]:
count    10.000000
mean      5.300000
std       1.159502
min       3.000000
25%       5.000000  →  [Quartile one/Q1]
50%       5.500000  ←  [Median/Q2]
75%       6.000000  →  [Quartile three/Q3]
max       7.000000
dtype: float64
```

Exhibit 6.1 Showing Q1, Q2 and Q3

From the above output you can see that we have the Median (50%) as 5.50, which is the Q2.

First Quartile: Q1 (25%) is 5.0 and third Quartile Q3: (75%) is 6.0.

Inter Quartile Range (IQR) = Q3-Q1

$$= 6.0 - 5.0$$

```
In [83]: 6.0-5.0
Out[83]: 1.0
```

Therefore, IQR is 1

6.2.3

Mode:

For Numeric data

```
In [43]: from scipy.stats import mode

In [51]: data = pd.read_csv('D:\stud_clean.csv')

In [52]: x = data.Attendance

In [53]: mode(x)
Out[53]: (array([ 97.]), array([ 6.]))
```

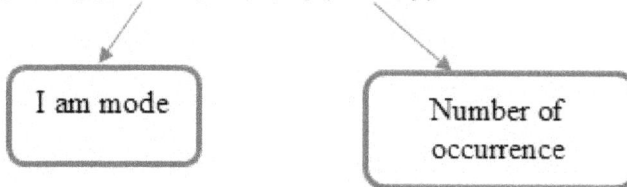

I am mode

Number of occurrence

Now let us find the mode of x.

Please refer previous examples to get the values of x.

```
In [7]: from scipy.stats import mode

In [8]: mode(x)
Out[8]: (array([ 3.]), array([ 4.]))
```

The output shows that Mode is 3 and it repeated 4 times

Mode for Text data

Find out the Most Popular Department in the College

```
In [65]: x = data.Dept

In [66]: mode(x)
Out[66]:
```

I am mode

Number of occurrence

```
(array(['Comm'],
       dtype='|S4'), array([ 48.]))
```

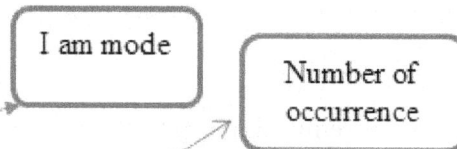

Most popular department in the aforementioned college data is Commerce, as it occurs 48 times.

Similarly, let us find most popular province in Canada

```
In [2]: canada = ('British Columbia','Ontario','Nova Scotia','Ontario','Alberta',
   ...: 'Ontario','Quebec','Ontario','Manitoba')

In [5]: mode(canada)
Out[5]:
(array(['Ontario'],
      dtype='|S7'), array([ 4.]))
```

Therefore, the popular Province is Ontario

6.3

Standard deviation:

Standard deviation is a measure of dispersion and commonly included as a part of preliminary analysis for various reasons. Here we can see how to get the standard deviation of the variables in our data set.

```
In [104]: std(marks)
Out[104]: 109.53264779580437
```

We could also find standard deviation for a set of numbers, which we put in directly.

```
In [11]: x=(12, 3, 4, 5, 6, 7, 8, 14, 15, 20)


In [12]: std(x)
Out[12]: 5.2952809179494906
```

6.4

Minimum, Maximum and Variance:

```
In [105]: min(marks)
Out[105]: 200

In [106]: max(marks)
Out[106]: 594

In [107]: var(marks)
Out[107]: 11997.400933159728
```

Now, we will find Min, Max and Variance of x, where x is same as above example (standard deviation).

Minimum

As you have already seen from the above illustrations, **Min** function will return the minimum value (lowest number) from a set of numbers

```
In [13]: min(x)
Out[13]: 3
```

Maximum

Max function will return maximum value (highest number) from a set of numbers

```
In [14]: max(x)
Out[14]: 20
```

Variance

```
In [15]: var(x)
Out[15]: 28.039999999999999
```

Similarly, you could also find Min, Max and Variance of any set of numbers.

Example 6.4

Use KLM retail sales data and compute Minimum and Maximum sales.

```
In [9]: sm = 5000, 5500, 6000, 6250, 6500

In [10]: min(sm)
Out[10]: 5000

In [11]: max(sm)
Out[11]: 6500
```

6.5

Range

As you already know, range is the difference between the highest and lowest value.

Let's find the rage of KLM sales data.

```
In [7]: sm = 5000, 5500, 6000, 6250, 6500
```

Now we will use min and max function to calculate highest and lowest value in sales.

```
In [10]: min(sm)
Out[10]: 5000
```

```
In [11]: max(sm)
Out[11]: 6500
```

Here we have minimum and maximum sales values. For easy computation of range, it is better to assign these results to a temporary container and then do the calculation. The following will illustrate the same:

```
In [12]: high = max(sm)
```

```
In [13]: high
Out[13]: 6500
```

Here we have assigned maximum sales to a variable named '**high**' and viewed the result.

Similarly, we will assign minimum sales to another variable named '**low**'.

```
In [14]: low=min(sm)
```

```
In [15]: low
Out[15]: 5000
```

Now it is simple; high-low will give us the range.

```
In [16]: high-low
Out[16]: 1500
```

So we have the range as $1500

However, if you want to use the result, you need to assign the computation to a temporary variable. The following is the example of the same:

```
In [21]: r =high-low
```

```
In [22]: r
Out[22]: 1500
```

6.6

Skewness and Kurtosis

In many cases, we often need measures of Skewness and Kurtosis to check the nature of distribution of our variables. This section talks about numerically identifying if there is skewness and also check for Kurtosis.

```
In [109]: marks.skew()
Out[109]: 0.038599826577723075

In [110]: marks.kurt()
Out[110]: -1.0000151247262243
```

6.7

Count: Python will count the number of non-NAN values in the column.

```
In [112]: gender = data.Gender

In [114]: gender.count()
Out[114]: 96
```

6.8

Cumulative sum

```
In [115]: cumsum(marks)
Out[115]:
0       475
1       778
2      1365
3      1768
4      2229
5      2681
```

If you want to use above output or want to save this output as a new column in the same data set, perform the following codes:

```
In [120]: csum = cumsum(marks)
```

When you type **csum** and press enter, you will have the output as shown in **cumsum(marks)**.

The following code will add the column to the data with the output of **csum**:

```
In [121]: data['Cum_sum'] = csum
```

In case you want to delete the same column, do the following:

```
In [124]: del data['Cum_sum']
```

6.9

Percentiles:

When we measure or quantify variables on a scale, we often need percentile to interpret the scores. We can see how to get a percentile of the scores that we are interested in.

In order to do this, first, we will import Numerical Python, or Numpy and assign Column Attendance to a temporary variable named x. The following code illustrates the same:

```
In [68]: import numpy as np

In [69]: x = data.Attendance
```

6.9.1

To calculate 50th percentile:

Now we will write and execute the code to get 50th percentile of x, which is Attendance.

```
In [70]: np.percentile(x, 50)
Out[70]: 68.414285715000005
```

6.9.2

60th percentile

Similarly, we find out 60th percentile of x, which again, attendance.

```
In [72]: np.percentile(x, 60)
Out[72]: 75.0
```

Note: In this Chapter we have made use of functions such as Mean, Median, Mode, Standard deviation and so on. They are not temporary containers. The difference between temporary containers and functions are: the temporary container is the one which we define, whereas functions are inbuilt and we could use it any time we want.

CHAPTER 7
Data Cleaning & Preparation

Data cleaning is essential for any quantitative research and often requires considerable time and effort to get it done. If we do analyses without giving due importance to data cleaning many of our output will not be reliable and even misleading. For instance, we have already seen in the section on Data entry in Python that 46 students have higher grade among all departments, but when we calculated department-wise it comes to 42. Here the results are not accurate.

While doing data cleaning especially with big data it is hectic to make corrections, replacements of the cell values, checking the outliers, managing missing values with average or other statistically appropriate data inputting methods. Here, Python is very helpful to get our work done with minimum effort and maximum accuracy particularly in case of big data, with a few clicks, we can make changes in large number of cells at a time and can avoid working on cell by cell.

7.1

Identifying & handling the Outliers

The first part is all about identifying if there is any outlier. In this example, we have to identify the outliers in Attendance and Sem_marks. In order to determine an outlier, we need to set a cut-off value depending on the data and situation. In this example, the maximum possible value for attendance is 100, and that of Sem_marks is 600. Any value about this cut- off may be treated as outliers. You can also do the same manually by taking a normal distribution and identifying the values above and below three standard deviations as outliers if the situation demands.

7.1.1

The following codes illustrate identifying the same:

```
In [7]: import numpy as np

In [8]: attendance[np.abs(attendance)>100]
Out[8]:
59    110
60    150
Name: Attendance, dtype: float64
```

Exhibit 7.1 displaying outliers with row location and value

Retrieving the whole record in Row 59 and 60 from data via the following code:

```
In [10]: data.ix[59]
Out[10]:
Studnt _ID        M196
Gender          Female
Dept           Science
Attendance         110
Sem_ Marks         654
Name               NaN
Name: 59, dtype: object

In [11]: data.ix[60]
Out[11]:
Studnt _ID        M199
Gender            Male
Dept           Science
Attendance         150
Sem_ Marks         277
Name            Mathew
Name: 60, dtype: object
```

Getting such detail will help us in decision-making at the time of data cleaning.

7.1.2

Once you have identified the outliers, you could either remove it or replace it with appropriate values depending on the scenario. In this example, we are replacing this with the mean value of the entire column.

The following code will serve you the purpose:

Scenario 1:

```
In [12]: attendance[np.abs(attendance)>100] = mean(attendance)
```

In order to see the output, you need to retrieve the respective row from the entire data, which you can see below:

```
In [16]: data.ix[59]
Out[16]:
Studnt _ID         M196
Gender           Female
Dept            Science
Attendance     68.82857
Sem_ Marks          654
Name                NaN
Name: 59, dtype: object
```

Scenario 2:

If you want to replace the outlier with Median the following code will suffice:

```
In [17]: median(attendance)
```

Scenario 3:

If you want to replace the outlier with any other specific value,(for example, 80) use the following:

```
In [18]: attendance[np.abs(attendance)>100] = 80
```

Value

7.2

Removing Duplicates

It is very much common in data entry that we tend to enter same record/data more than once. It is just a human error, as it occurs while doing data entry, especially when large amount of data is involved. Therefore, we face the problem of duplication in our data. If you check it manually, it takes much time, and often you miss many. In this section, we talk about handling the issue of duplicates.

In this book, we identify duplicates based on a unique/primary key (Studnt_ID). Using Python, we will find a replication of the same ID if any and will remove the same.

```
In [39]: data.drop_duplicates(['Stud_id'])
Out[39]:
<class 'pandas.core.frame.DataFrame'>
Int64Index: 102 entries, 0 to 106
Data columns (total 6 columns):
Stud_id       102  non-null values
Gender         99  non-null values
Dept          100  non-null values
Attendance    100  non-null values
Sem_ Marks    101  non-null values
Name           50  non-null values
dtypes: float64(2), object(4)
```

Here you have the data with no duplicate records.

7.3

Correcting Errors

In order to correct errors in variable you need to do the following:

In case of string variable, spelling correction may be done with the following codes:

14	C164	Male	Science	40	258	Atul
15	C152	Female	Comms	69	282	Millen
16	M188	Male	Commerce	0	206	Roshan
25	A107	Male	Art	57	359	Susan
26	C153	Female	Commerce	0	399	Victor

Scenario 1:

In the above data you can see a few errors such in rows 15 and 25. We could correct the same via entering the following Python code:

```
In [13]: dept = data.Dept
```

```
In [14]: dept.replace(['Art', 'Comms'], ['Arts', 'Commerce'])
```

```
In [15]: dept.ix[25]
Out[15]: 'Arts'
```

Here, we assigned a variable named dept for the column Dept in the data (See In[13]). Then we replaced 'Art' and 'Comms' with 'Arts' and 'Commerce' respectively.

After this, we need to replace the existing Dept column with the newly edited one using the following code:

```
In [18]: data.Dept =dept
```

To see the edited data, give the following code:

```
In [19]: data.ix[25]
Out[19]:
Stud_id        A118
Gender         Male
Dept           Arts
Attendance       89
Sem_ Marks      443
Name          Anuja
Name: 25, dtype: object
```

Scenario 2:

If you want to replace number do the following:

```
In [37]: attendance = data.Attendance

In [38]: newattendance = attendance.replace(0, mean(attendance))

In [42]: data.Attendance = newattendance
```

Now, we have replaced zero value in attendance with mean value.

If you already know the mean value, or if you want to enter any other value, you give same instead of mean (attendance).

For example: Attendance.replace (0, 30)

Here, the first value inside the bracket is the value that to be replaced with the second one.

> You can save the data at this stage. Please do not forget the code
>
> data.to_csv ('F: \name.csv')

7.4

Handling Missing Values: Data imputation

The missing values are another area to be handled scientifically in data analysis. Missing values can negatively affect the accuracy of the results if it is not handled carefully using statistically valid methods.

Suppose you want to impute missing values with computed values or specific values, do the following:

```
In [46]: attendance = data.Attendance

In [47]: fill = attendance.fillna(attendance.mean())

In [48]: data.Attendance = fill
```

Here in the first step, we stored Column Attendance in a variable called attendance. In the second step, we assigned a new variable 'fill', and performed the process of filling the missing values with the mean value of the same column and the results are also stored in 'fill'. In the third step, we replaced the existing Attendance column in the data with new values which we have computed and stored in Fill at Step 2.

Suppose you want to replace with a specific number, say 30, the code will be modified as:

In [49]: fill = attendance.fillna (30)

7.4.1

Filling missing string

We give different scenarios and show how to approach them.

Scenario 1:

Suppose, you want to fill the whole column with a specific word then do the following: Here we are filling the missing values in the variable column **'Gender'** with **'Female'**.

```
In [70]: gender = data.Gender

In [71]: fill = gender.fillna(str('Female'))

In [72]: data.Gender = fill
```

Scenario 2:

At this time, we want to replace specific string cells with specific words. In this example, there are a few missing values in 'Dept'. We want to fill in stud_id M198 with Arts.

```
In [78]: dept = data.Dept

In [79]: dept.ix[42]
Out[79]: nan

In [80]: dept.ix[42] = 'Arts'

In [81]: dept.ix[42]
Out[81]: 'Arts'
```

In the above mentioned code, first one is for taking out the particular column and in this example, it is 'Dept. The second code is for retrieving a particular cell value in Dept. (42nd). The output shows there is a missing value. Then we impute the missing value with 'Arts'. The Code is shown in [81] is to check if the modification has been done.

```
In [82]: data.Dept=dept
```

This code is to replace the existing column Dept with newly imputed column to the original data.

7.5

Dropping Records with missing values

This section talks about how to drop all the rows with at least one missing value which was impossible to fill. The following code illustrates the same:

```
In [88]: droping = data.dropna()

In [89]: data=droping
```

Here, data.dropna() implies dropping the missing values from the data. In order to use this result, we save this in a variable called 'droping'. Now the variable 'dropping' has the original data after dropping the remaining missing values. In the second step, it implies that, we are storing the newly edited data in the variable 'data.'

Now it is time to save the data by entering the following code:

```
In [91]: data.to_csv('F:\stud_clean.csv')
```

Now you can open the stud_clean from the saved folder/drive.

You may save the data at different stages of this process at your convenience

CHAPTER 8
Data Visualization

Data Visualization is an integral part of data processing and analysis. It helps to understand how the large volume of data can be displayed using various data visualization methods. It gives us the properties of data and the pattern of their distribution across various criteria. Python helps to display data more conveniently and efficiently than many other available methods of data visualization. This chapter talks on how to display your data using various methods and techniques.

Use stud_clean.csv

8.1

Histogram:

We all are familiar with histograms, and we know how to draw manually for our data. In this section, you will learn on how to do it with the help of Python. In order to draw a histogram, we need to import necessary modules such as **matplotlib** and **matplotlib.pyplot**. In this section, we have imported it as mlab and plt respectively. However, you could do import it as any name of your choice.

Draw a histogram of Attendance

The following codes illustrates the same:

```
In [178]: import numpy as np
```

```
In [179]: import matplotlib.mlab as mlab
```

```
In [180]: import matplotlib.pyplot as plt
```

```
In [181]: x = data.Attendance
```

In the aforementioned code, we have assigned column Attendance to a temporary variable named 'x'.

```
In [184]: n, bins, patches = plt.hist(x, bins=20, normed = 1, facecolor = 'blue', alpha=0.5)
```

When you press enter, you will get the following output. Here 'bins' implies the frequency. In this case, it is frequency of the variable 'attendance'.

To make you understand, we are giving you an example:

Suppose say, data x has 1, 2, 2, 3, 3, 3, 4, 5, 6, 7 and in total you can see, we have 10 numbers. But bins will be 7, because, a few numbers are being repeated. However, in case of big data, you can enter any number like 10 or 20, and you could tweak it based on the output.

Alpha =0.5 is just for the colour adjustments. It has nothing to do with any calculations. You could draw a histogram without alpha =0.5. Or any number.

Now we will view the histogram of Attendance.

Normed could be either True or False, or '1' as in this example.

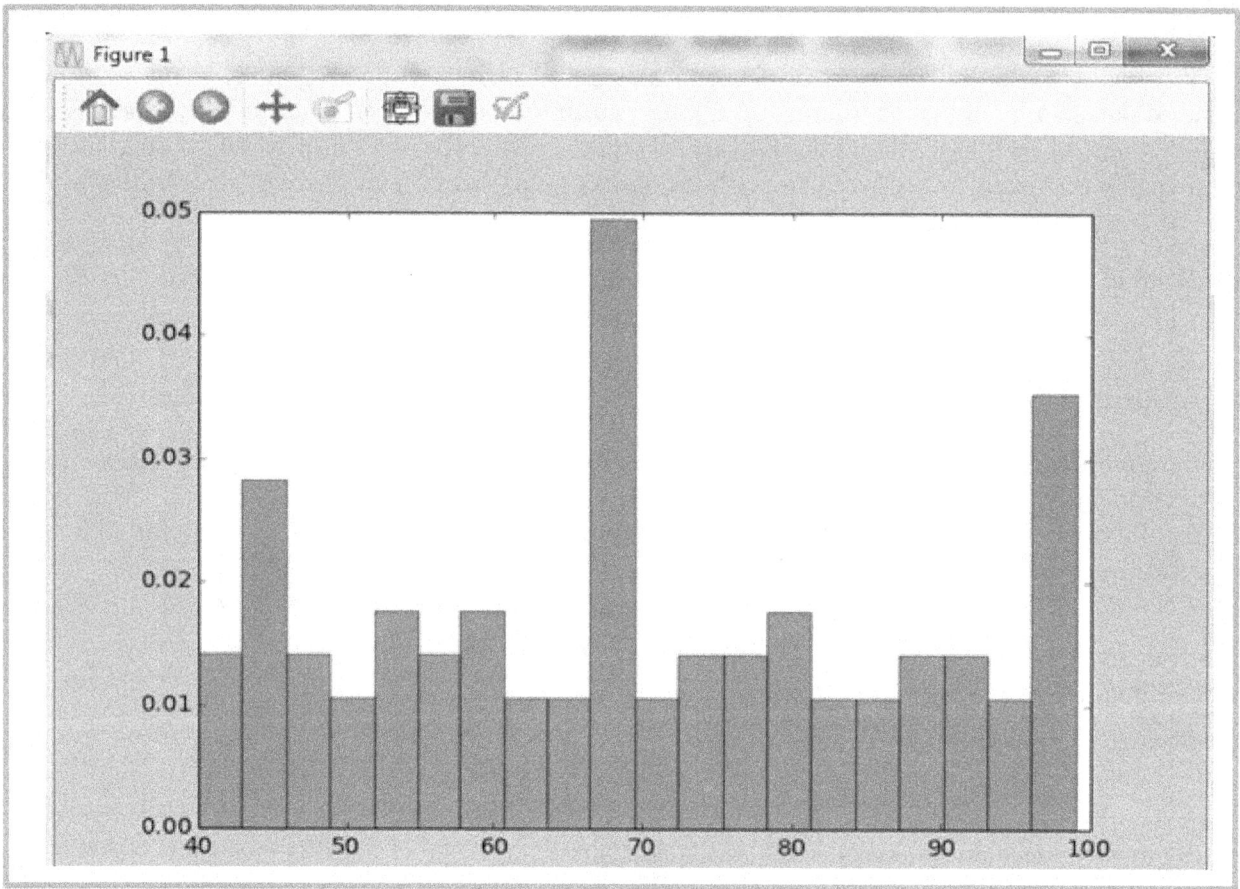

Exhibit 8.1 Histogram

8.1.1

Adding Goodness of Fit

Following code will illustrate on how to add goodness of fit:

```
In [185]: mu = mean(x)

In [186]: sigma = std(x)

In [187]: y = mlab.normpdf(bins, mu,sigma)
```

  Here **mu** is the Mean, **sigma** is the Standard Deviation. We have computed and stored the values of mean, standard deviation in mu and sigma respectively. Here, we have made use of functions: mean and standard deviation, to compute mean and standard deviation.

8.1.2

Plotting Goodness of Fit:

The following code will plot goodness of Fit on the graph:

```
In [191]: plt.plot(bins, y, 'r--')
Out[191]: [<matplotlib.lines.Line2D at 0x7fabe90>]
```

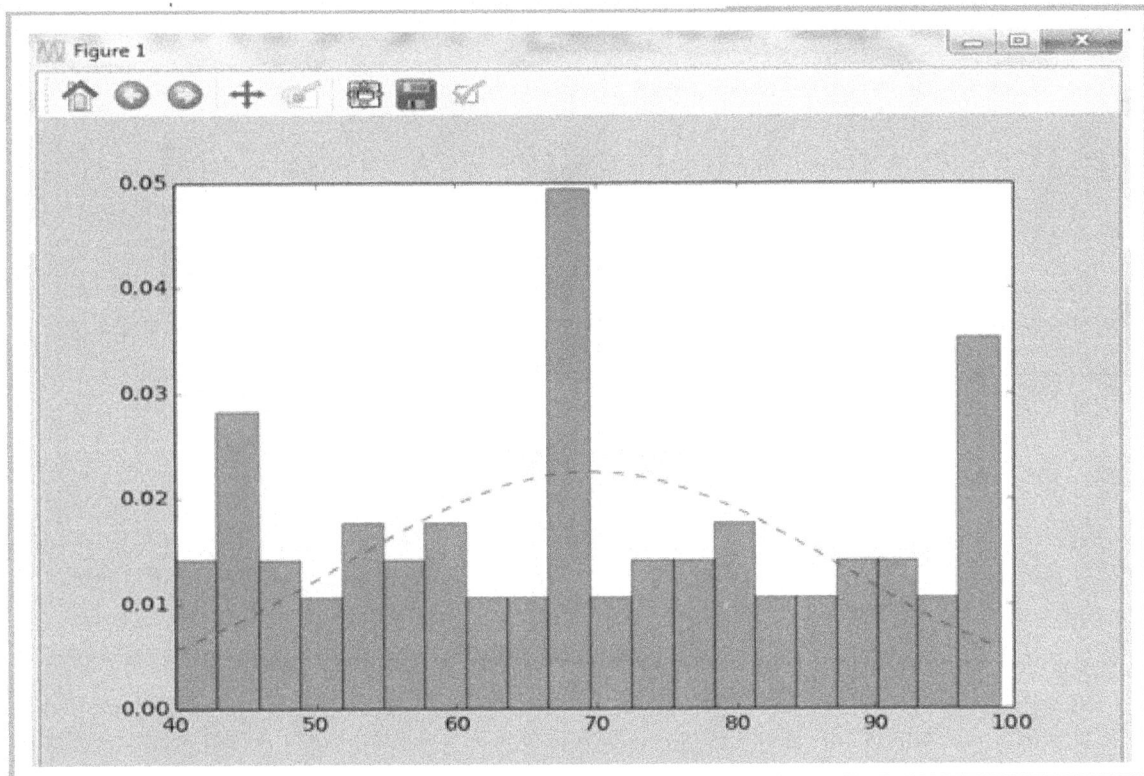

Exhibit 8.2 histogram with goodness of fit

Adding axis and chart titles:

Now that we have a histogram with goodness of fit. Let us add axis and chart titles apart from tweaking the chart for space adjustments.

The following code helps you to adjust the chart to provide enough space for y label:

```
In [21]: plt.subplots_adjust(left=0.15)
```

Title:

```
In [20]: plt.title('Histogram of Attendance: $\mu=69.6$, $\sigma=17.7$', color = 'red')

In [22]: plt.xlabel('Attendance', color='red')

In [23]: plt.ylabel('probability', color = 'red')
```

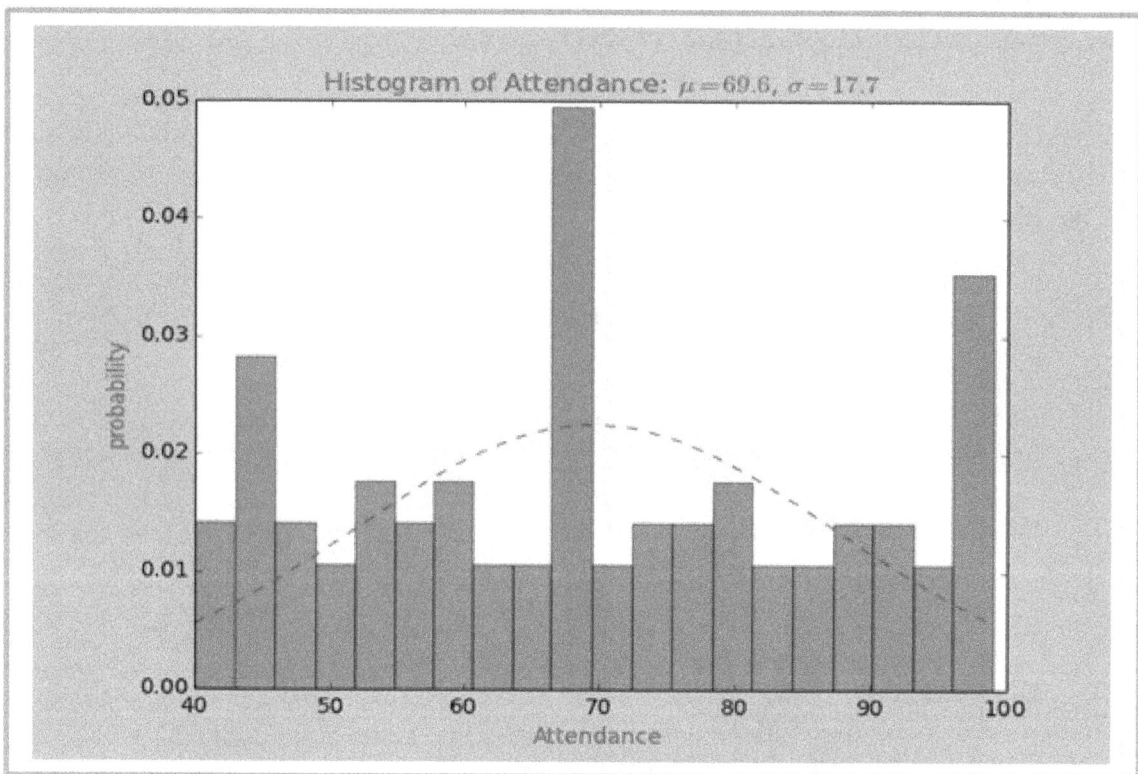

Exhibit 8.3 histogram with goodness of fit and chart labels

You can save the figure directly using the save option at the top of the figure itself.

Steps in drawing histogram with goodness of fit at a glance:

- ➢ **Importing necessary modules**
- ➢ **Select variable to draw histogram; in this example, x=data.Attendance.**
- ➢ **Plot the graph**
- ➢ **Add goodness of fit**
- ➢ **Add chart titles**

8.2

Pie Chart

Use pivot.csv for this purpose.

This section will guide you to draw a simple pie chart.

```
In [200]: pdata = pd.read_csv('F:\pivot.csv')
```

```
In [201]: pdata
Out[201]:
```

	Dept	Count
0	Arts	28
1	Commerce	48
2	Science	20

Before loading pivot.csv data, which is previously saved, we advise you to give column name as 'Dept' and 'Count' respectively . Since we have already imported **matpolib.lib** and **pyplot**, you need not import it again.

```
In [202]: labels = pdata.Dept
```

```
In [203]: size = pdata.Count
```

```
In [204]: colors = ['Green', 'Blue', 'Red']
```

```
In [205]: explode = (0, 0.1, 0)
```

In explode, 0.1 implies, Commerce (second position) will explode (Explode is one of the Pie chart features in Python)

The following code will plot the pie chart:

```
In [209]: plt.pie(size, explode = explode, labels = labels, colors = colors,
     ...: autopct='%1.1f%%', shadow = True, startangle = 0)
```

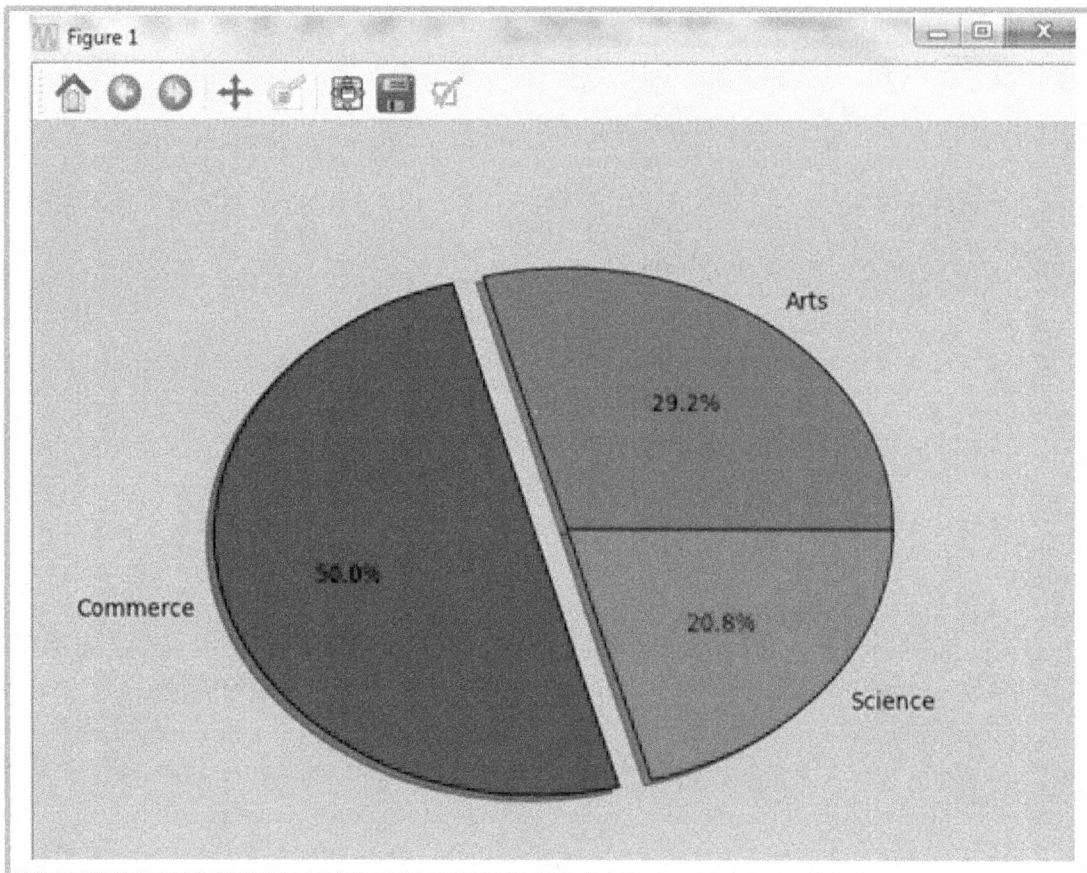

Exhibit 8.4 Pie chart

8.3

Drawing a Scatter Plot

In order to draw a scatter plot, first we will assign two variables to two temporary containers namely, column 'Attendance' to 'x' and column 'Sem_marks' to 'y' using the following codes:

```
In [220]: x = data.Attendance
```

```
In [221]: y = data.Sem_marks
```

The following codes will plot scatter diagram

```
In [222]: plt.scatter(x, y)
Out[222]: <matplotlib.collections.PathCollection at 0x7f140b0>
```

Now we will add labels of x and y axis

```
In [223]: plt.xlabel('Attendance', color='r')
Out[223]: <matplotlib.text.Text at 0x792d270>
```

```
In [225]: plt.ylabel('Semester Marks', color = 'r')
Out[225]: <matplotlib.text.Text at 0x7f0c1f0>
```

8.3.1

Adding Title on the Plot:

```
In [227]: plt.title('Scatter Plot', color = 'r')
Out[227]: <matplotlib.text.Text at 0x7f1ddb0>
```

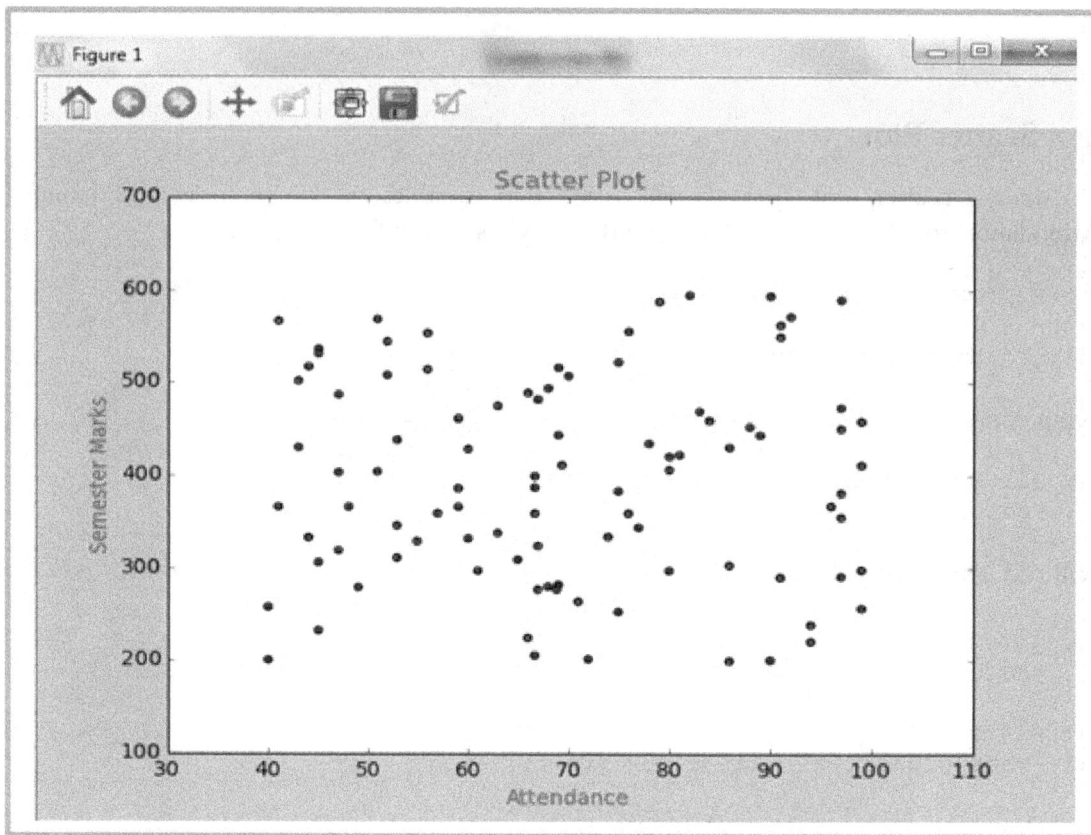

Exhibit 8.5 Scatter plot

8.4

Drawing a Bar chart

Drawing a bar char is very simple and easy. Before we plot, we will view the data.

```
In [233]: pivot
Out[233]:
Dept
Arts        28
Commerce    48
Science     20
```

The following code will help you to draw a bar chart in using Python:

```
In [234]: pivot.plot(kind='bar', rot=0)
```

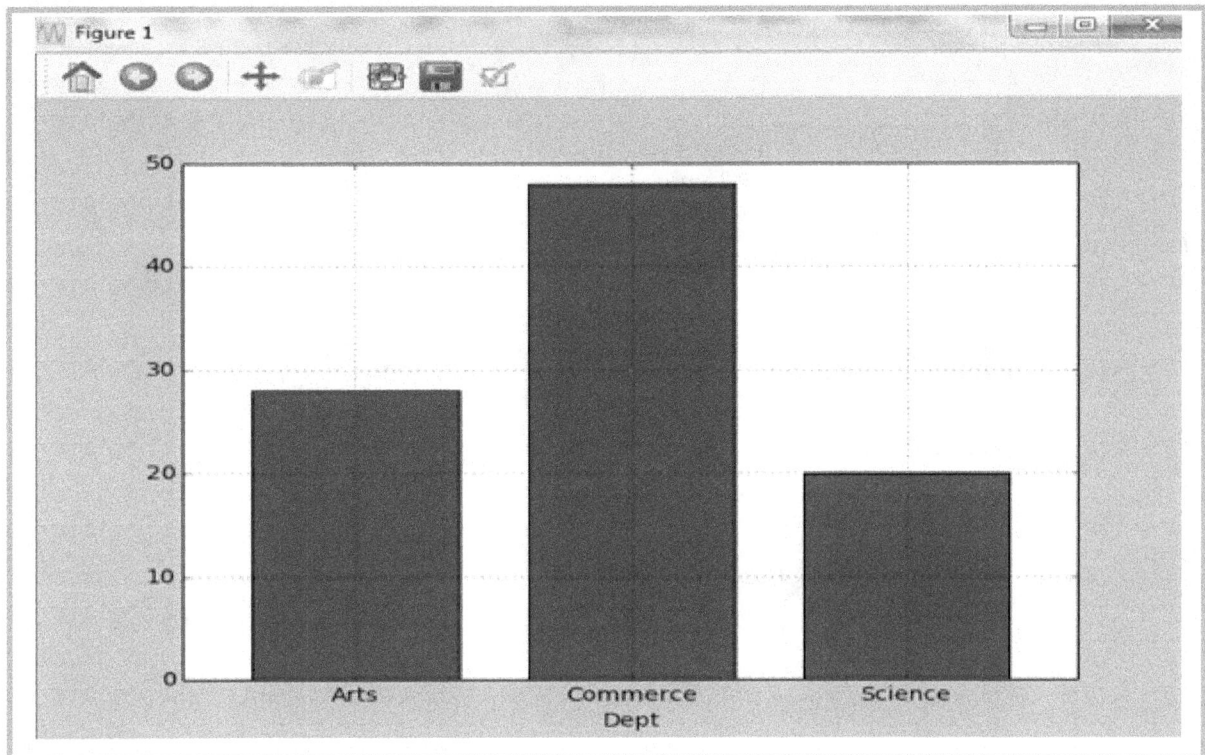

Exhibit 8.6 Bar chart

8.5

Plotting a Horizontal bar chart for the same data

If you want to draw a horizontal bar chart instead of a vertical one, use the following steps:

```
In [236]: pivot.plot(kind='barh', rot = 0, color = 'g')
```

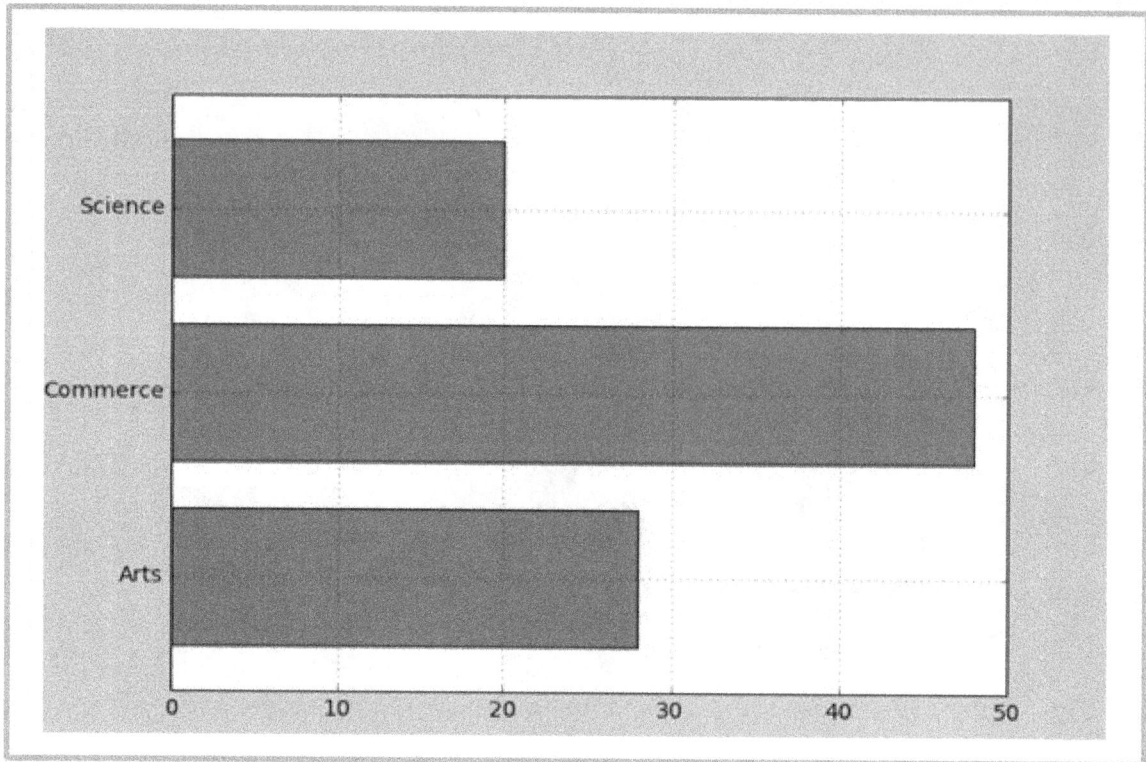

Exhibit 8.7 Horizontal bar chart

Labelling can be done in the same way as that of the Scatter plot.

8.6

Drawing a Stacked Bar Plot

Here you will learn how to make a stacked bar plot with the help of Python.

8.6.1

For this purpose we will cross tab 'Department' and 'Gender'.

```
In [52]: tab = pd.crosstab(data.Dept, data.Gender, margins=True)
```

```
In [53]: tab
Out[53]:
```

Gender	Female	Male	All
Dept			
Arts	17	11	28
Commerce	27	21	48
Science	9	11	20
All	53	43	96

For plotting purpose, we don't need the column 'All', so using the following code we shall remove the column.

```
In [56]: del tab['All']
```

```
Out[57]:
```

	Female	Male
Dept		
Arts	17	11
Commerce	27	21
Science	9	11
All	53	43

8.6.2

Plotting a Stacked Horizontal Bar Chart:

Now we can make stacked horizontal bar chart with the same data.

```
In [59]: tab.plot(kind='barh', stacked=True, alpha=0.5)
```

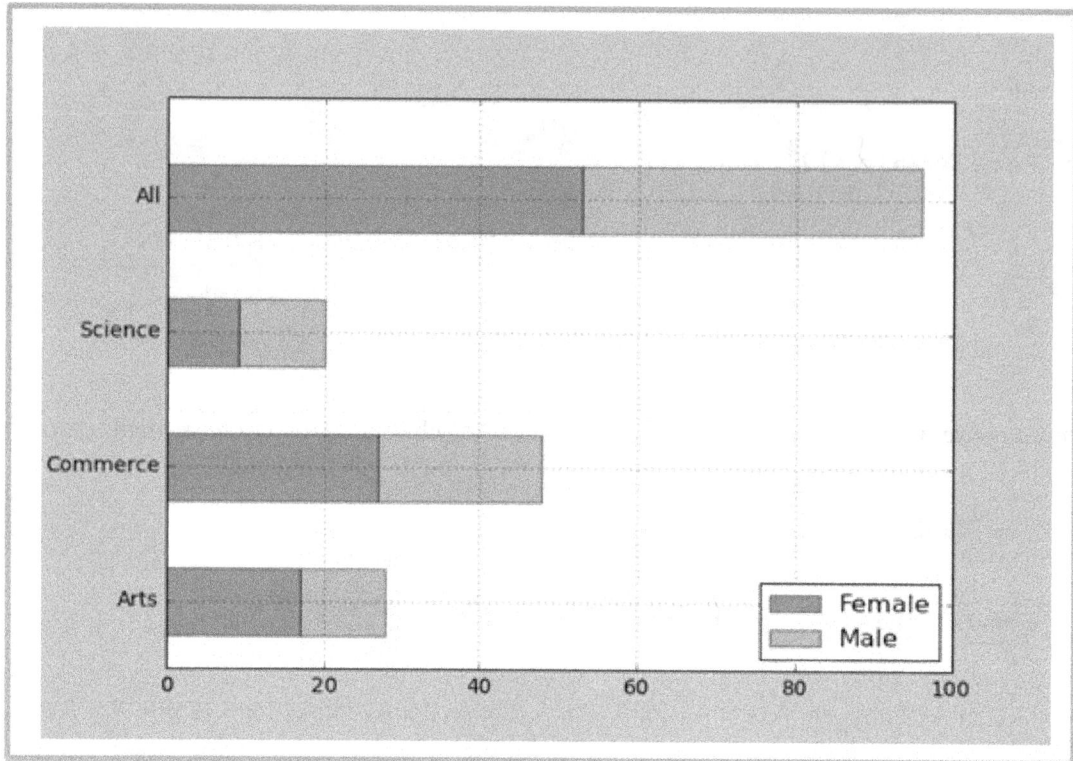

Exhibit 8.8 stacked horizontal bar chart

8.6.3

If you want the chart vertically, enter the following code:

```
In [62]: tab.plot(kind='bar',rot = 0, stacked=True, alpha=0.5)
```

8.6.4

Giving the labels:

```
In [65]: plt.title('Count of Male and Female across Departments', color='Blue')
In [66]: plt.ylabel('Count', color='blue')
In [67]: plt.xlabel('Department', color='blue')
```

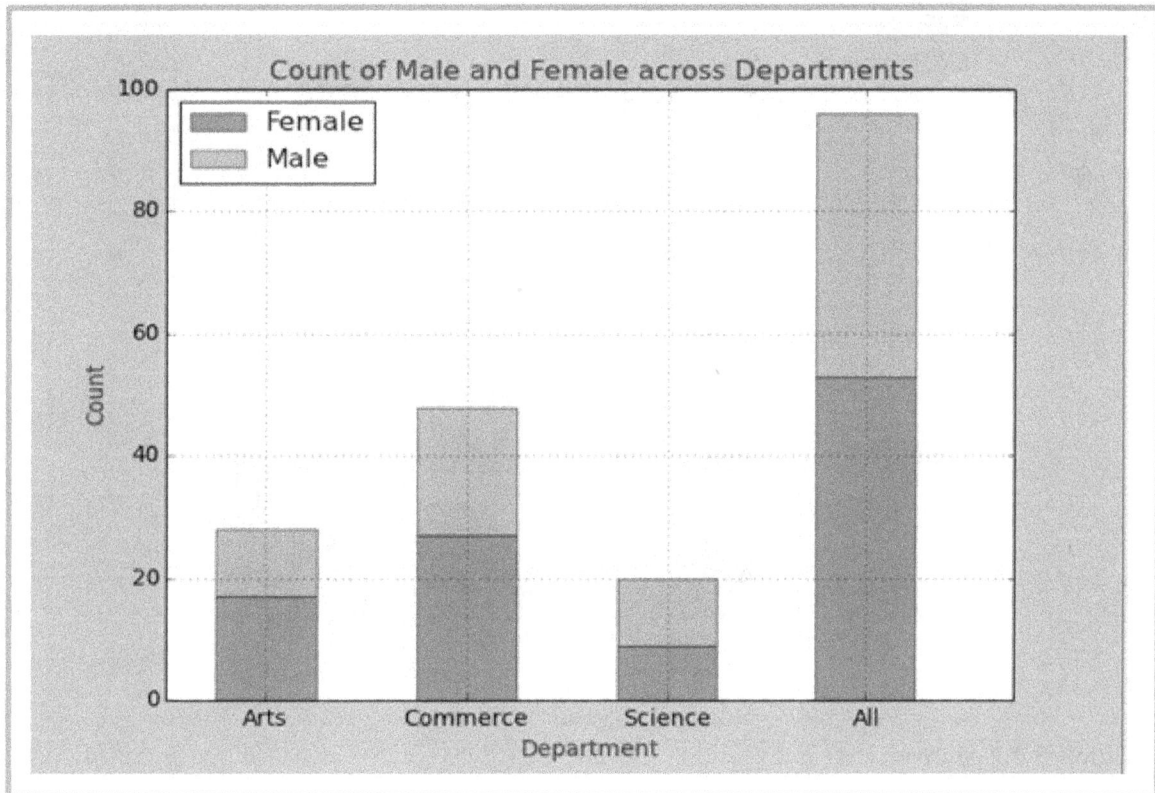

Exhibit 8.9 Stacked bar chart

8.7

Yet another way of presenting the same data:

We have some other ways to present our data, which will give more flexibility for the readers to use the codes for the same purpose.

```
In [71]: tab.plot(kind='bar', rot=0)
```

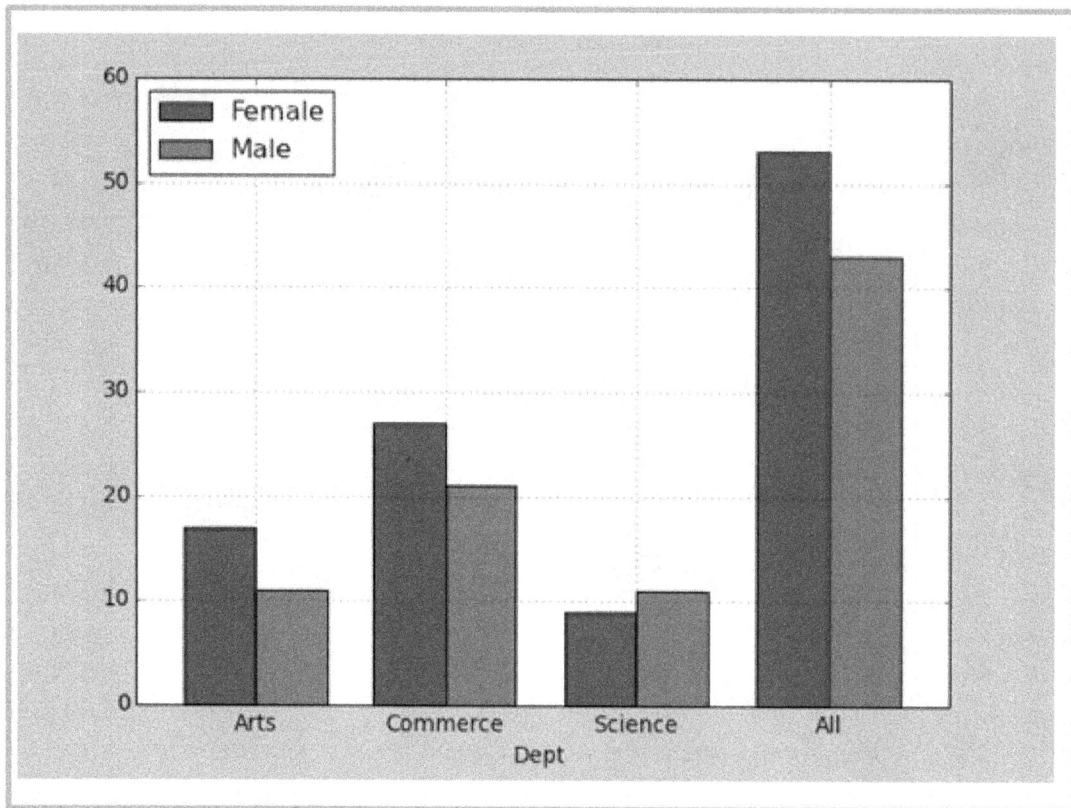

Exhibit 8.9 bar chart

8.8

Drawing a line graph:

This section will guide you to make a line graph using Python

For this, you need to import **wxyz_ca.xlsx**, an apparel company who has stores in Canada and India. This data is from their Canadian database. Remember, before loading data, you should first import **pandas** unless it is already imported. Along with that, you should import matplotlib and pyplot, which supports visualization.

```
In [99]: data = pd.read_excel('D:\wxyz_ca.xlsx', 'Sheet1')

In [94]: data
Out[94]:
```

	Year	Sales	City
0	2000	50000	Dryden
1	2001	60000	Mississauga
2	2002	75000	Toronto
3	2003	100000	Kingston
4	2004	125000	North Bay
5	2005	150000	Pickering

Drawing the chart

```
In [98]: plt.plot(data.Year, data.Sales, color='g', linestyle='dashed', marker = '*')
```

After typing the code, press enter, you will get the output.

After adding the titles the output will be shown as given below:

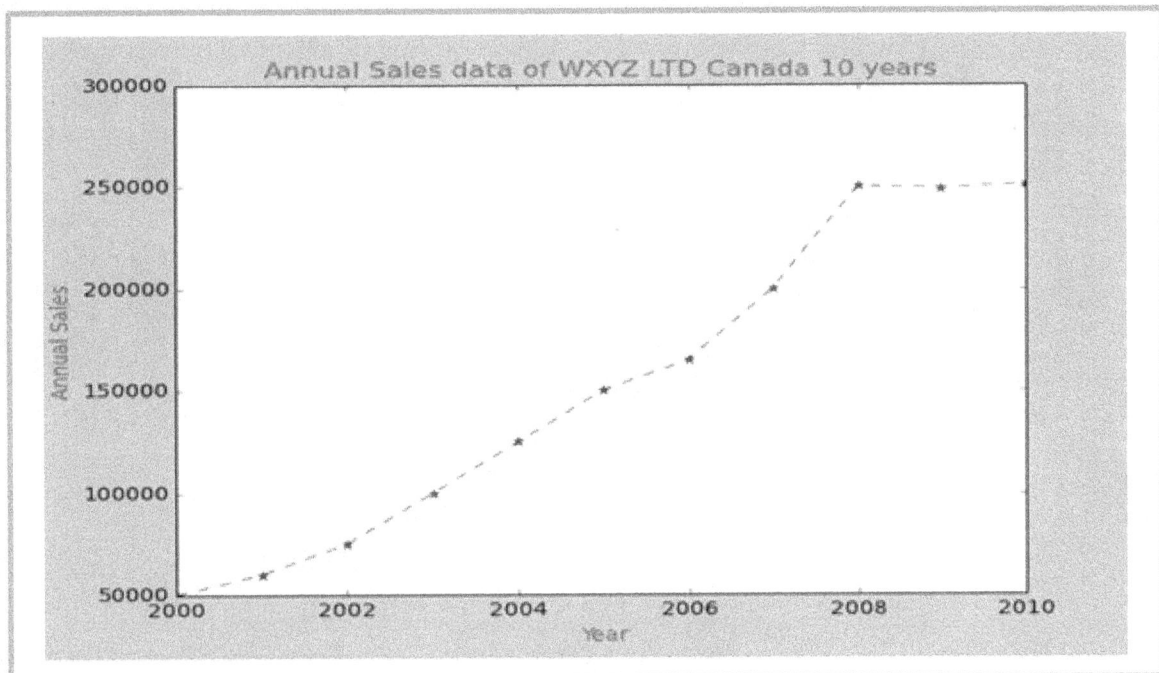

Exhibit 8.10 Line graph

8.9

Drawing a Steps-Post for Data Wxyz_Ca.Xlsx

Now we can learn how to make a step-post for our data.

```
In [15]: plt.plot(data.Year, data.Sales, 'g-',drawstyle='steps-post', label ='steps-post')
```

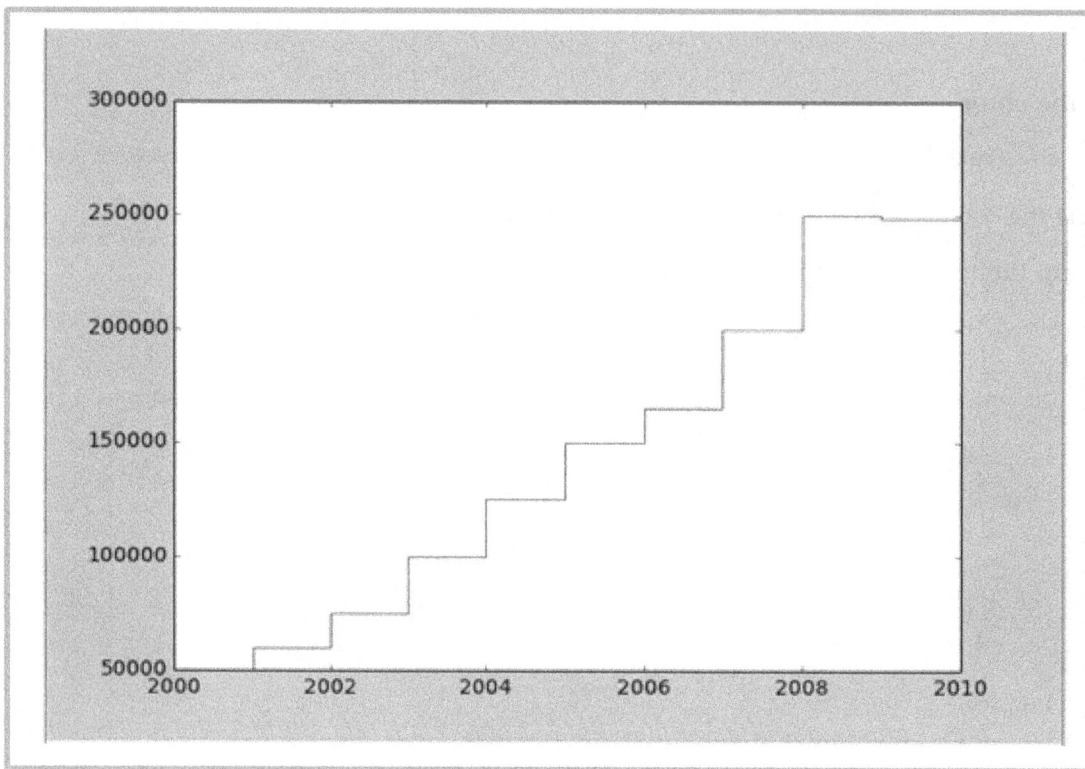

Exhibit 8.11 Steps – post chart

8.10

Line Plot with Steps Plot

This section will help you to combine both line and steps plots together.

```
In [7]: plt.plot(data.Year, data.Sales, 'g-',
                drawstyle='steps-post', label='Default')
```

Adding line with steps-post

```
In [8]: plt.plot(data.Year, data.Sales, 'r--')
```

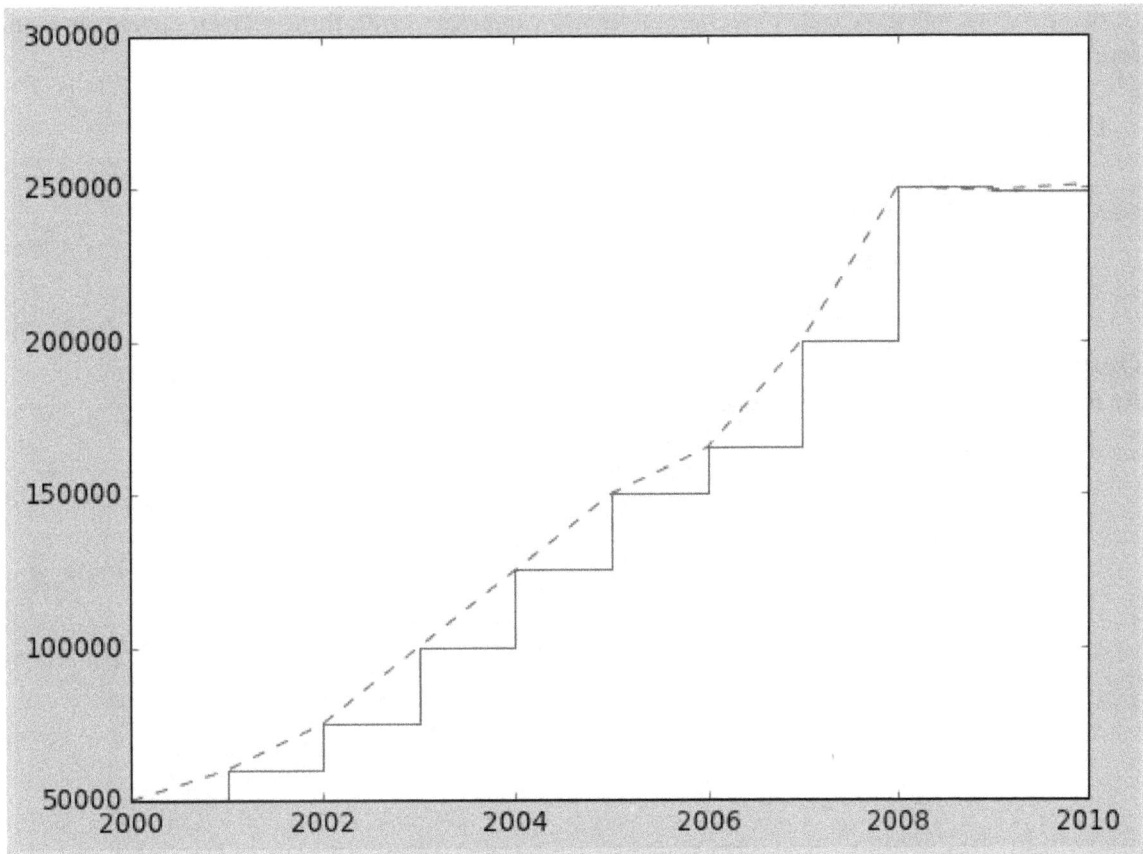

Exhibit 8.12 Line with Steps-post

8.11

Creating multiple charts on a single frame:

For the same data, we are going to draw scatter plot and line chart on a single frame using the following codes:

1. **Creating a Frame:**

   ```
   In [120]: frame=plt.figure()
   ```

2. **Creating chart areas:**

   In this case, we will have only two charts, but you can create up to three to four charts on a single frame.

   Code for chart1 and 2:

   ```
   In [121]: diag1 = frame.add_subplot(2, 2, 1)
   In [122]: diag2=frame.add_subplot(2, 2, 2)
   In [123]: diag1
   In [124]: diag2
   ```

   Output 1:
   At this point the output will look like this:

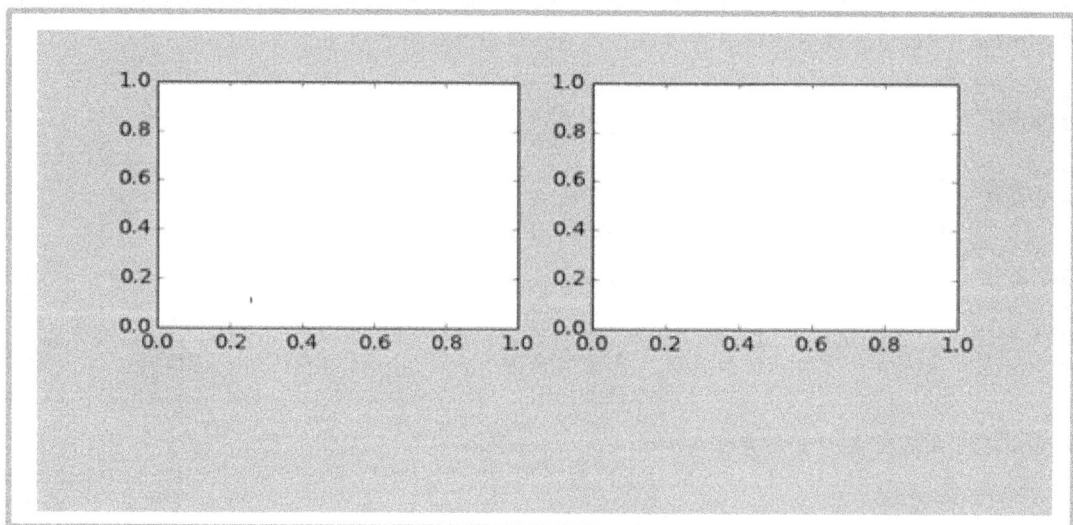

Exhibit 8.12 Frames

Drawing scatter plot and Line graph

When we plot a graph, without mentioning the chart area, it will automatically use the last area in the frame. In this example, the scatter plot will be on the second chart area.

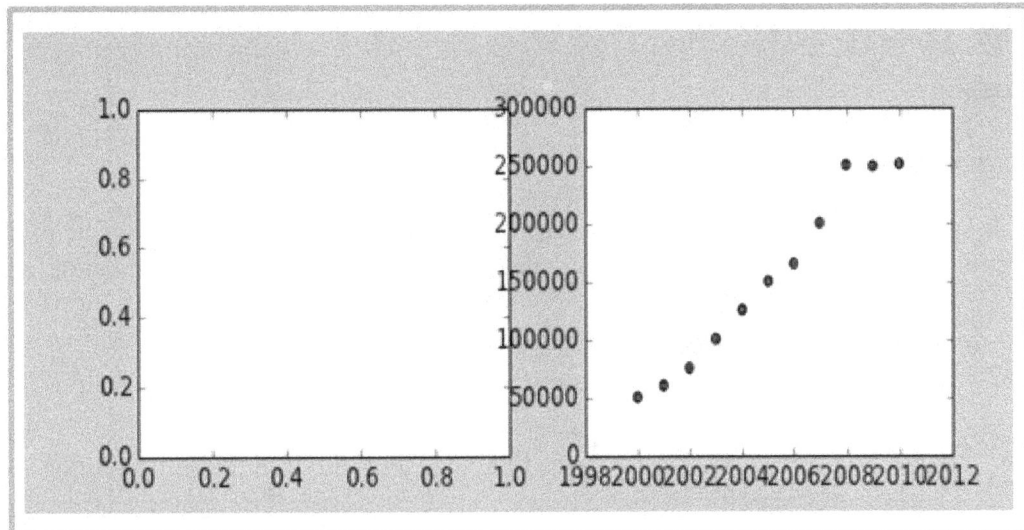

Exhibit 8.13 Frame with Scatter plot

Now we will draw a line graph for the same data. In order to draw a plot on a particular subplot or a chart area with in a frame, you need to specify the area.

```
In [133]: diag1.plot(data.Year, data.Sales, color='g', linestyle='dashed', marker='*')
```

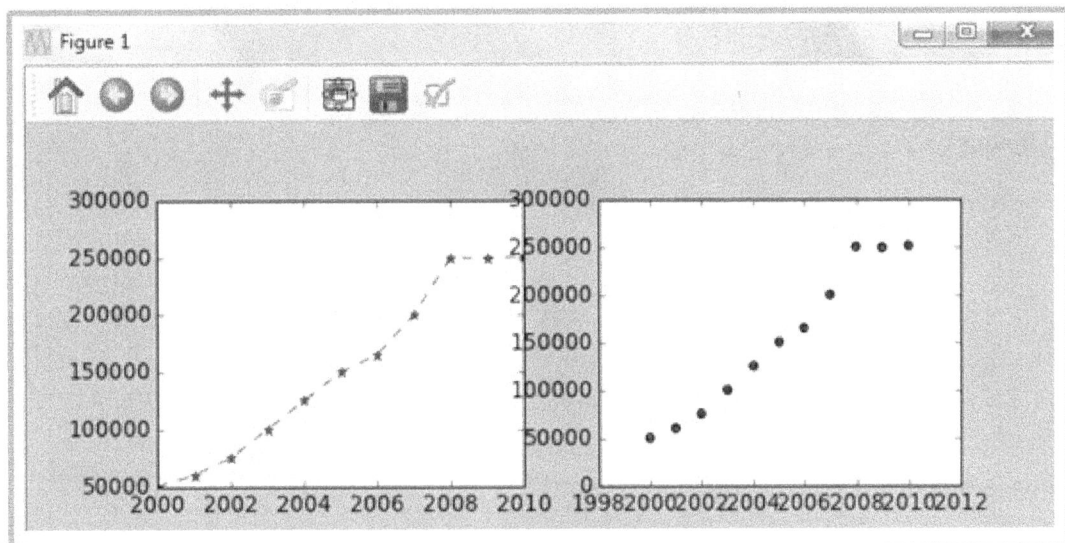

Exhibit 8.14 Frame with multiple charts

Maximise this window for a better view of the frame and output.

8.12
Histogram of data

Use stud_clean.csv for the purpose

This section will help us to draw a histogram with ease. **'.hist()'** will be very helpful if you want to see the distribution of the data. Here we make a histogram of attendance and **sem_marks**.

```
In [2]: data = pd.read_csv('F:\stud_clean.csv')
In [3]: data.head(2)
Out[3]:
```

	Stud_id	Gender	Dept	Attendance	Sem_marks	Name
0	M197	Female	Science	63	475	Ritu
1	M181	Male	Commerce	86	303	Victor

Selecting the required columns

```
In [4]: cols = ['Attendance', 'Sem_marks']
```

Making a new data with these columns

```
In [5]: ndata = data[cols]
```

Histogram

```
In [6]: ndata.hist()
```

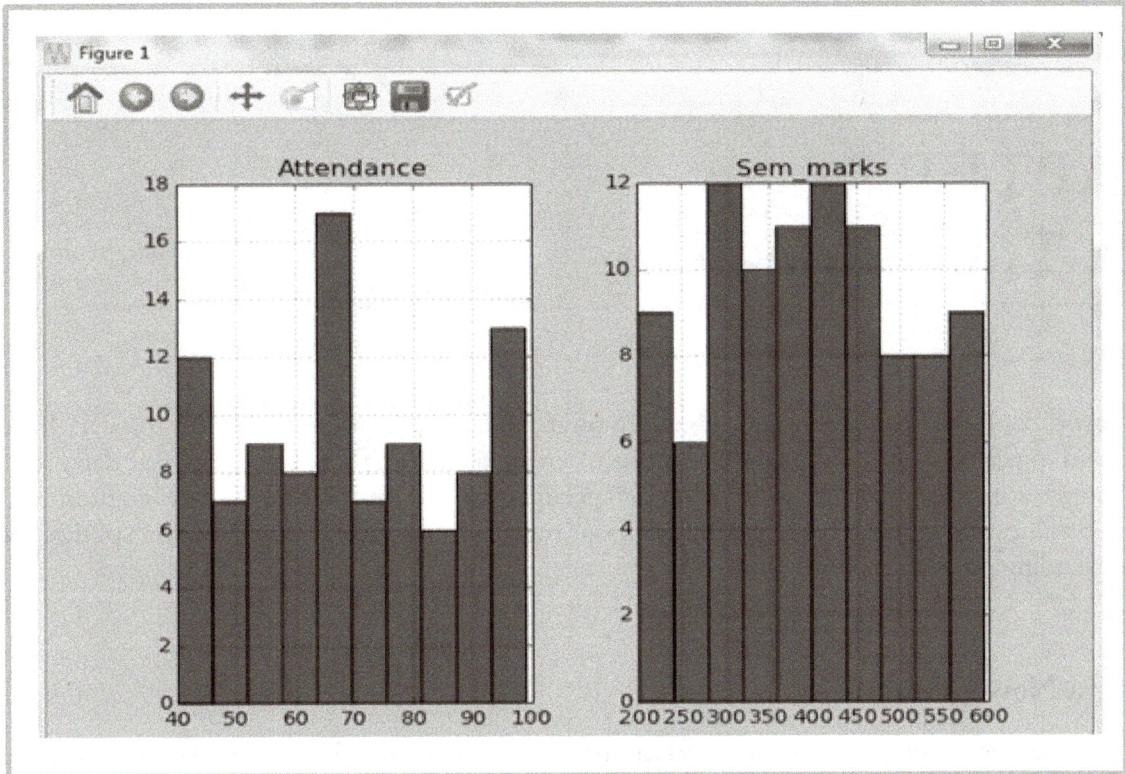

Exhibit 8.15 Simple histogram

CHAPTER 9
Data Transformation

When we work with data for rigorous analyses, we often find it necessary to transform the data for various statistical and logical reasons. Sometimes, we need to create a new column with a derived data; sometimes we may apply some statistical equations on a specific variable and create a new column with that transformed values and so on. This chapter is all about transforming data so as to perform specific statistical analysis depending on your needs.

9.1

Creating a New Column:

You can create a new column in two ways; you can try both and find which one you like the most.

1. Using this step, we can append a column to the end of an existing table. (Use wxyz_ca.xlsx).

```
In [31]: data
Out[31]:
```

	Year	Sales	City	Mkt_exp
0	2000	50000	Dryden	10000
1	2001	60000	Mississauga	12000
2	2002	75000	Toronto	13500
3	2003	100000	Kingston	16000

The following code will add a new column and their values:

```
In [34]: data['Best_emp'] = ['Brits', 'Anne', 'Joa', 'Thomas', 'Cris',
    ...: 'Joe', 'Mat', 'Mark', 'Tom', 'Gim', 'Peter']

In [33]: data
Out[33]:
```

	Year	Sales	City	Mkt_exp	Best_emp
0	2000	50000	Dryden	10000	Brits
1	2001	60000	Mississauga	12000	Anne
2	2002	75000	Toronto	13500	Joa

9.1.1

If you want to enter a column on a particular location, then do the following:

In this example, we are adding a column to the third position (remember, Python counts column from 0)

```
In [38]: data.insert(3, 'Best_emp', ['Brits', 'Anne', 'Joa', 'Thomas', 'Cris', 'Joe', 'Mat', 'Mark', 'Tom', 'Gim', 'Peter'],
    ...: allow_duplicates = False)

In [39]: data
Out[39]:
```

	Year	Sales	City	Best_emp	Mkt_exp
0	2000	50000	Dryden	Brits	10000
1	2001	60000	Mississauga	Anne	12000
2	2002	75000	Toronto	Joa	13500

It is advisable not to enter the data or text as above in the case of a large data set. Instead, you could create an empty column, and, using excel you could do the same. Simultaneously, you could create a new column with new values based on an existing column/value. You can see similar examples in the following chapters.

9.2

How to Delete a Column:

In this section, you will learn in detail on deleting single and multiple columns.

To delete a particular column:

```
In [41]: del data['Best_emp']

In [42]: data
Out[42]:
```

	Year	Sales	City	Mkt_exp
0	2000	50000	Dryden	10000
1	2001	60000	Mississauga	12000
2	2002	75000	Toronto	13500

9.3

How to Delete Multiple Columns:

Here you will learn to delete few columns together.

In this example, we will delete column 'city' and 'Best_emp'.

```
In [49]: data.drop(['City', 'Best_emp'], axis=1)
Out[49]:
```

	Year	Sales	Mkt_exp
0	2000	50000	10000
1	2001	60000	12000
2	2002	75000	13500

9.4

How to Create an Empty Column in Python

Here, you keep in mind that we will not have any empty column in Python, if we import data from another format such as Excel; it is represented as NaN. However, if we create an empty column in Python, it will not be displayed as NaN.

```
In [5]: data['Emp'] = ' '

In [6]: data.head(3)
```

```
Out[6]:
```

	Year	Sales	City	Mkt_exp	Emp
0	2000	50000	Dryden	10000	
1	2001	60000	Mississauga	12000	
2	2002	75000	Toronto	13500	

Now we have created an empty column as ''.This implies that anything we enter in this column will be treated as text. So if you want to make an empty column which will need to be filled with numeric data, it is better to enter any number. For example, data ['Emp'] = 000.

9.5

Filtering

This section deals with retrieving specific information from a data set as per your requirements. Filtering is a blessing, I would say, especially when you deal with a large amount of data. Filtering will allow you to get what you actually want.

How to retrieve specific data based on a condition

In this example, we want to retrieve data with sales greater than $ 165000.

```
In [7]: data[data['Sales']>165000]
```

Out[7]:

	Year	Sales	City	Mkt_exp	Emp
7	2007	200000	Kitchener	20000	
8	2008	250000	Brantford	21200	
9	2009	249000	Ottawa	21000	
10	2010	251000	Oshawa	21100	

Remember the logic 'data[data['Sales']>165000. The code will look in the sales column for sales greater than $ 165000 and then display the information.

9.6

How to enter values in a particular Cell in Python

There are occasions that we need to make changes on particular text or number with in a cell/row. In this example, we want to change city Markham to Vaughan.

```
In [55]: city = data.City

In [56]: city.ix[6] = 'Vaughan'

In [57]: data.city=city
```

In the following data, you will notice the empty column Emp is being displayed with NaN, because we have filled the column with a single text. The same thing is applicable while doing with a number. You can fill with a single value of any digit.

```
In [13]: data['Emp'] = 'NaN'

In [58]: data
Out[58]:
```

	Year	Sales	City	Best_emp	Mkt_exp	Emp
0	2000	50000	Dryden	Brits	10000	NaN
1	2001	60000	Mississauga	Anne	12000	NaN
2	2002	75000	Toronto	Joa	13500	NaN
3	2003	100000	Kingston	Thomas	16000	NaN
4	2004	125000	North Bay	Cris	17000	NaN
5	2005	150000	Pickering	Joe	19000	NaN
6	2006	165000	Vaughan	Mat	19500	NaN

9.7

How to change a particular row of the data:

Here we want to make changes in row [0] by changing Best_emp, and Mkt_exp with new values.

```
In [70]: data.ix[0] = [2000, 50000, 'Dryden', 'Bob',10500]

In [71]: data
Out[71]:
```

	Year	Sales	City	Best_emp	Mkt_exp	Emp
0	2000	50000	Dryden	Bob	10500	NaN
1	2001	60000	Mississauga	Anne	12000	NaN

If you want to change the entire row value, you can do the same. You need not code NaN value, if any.

You can delete column Emp.

9.8

Creating New Variables Using IF Statements from Existing Variables

In this section, you will work with conditional statements such as **IF** statement and **Loop** statements such as **For**. You should not forget about indentation while performing such statements. If the indentation is not properly aligned even by a single space, you will get an error.

Then we can create categories of a continuous variable using IF statements in Python. You have to write a small program for this purpose.

Now we will create a new variable based on Sales using the following conditions:

9.8.1

Conditions:

Sales less than $ 99999 will be coded as '1'

Sales $ 100,000 – $ 149999 will be '2'

Sales $ 150000 and above will be 3

Here '1' implies Low Sales, '2' implies 'Medium sales', and '3' implies High Sales'

9.8.2

In order to do this, create an empty column after sales (position =2) as below:

```
In [76]: data.insert(2, 'Sales_cat', 'Nan', allow_duplicates=False)

In [77]: data
Out[77]:
```

	Year	Sales	Sales_cat	City	Best_emp	Mkt_exp
0	2000	50000	Nan	Dryden	Bob	10500
1	2001	60000	Nan	Mississauga	Anne	12000

Next you should write the following code:

```
In [79]: cat= data.Sales_cat

In [81]: sales = data.Sales
```

The above code assign column 'Sales_cat' as 'cat' and column 'Sales' as 'sales' for further proceedings will be easier and make the variable name shorter.

9.8.3

```
In [6]: j =0

In [7]: for i in sales:
   ...:      if i <=99999:
   ...:          cat.ix[j] = 1
   ...:      elif i>=100000 and i<=149999:
   ...:          cat.ix[j] = 2
   ...:      else:
   ...:          cat.ix[j] =3
   ...:      j=j+1
   ...: print 'job done'

In [85]: data
Out[85]:
```

	Year	Sales	Sales_cat	City	Best_emp	Mkt_exp
0	2000	50000	1	Dryden	Bob	10500
1	2001	60000	1	Mississauga	Anne	12000
2	2002	75000	1	Toronto	Joa	13500
3	2003	100000	2	Kingston	Thomas	16000
4	2004	125000	2	North Bay	Cris	17000
5	2005	150000	3	Pickering	Joe	19000

Note:

When we say 'For I in cat' it implies each and every row element/values with in the variable Sales.

Initially we assigned j = 0 which implies that its 0th row in Python. (in real, first row in the data).

'For' Loop statement automatically iterates with in a the column till the last element.

cat.ix[j] implies 0th row of column Sales_cat in the beginning.

When we say if i<=99999, the code will iterates with in Sales and check for such values. For example 50,000 is less than 99999, and therefore the code will assign 1 to row 0 of Sales_cat. Similarly it checks for all the conditions and assign the values we have already specified.

J = j+1 . At this stage, j will be equal to 1 [0+1] because J was 0 at the start. Similarly next time, j will be equal to 2 (1+1).

This program will run until j or row values are less than 11.

> **For i** implies each and every element or values with in a variable.
>
> Please do not forget to intend the codes properly.
>
> pl

9.9

Creating new variable based on existing variable using 'Recoding'

Recode Medium and High Sales to '2', and retain low sales '1' as it is in a new Column.

Step 1:

Create an empty row named 'Recode' to the data after Sales_cat.

```
In [93]: data.insert(3, 'Recode', 'NaN', allow_duplicates= False)
```

```
In [94]: data
Out[94]:
```

	Year	Sales	Sales_cat	Recode	City	Best_emp	Mkt_exp
0	2000	50000	1	NaN	Dryden	Bob	10500
1	2001	60000	1	NaN	Mississauga	Anne	12000
2	2002	75000	1	NaN	Toronto	Joa	13500
3	2003	100000	2	NaN	Kingston	Thomas	16000

Step 2:

Assign Column 'Sales_cat' to variable 'cat'.

```
In [95]: cat = data.Sales_cat
```

Step 3:

In a new variable 'recode', we perform recoding:

```
In [96]: recode = cat.replace([2, 3], 2)

In [97]: recode
Out[97]:
0    1
1    1
2    1
3    2
```

Step 4:

Appending recode to column 'Recode'. This implies that, we equate recode with Column Recode as shown below.

```
In [98]: data['Recode'] = recode
```

View the data:

```
In [99]: data
Out[99]:
```

	Year	Sales	Sales_cat	Recode	City	Best_emp	Mkt_exp
0	2000	50000	1	1	Dryden	Bob	10500
1	2001	60000	1	1	Mississauga	Anne	12000

9.10

Creating New Variable by Manipulating the Values of an Existing Variable

Use wxyz_ca.xlsx for the purpose

This section, you will learn how to create a new variable based on an existing variable. In marketing research and social science, and in all other related areas, this is an important task, when it comes to data analytics. And yes, Python helps us to do the same with much ease.

```
In [70]: data.head(3)
Out[70]:
```

	Year	Sales	City	Mkt_exp
0	2000	50000	Dryden	10000
1	2001	60000	Mississauga	12000
2	2002	75000	Toronto	13500

Here we are creating a new variable by making marketing expense (Mkt_exp) in percentage.

Step 1: assign the column Mkt_exp to a temporary container.

```
In [73]: mktexp = data.Mkt_exp
```

Step 2: find the total of marketing expense.

```
In [79]: sum(mktexp)
Out[79]: 190300.0
```

Perform the calculation for finding the percentage.

```
In [80]: cal = mktexp/190300.0*100.0
```

We have stored the calculation to a variable 'cal'. In step 2, we have found the sum of the column Mkt_exp. Then, we defined a formula as mktexp/190300*100. Now, when we execute the formula, it will divide each value in the column Mkt_exp and replace it with the result. The final output is being given below:

```
In [81]: data['Exp_percentage'] = cal
```

```
Out[82]:
```

	Year	Sales	City	Mkt_exp	Exp_percentage
0	2000	50000	Dryden	10000	5.254861
1	2001	60000	Mississauga	12000	6.305833
2	2002	75000	Toronto	13500	7.094062

Please note that when you enter numbers in Python, you need to enter with decimal. For e.g. If you want to enter 100, type it as 100.0. Otherwise, the output might not be properly displayed in certain cases.

9.11

Making a new data with selected variables from an existing data

This section is about making a new data set from an existing data set. Being researchers and business analysts, we tend to deal with huge amount of data with a large number of variables. Maybe for your study/analysis, you might not require all the variables that are available within a particular data set. For example, you might have a data set with 30 variables and for your analysis; you might need around 10 variables at this time. The presence of so many unwanted fields/variables could cause confusion or difficulty in dealing with data analysis for our study and at the same time, it's tough to handle. This particular section talks about how to get those variables from an existing data set and make it a new data set. Once we have exactly what we wanted, we could handle our analysis and data management with ease.

Load datanew.csv

	Stud_id	Gender	Gen	Dept	Attendance	Att_odr	Sem_marks	Name
0	M197	Female	0	Science	63	3	475	Ritu
1	M181	Male	1	Commerce	86	3	303	Victor
2	S137	Female	0	Commerce	79	3	587	Daven

9.11.1

Selecting Required Columns/Variables.

For this example, we need variables such as 'Stud_id', 'Gen', and 'Att_odr'. So we take out these variables from the data named datanew.csv, and make a new data.

```
In [36]: cols = ['Stud_id', 'Gen', 'Att_odr']

In [37]: d1= data[cols]

In [38]: d1.head(2)
Out[38]:
```

	Stud_id	Gen	Att_odr
0	M197	0	3
1	M181	1	3

9.11.2

Saving to Excel

```
In [39]: d1.to_csv('F:\d1.csv')
```

Similarly, you could extract specific variables from a data set with a large number of variables.With the extracted variables, yo could easily make a new data set and save the same. Then open the new data, for your further analysis. In this case, if you want to further analysis, you have to open **d1.csv**.

9.12

Merging two files:

We researchers often find hard to merge files and make it one data for our data analysis purpose.
WXYZ LTD has its business in Canada and India, and they have two different files having similar data. For further analysis, we merge these files.

Step 1:

In 'data' open wxyz_ca.xlsx

In 'data1' open wxyz_ind.xlsx

Step2: create a common variable named 'Region' with values Canada in data and India in **data1**.

```
In [123]: data.insert(0, 'Region', 'Canada', allow_duplicates = False)
```

```
In [124]: data
Out[124]:
```

	Region	Year	Sales	City	Mkt_exp
0	Canada	2000	50000	Dryden	10000
1	Canada	2001	60000	Mississauga	12000

```
In [125]: data1.insert(0, 'Region', 'India', allow_duplicates = False)
```

```
In [126]: data1
Out[126]:
```

	Region	Year	Sales	City	Mkt_exp
0	India	2000	75000	Banglore	5000
1	India	2001	100000	Trivandrum	10000

9.13

Merging Two Files: Top Bottom

```
In [2]: merged = pd.merge(data, data1, on=['Region',
   ...: 'Year', 'Sales', 'City', 'Mkt_exp'], how = 'outer')
```

```
In [128]: merged
Out[128]:
```

	Region	Year	Sales	City	Mkt_exp
0	Canada	2000	50000	Dryden	10000
1	Canada	2001	60000	Mississauga	12000
2	Canada	2002	75000	Toronto	13500
3	Canada	2003	100000	Kingston	16000
9	Canada	2009	249000	Ottawa	21000
10	Canada	2010	251000	Oshawa	21100
11	India	2000	75000	Banglore	5000

At this point, you can save the file.

9.14

Merging Side by side:

For this delete columns 'Region', City' and 'Mkt_exp; from 'data1' (refer previous chapters on how to delete multiple columns). Once you perform this step, you will get the following output:

```
In [138]: data1
Out[138]:
```

	Year	Sales
0	2000	75000
1	2001	100000
2	2002	150000

Here is the code for merging on left side:

```
In [141]: mergeL = pd.merge(data, data1, on=['Year'], how='left')

In [142]: mergeL
Out[142]:
```

	Region	Year	Sales_x	City	Mkt_exp	Sales_y
0	Canada	2000	50000	Dryden	10000	75000
1	Canada	2001	60000	Mississauga	12000	100000

9.15

Dummy Variables

Here we are making dummy variable on 'Region'. This is done on the merged data.

To proceed further, please import data we saved after merging based on top bottom.

```
In [128]: merged
Out[128]:
```

	Region	Year	Sales	City	Mkt_exp
0	Canada	2000	50000	Dryden	10000
1	Canada	2001	60000	Mississauga	12000
2	Canada	2002	75000	Toronto	13500
3	Canada	2003	100000	Kingston	16000
9	Canada	2009	249000	Ottawa	21000
10	Canada	2010	251000	Oshawa	21100
11	India	2000	75000	Banglore	5000

Making dummies and viewing the same:

```
In [148]: dummies = pd.get_dummies(merged['Region'])
```

```
In [149]: dummies
Out[149]:
```

	Canada	India
0	1	0
1	1	0
2	1	0
3	1	0.

Appending the dummies to the data

```
In [151]: merged = merged.join(dummies)
```

```
In [152]: merged
Out[152]:
```

	Region	Year	Sales	City	Mkt_exp	Canada	India
0	Canada	2000	50000	Dryden	10000	1	0
1	Canada	2001	60000	Mississauga	12000	1	0
2	Canada	2002	75000	Toronto	13500	1	0
11	India	2000	75000	Banglore	5000	0	1
12	India	2001	100000	Trivandrum	10000	0	1

9.16

Unique, Mapping & Merging

This section deals with few easy to use Python features, such as Unique and Mapping. We shall also transform data, and merge the same.

9.16.1

Unique

Here we shall learn a new function named 'Unique'. When applied, it will return unique characters/numbers, depends on the type of data.

Load torlib.xlsx.

```
In [6]: data = pd.read_excel('D:/torlib.xlsx', 'Sheet1')
```

You could view the data.

	Bcode	Book Name	Author	Publisher	Year
0	B101	Alice in Wonderland	Lewis Carrol	Macmillan	1865
1	B102	Beauty and the Beast	Jeanne	Buki Editions	1740
2	B103	Cinderella	Anne Anderson	Domain Books	2004
3	B104	Winter (The Lunar Chronicles)	Marissa Meyer	Feiwel and Friends	2015
4	B105	The Game of Logic	Lewis Carrol	Macmillan	1886
5	B106	Sapphire Blue (Precious stone trilogy)	Kerstin Gier	Henry Holt	2012
6	B105	Lion Heart	A.C.Gaughen	Bloomsburry	2015
7	B108	Shades of Earth	Beth Revis	Razorbill	2013
8	B109	The Fractured Light	Ammie Kaufman	Disney	2015
9	B110	Scarlett	Marissa Meyer	Feiwel and Friends	2013

Well, now we want to display the list of Authors from the data, we could easily display it by the Column 'Author'. However, a few names are repeating. 'Unique,' will help to get the unique names, which in turn implies you get the author names with no repetition.

Text data

Following shall illustrate the same:

```
In [8]: ub = data.Author.unique()
```
             ↓   ↓
        Column name   Function

Now, we shall type **ub** and press enter, you will get the result.

```
In [9]: ub
Out[9]:
array([u'Lewis Carrol', u'Jeanne', u'Anne Anderson', u'Marissa Meyer',
       u'Kerstin Gier', u'A.C.Gaughen ', u'Beth Revis', u'Ammie Kaufman'], dtype=object)
```

Well, In case you want in a row-column format, you need to convert the arrays using **data frame**. As you know, we will import 'pandas Data Frame' to convert arrays.

```
In [33]: from pandas import DataFrame
```

```
In [34]: nam = pd.DataFrame(ub)
```

Type **nam** and press enter; you will get the following result:

```
In [35]: nam
Out[35]:
```

	0
0	Lewis Carrol
1	Jeanne
2	Anne Anderson
3	Marissa Meyer
4	Kerstin Gier
5	A.C.Gaughen
6	Beth Revis
7	Ammie Kaufman

Now let us change the Column name from '0' to 'Author Name'.

```
In [36]: nam.columns =['Author Name']
```

```
In [37]: nam
Out[37]:
```

	Author Name
0	Lewis Carrol
1	Jeanne
2	Anne Anderson
3	Marissa Meyer
4	Kerstin Gier
5	A.C.Gaughen
6	Beth Revis
7	Ammie Kaufman

Numeric Data

Now we shall see the same, in a numerical data. Here we shall make use of column 'Year' from the data.

```
In [70]: u = data.Year.unique()
```

```
In [71]: u
Out[71]: array([ 1865.,   1740.,   2004.,   2015.,   1886.,   2012.,   2013.])
```

Converting to table format.

```
In [72]: ud = pd.DataFrame(u)
```

```
In [73]: ud
Out[73]:
```

	0
0	1865
1	1740
2	2004
3	2015
4	1886
5	2012
6	2013

You can give the column name as 'Year'.

```
In [74]: ud.columns = ['Year']
```

```
In [75]: ud
Out[75]:
```

	Year
0	1865
1	1740
2	2004
3	2015
4	1886
5	2012
6	2013

Giving column Names at the time of converting arrays to Data Frame

Let us take the above example of year.

```
In [27]: ud = pd.DataFrame(u, columns = ['Year'])
```

You can see that u is the temporary variable containing the data with the unique year (the result of unique() function). Moreover, we are giving column label at the time of converting arrays into a data frame.

```
In [28]: ud
Out[28]:
```

	Year
0	1865
1	1740
2	2004
3	2015
4	1886
5	2012
6	2013

9.16.2

Changing column title of multiple columns

This section illustrates how to change names of multiple columns of a data set.

Remember, we have imported data torlib.xlsx, in a temporary container 'data.'

Now if you type data and press enter, you could view the data. Let's view a part of the data.

```
In [56]: data.head(2)
Out[56]:
```

	Bcode	Book Name	Author	Publisher	Year
0	B101	Alice in Wonderland	Lewis Carrol	Macmillan	1865
1	B102	Beauty and the Beast	Jeanne	Buki Editions	1740

We shall change 'Book Name' to 'Title' and 'Publisher' to 'Publisher name'.

```
In [18]: data.rename(columns = {'Book Name': 'Title', 'Publisher': 'Publisher name'}, inplace=True)
```

Now let's view a part of the data.

```
In [64]: data.head(1)
```
Out[64]:

	Bcode	Title	Author	Publisher Name	Year
0	B101	Alice in Wonderland	Lewis Carrol	Macmillan	1865

9.17

Mapping

"A map is a type of fast key lookup data structure that offers a flexible means of indexing into its individual elements." This definition is from mathworks.com.

When we talk about map/mapping, the data will have two factors such as 'Key' and 'Value'. Values could be repeated, but the key will be unique, and each key will have its corresponding value.

Example 9.1

Let us examine torlib.xlsx. If you have not imported the data, please do import it. Now, we are showing you a part of the data

```
In [110]: data.head(3)
```
Out[110]:

	Bcode	Book Name	Author	Publisher	Year
0	B101	Alice in Wonderland	Lewis Carrol	Macmillan	1865
1	B102	Beauty and the Beast	Jeanne	Buki Editions	1740
2	B103	Cinderella	Anne Anderson	Domain Books	2004

In order to make you understand Key and Value, when it comes to mapping, let's make a new data out of the same.

Selecting columns 'Book Name' and 'Author'.

```
In [111]: c = ['Book Name', 'Author']
```

Making a new data.

```
In [112]: newdata = data[c]
```

Viewing the data.

```
In [114]: newdata
Out[114]:
```

	Book Name	Author
0	Alice in Wonderland	Lewis Carrol
1	Beauty and the Beast	Jeanne
2	Cinderella	Anne Anderson
3	Winter (The Lunar Chronicles)	Marissa Meyer
4	The Game of Logic	Lewis Carrol
5	Sapphire Blue (Precious stone trilogy)	Kerstin Gier
6	Lion Heart	A.C.Gaughen
7	Shades of Earth	Beth Revis
8	The Fractured Light	Ammie Kaufman
9	Scarlett	Marissa Meyer

In this example, Book name is the Key and Author is the corresponding value which in turn implies a dictionary. In a dictionary, there will not be repetition for 'Key'. A dictionary is like an array, with a key and a corresponding value or values. There could be multiple values for a Key, but cannot have multiple keys for a value.

An example on how to make a dictionary is as follows:

```
In [118]: abc = {'Salary':'2000$', 'Address':'Progress, Canada'}


In [119]: abc
Out[119]: {'Address': 'Progress, Canada', 'Salary': '2000$'}
```

This is a small example of dictionary. It will have curly brackets. Simultaneously, we could convert any given data to a dictionary, which we will see in coming sections.

Now we have made a new data with the key as 'Book name' and value as 'Author'.

Now we shall do a simple mapping.

First and foremost, let us separate the key column which is book name.

```
In [120]: col = newdata['Book Name']
```

Now we have the column book name, which will be used to map with 'Author'.

Now we shall convert the new data into arrays.

In order to make it into arrays, first and foremost, you need to import numpy,(import numpy as np) and then follow these steps.

```
In [121]: ara = np.array(newdata)
```

Viewing the arrays

```
In [122]: ara
Out[122]:
array([[u'Alice in Wonderland', u'Lewis Carrol'],
       [u'Beauty and the Beast', u'Jeanne'],
       [u'Cinderella', u'Anne Anderson'],
       [u'Winter (The Lunar Chronicles)', u'Marissa Meyer'],
       [u'The Game of Logic', u'Lewis Carrol'],
       [u'Sapphire Blue (Precious stone trilogy)', u'Kerstin Gier']
       [u'Lion Heart', u'A.C.Gaughen '],
       [u'Shades of Earth', u'Beth Revis'],
       [u'The Fractured Light', u'Ammie Kaufman'],
       [u'Scarlett', u'Marissa Meyer']], dtype=object)
```

Now we shall convert these arrays in to a dictionary

```
In [123]: d = dict(ara)
```

Viewing the dictionary

```
In [124]: d
Out[124]:
{u'Alice in Wonderland': u'Lewis Carrol',
 u'Beauty and the Beast': u'Jeanne',
 u'Cinderella': u'Anne Anderson',
 u'Lion Heart': u'A.C.Gaughen ',
 u'Sapphire Blue (Precious stone trilogy)': u'Kerstin Gier',
 u'Scarlett': u'Marissa Meyer',
 u'Shades of Earth': u'Beth Revis',
 u'The Fractured Light': u'Ammie Kaufman',
 u'The Game of Logic': u'Lewis Carrol',
 u'Winter (The Lunar Chronicles)': u'Marissa Meyer'}
```

Now let us map the key, which is the Column 'book name' with a dictionary so that it will match its corresponding value. In this example, it is the Author names.

```
In [130]: result = col.map(d)
```

Now we shall see the mapped result.

```
In [131]: result
Out[131]:
0       Lewis Carrol
1             Jeanne
2      Anne Anderson
3      Marissa Meyer
4       Lewis Carrol
5        Kerstin Gier
6        A.C.Gaughen
7         Beth Revis
8      Ammie Kaufman
9      Marissa Meyer
Name: Book Name, dtype: object
```

Now let us analyse the mapped result with our data, key and value.

KEY

```
In [134]: col
Out[134]:
0                        Alice in Wonderland
1                     Beauty and the Beast
2                                 Cinderella
3                  Winter (The Lunar Chronicles)
4                            The Game of Logic
5        Sapphire Blue (Precious stone trilogy)
6                                 Lion Heart
7                             Shades of Earth
8                         The Fractured Light
9                                   Scarlett
Name: Book Name, dtype: object
```

Location in the Column

VALUE

```
In [133]: result
Out[133]:
0        Lewis Carrol
1              Jeanne
2      Anne Anderson
3      Marissa Meyer
4        Lewis Carrol
5        Kerstin Gier
6        A.C.Gaughen
7          Beth Revis
8      Ammie Kaufman
9      Marissa Meyer
Name: Book Name, dtype: object
```

Mapped based on Key and location of Key

	Book Name	Author
0	Alice in Wonderland	Lewis Carrol
1	Beauty and the Beast	Jeanne
2	Cinderella	Anne Anderson
3	Winter (The Lunar Chronicles)	Marissa Meyer
4	The Game of Logic	Lewis Carrol
5	Sapphire Blue (Precious stone trilogy)	Kerstin Gier
6	Lion Heart	A.C.Gaughen
7	Shades of Earth	Beth Revis
8	The Fractured Light	Ammie Kaufman
9	Scarlett	Marissa Meyer

Exhibit 9.1 Mapped output

In the output above, we have mapped Value (Author name) with Key (Book Name) and along with its location, For example, we have at the 3rd location; book 'Winter' written by 'Marissa Meyer'. This is a case of simple mapping.

Example 9.2

The beauty of Mapping:

Suppose, you have a large data with text and its corresponding values, where, you have so much of repetition in the text, but corresponding values are different. Probably, there are only 40 texts, but because of its repetition, it is 100, but with different values. The beauty of mapping lies here. Let us consider data torlib.xlsx. Remember, in the previous example, we have made Book Name as Key and Author as value. In this case, we shall make Author as Key and Book Name as Value.

Let us consider the new data set we made from torlib.xlsx. If you have not created, please do follow the steps and continue the rest.

Creating new data

```
In [145]: newdata = data[newc]
```

```
In [122]: newdata
Out[122]:
```

	Book Name	Author
0	Alice in Wonderland	Lewis Carrol
1	Beauty and the Beast	Jeanne
2	Cinderella	Anne Anderson
3	Winter (The Lunar Chronicles)	Marissa Meyer
4	The Game of Logic	Lewis Carrol
5	Sapphire Blue (Precious stone trilogy)	Kerstin Gier
6	Lion Heart	A.C.Gaughen
7	Shades of Earth	Beth Revis
8	The Fractured Light	Ammie Kaufman
9	Scarlett	Marissa Meyer

Here, we have Key as Author and Value as Book Name. The shaded areas are of those authors whose names are repeated. Accordingly, we have Lewis Carrol and Marissa Meyer, but with different books. Also, remember, there should not be any repetition in the Key whereas, in the example, we do have such repetitions.

Here we need author names without repetitions, but, it should have all their works. We shall make the Key as a separate column using the technique Unique.

```
In [147]: u = newdata.Author.unique()
```

Now let's view the result by typing **u** and pressing enter.

```
In [148]: u
Out[148]:
array([u'Lewis Carrol', u'Jeanne', u'Anne Anderson', u'Marissa Meyer',
       u'Kerstin Gier', u'A.C.Gaughen ', u'Beth Revis', u'Ammie Kaufman'], dtype=object)
```

The output is an array. Let us make it into a table format. In order to do that, first, we need to import pandas Data Frame.

```
In [10]: from pandas import DataFrame
```

```
In [11]: utab = pd.DataFrame(u, columns = ['Authors'])

In [12]: utab
Out[12]:
```

	Authors
0	Lewis Carrol
1	Jeanne
2	Anne Anderson
3	Marissa Meyer
4	Kerstin Gier
5	A.C.Gaughen
6	Beth Revis
7	Ammie Kaufman

Now we have the author names without any repetition. The ultimate aim is to map author names (key) with book name (value).

Now, we need to make a dictionary. To do this, first, let us convert the newdata into arrays.

```
In [14]: ara = np.array(newdata)

In [128]: ara
Out[128]:
array([[u'Alice in Wonderland', u'Lewis Carrol'],
       [u'Beauty and the Beast', u'Jeanne'],
       [u'Cinderella', u'Anne Anderson'],
       [u'Winter (The Lunar Chronicles)', u'Marissa Meyer'],
       [u'The Game of Logic', u'Lewis Carrol'],
       [u'Sapphire Blue (Precious stone trilogy)', u'Kerstin Gier'],
       [u'Lion Heart', u'A.C.Gaughen '],
       [u'Shades of Earth', u'Beth Revis'],
       [u'The Fractured Light', u'Ammie Kaufman'],
       [u'Scarlett', u'Marissa Meyer']], dtype=object)
```

When we make a dictionary, remember that it will not allow any repetition in the 'Key' and the corresponding value of repeated key. In other words, we will miss, one of the repeated records. For example, we have Lewis Carrol, for Alice in Wonderland and the game of logic. When we make a dictionary, we will lose one of those. The following will illustrate it:

```
In [16]: dict(ara)
Out[16]:
{u'A.C.Gaughen ': u'Lion Heart',
 u'Ammie Kaufman': u'The Fractured Light',
 u'Anne Anderson': u'Cinderella',
 u'Beth Revis': u'Shades of Earth',
 u'Jeanne': u'Beauty and the Beast',
 u'Kerstin Gier': u'Sapphire Blue (Precious stone trilogy)'
 u'Lewis Carrol': u'The Game of Logic',
 u'Marissa Meyer': u'Scarlett'}
```

Here you can notice, you have missed a few repeated records. Under these circumstances, we will do a coding, which will help us to get all the records, even if it is repeating, into the dictionary.

```
In [17]: from collections import defaultdict
```

Before proceeding further, we shall store the result of **dict(ara)**, which is the dictionary into a temporary variable named **dct**.

```
In [18]: dct = dict(ara)
```

If you type **dct** and press enter, you will get the output as you have already seen for dict(ara).

Now we shall write the code to iterate within the dictionary and group repeated items and make a new dictionary out of it.

```
In [133]: newdict = defaultdict(list)
```

Temporary variable **newdict** implies the new dictionary.

```
In [134]: for key, value in sorted(dct.iteritems()): newdict[value].append(key)
```

Let us view the output.

```
In [135]: newdict
Out[135]: defaultdict(<type 'list'>, {u'Anne Anderson': [u'Cinderella'], u'Ammie Kaufman': [u'The Fractured Light'], u'A.C.Gaughen ': [u'Lion
Heart'], u'Beth Revis': [u'Shades of Earth'], u'Kerstin Gier': [u'Sapphire Blue (Precious stone trilogy)'], u'Marissa Meyer': [u'Scarlett',
u'Winter (The Lunar Chronicles)'], u'Lewis Carrol': [u'Alice in Wonderland', u'The Game of Logic'], u'Jeanne': [u'Beauty and the Beast']})
```

Now we have a new dictionary with repeated items are being grouped accordingly. For example, we have Author Marissa Meyer with two books, namely Scarlett and Winter.

In the above code (for key, value), the key is Author and Value is Book names. The code will sort the data and group the items, and we will get the following output.

Now, we shall see the beauty of mapping.

Remember, we have already saved unique author names in a temporary variable named utab. We shall view the same before we proceed further.

```
In [137]: utab
Out[137]:
```

	Authors
0	Lewis Carrol
1	Jeanne
2	Anne Anderson
3	Marissa Meyer
4	Kerstin Gier
5	A.C.Gaughen
6	Beth Revis
7	Ammie Kaufman

The following code will return the Mapped data.

```
In [144]: mdata = utab.Authors.map(newdict)
```

Now, we are performing mapping in a temporary variable named **mdata**.

Utab.Authors implies column in the **Utab**, as shown above, and we are mapping the same with that of new dictionary, which is stored in **newdict**.

```
In [145]: mdata
Out[145]:
0      [Alice in Wonderland, The Game of Logic]
1                       [Beauty and the Beast]
2                                  [Cinderella]
3      [Scarlett, Winter (The Lunar Chronicles)]
4      [Sapphire Blue (Precious stone trilogy)]
5                                  [Lion Heart]
6                             [Shades of Earth]
7                          [The Fractured Light]
```

Here, we list of books mapped with the row location of respective author. Let us view it in table format.

```
In [152]: tabdata = pd.DataFrame(mdata, columns = ['Book Name'])
```

Displaying the output.

```
In [153]: tabdata
Out[153]:
```

	Book Name
0	[Alice in Wonderland, The Game of Logic]
1	[Beauty and the Beast]
2	[Cinderella]
3	[Scarlett, Winter (The Lunar Chronicles)]
4	[Sapphire Blue (Precious stone trilogy)]
5	[Lion Heart]
6	[Shades of Earth]
7	[The Fractured Light]

Now, let us analyze mapping in detail along with the outputs.

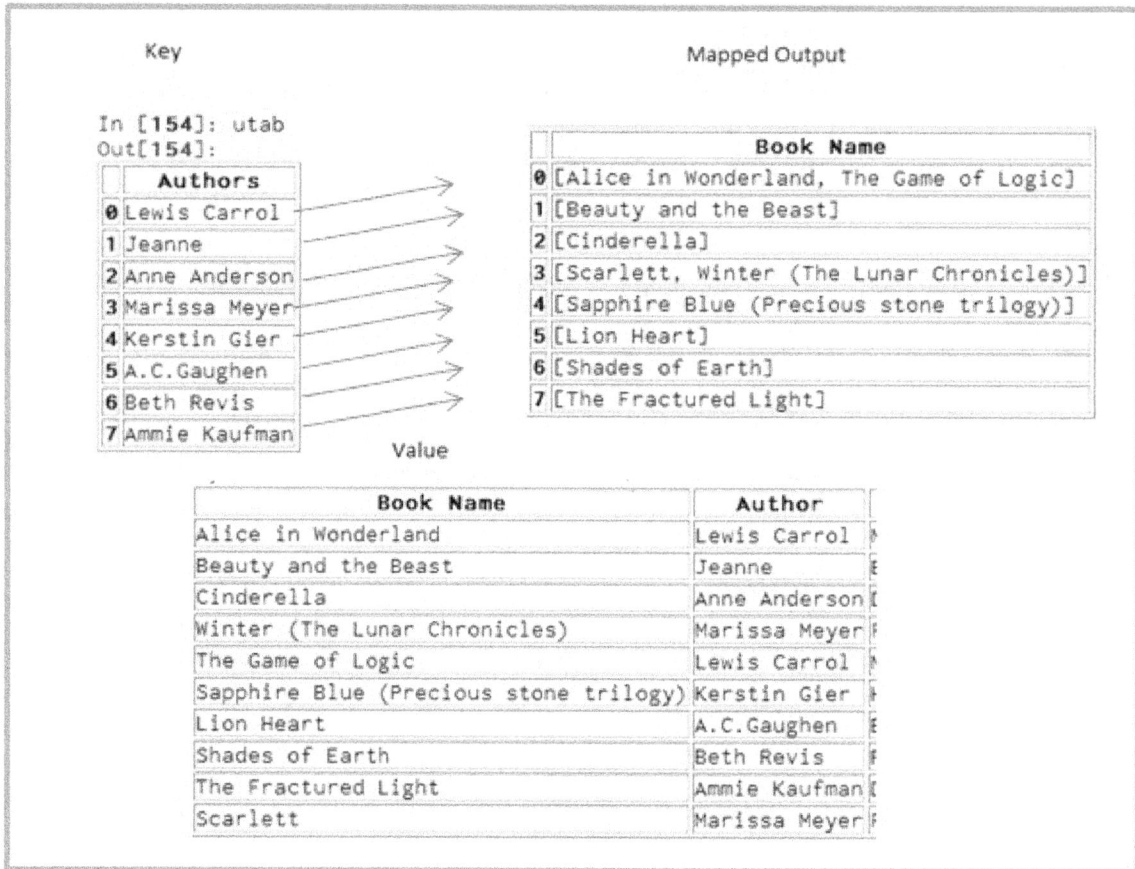

| Key | Mapped Output |

```
In [154]: utab
Out[154]:
```

	Authors
0	Lewis Carrol
1	Jeanne
2	Anne Anderson
3	Marissa Meyer
4	Kerstin Gier
5	A.C.Gaughen
6	Beth Revis
7	Ammie Kaufman

	Book Name
0	[Alice in Wonderland, The Game of Logic]
1	[Beauty and the Beast]
2	[Cinderella]
3	[Scarlett, Winter (The Lunar Chronicles)]
4	[Sapphire Blue (Precious stone trilogy)]
5	[Lion Heart]
6	[Shades of Earth]
7	[The Fractured Light]

Value

Book Name	Author	
Alice in Wonderland	Lewis Carrol	
Beauty and the Beast	Jeanne	
Cinderella	Anne Anderson	
Winter (The Lunar Chronicles)	Marissa Meyer	
The Game of Logic	Lewis Carrol	
Sapphire Blue (Precious stone trilogy)	Kerstin Gier	
Lion Heart	A.C.Gaughen	
Shades of Earth	Beth Revis	
The Fractured Light	Ammie Kaufman	
Scarlett	Marissa Meyer	

Exhibit 9.2 beauty of mapping

The above is the mapped output along with key and values. Accordingly, we have at '0' location, Author Lewis Carrol with two books and so on.

The following figure explains how the aforementioned mapping took place.

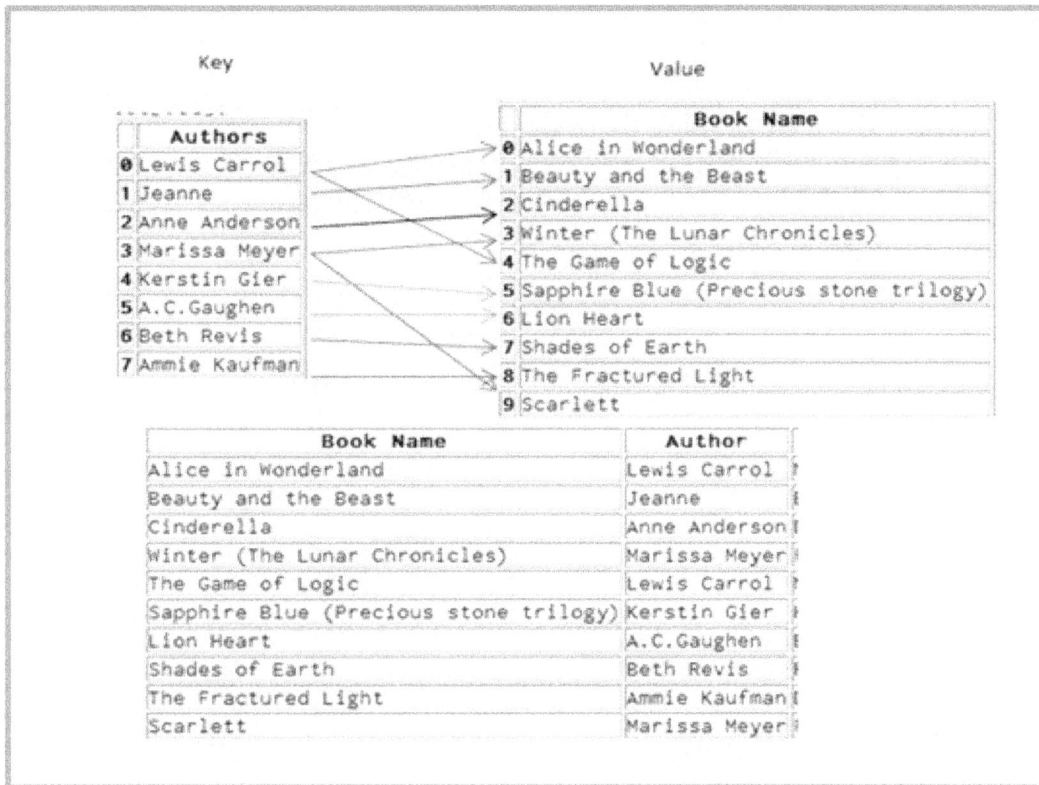

Exhibit 9.3 Mapping

We have given the original data so that you could verify the output.

This is the beauty of Mapping, where, you can get the data in a very meaningful manner, at a glance. For example, let us view the final output here:

Exhibit 9.4 mapped output

While looking at the output, and comparing with the Authors, we could get at a glance that, '0' refers to Lewis Carrol with two books named 'Alice in Wonderland' and 'The game of logic.'

Similarly, we have at location 3, two books, Scarlett, and Winter, which corresponds to Marissa Meyer. Guess that makes our life easier, especially when you deal with huge amount of data!!

Example 9.3

To proceed further, please import data **worldcup.xlsx**. Please import pandas (if you haven't already) before proceeding with the following code:

```
In [101]: data = pd.read_excel('D:/worldcup.xlsx', 'Sheet1')
```

Displaying the data

```
In [102]: data
Out[102]:
```

	Year	Team
0	1975	West Indies
1	1979	West Indies
2	1983	India
3	1987	Australia
4	1992	Pakistan
5	1996	Srilanka
6	1999	Australia
7	2003	Australia
8	2007	Australia
9	2011	India
10	2015	Australia

Here, we have the key as Team and value as Year.

Now we shall pull out unique team.

```
In [103]: un = data.Team.unique()
```

```
In [104]: un
Out[104]: array([u'West Indies ', u'India', u'Australia', u'Pakistan', u'Srilanka'], dtype=object)
```

Let us make the arrays more beautiful by converting to data frame

```
In [105]: from pandas import DataFrame
```

```
In [106]: unq = pd.DataFrame(un, columns = ['Teams'])
```

```
In [107]: unq
Out[107]:
```

	Teams
0	West Indies
1	India
2	Australia
3	Pakistan
4	Srilanka

Converting the entire data into arrays, so that we could make a dictionary.

Before proceeding further, please import **numpy** as **np**

```
In [108]: ara = np.array(data)
```

```
In [109]: ara
Out[109]:
array([[1975.0, u'West Indies '],
       [1979.0, u'West Indies '],
       [1983.0, u'India'],
       [1987.0, u'Australia'],
       [1992.0, u'Pakistan'],
       [1996.0, u'Srilanka'],
       [1999.0, u'Australia'],
       [2003.0, u'Australia'],
       [2007.0, u'Australia'],
       [2011.0, u'India'],
       [2015.0, u'Australia']], dtype=object)
```

Making a dictionary:

```
In [110]: dct = dict(ara)
```

```
In [111]: dct
Out[111]:
{1975.0: u'West Indies ',
 1979.0: u'West Indies ',
 1983.0: u'India',
 1987.0: u'Australia',
 1992.0: u'Pakistan',
 1996.0: u'Srilanka',
 1999.0: u'Australia',
 2003.0: u'Australia',
 2007.0: u'Australia',
 2011.0: u'India',
 2015.0: u'Australia'}
```

Now we shall write the codes to make a new dictionary out of it.

```
In [112]: from collections import defaultdict
```

```
In [113]: newd = defaultdict(list)
```

```
In [115]: for key, value in sorted(dct.iteritems()): newd[value].append(key)
```

Now we shall view the new dictionary:

```
In [116]: newd
Out[116]: defaultdict(<type 'list'>, {u'Pakistan': [1992.0], u'Australia': [1987.0, 1999.0, 2003.0, 2007.0, 2015.0], u'India': [1983.0,
2011.0], u'West Indies ': [1975.0, 1979.0], u'Srilanka': [1996.0]})
```

Now let us map it

```
In [117]: mdata = unq.Teams.map(newd)
```

Where **unq** is the unique team name, which we have done at the beginning of this exercise, **newd** is the new dictionary and using map function, we have mapped it. Now let us view the mapped output:

```
In [118]: mdata
Out[118]:
0                              [1975.0, 1979.0]
1                              [1983.0, 2011.0]
2    [1987.0, 1999.0, 2003.0, 2007.0, 2015.0]
3                                      [1992.0]
4                                      [1996.0]
Name: Teams, dtype: object
```

Converting the mapped data to table format.

```
In [119]: tab = pd.DataFrame(mdata, columns = ['Year of Win'])
```

Displaying the data:

```
In [120]: tab
Out[120]:
```

	Year of Win
0	[1975.0, 1979.0]
1	[1983.0, 2011.0]
2	[1987.0, 1999.0, 2003.0, 2007.0, 2015.0]
3	[1992.0]
4	[1996.0]

Now let us examine the output:

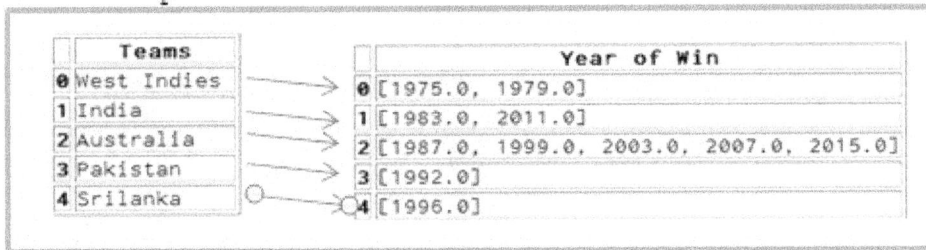

	Teams			Year of Win
0	West Indies	→	0	[1975.0, 1979.0]
1	India	→	1	[1983.0, 2011.0]
2	Australia	→	2	[1987.0, 1999.0, 2003.0, 2007.0, 2015.0]
3	Pakistan	→	3	[1992.0]
4	Srilanka	○→○	4	[1996.0]

Exhibit 9.4 Mapped output

In the figure, we have at location/row 2, Australia winning world cups in the year 1987, 1999, 2003, 2007 and 2015. Similarly at row 1, we have year 1983 and 2011 and corresponds to India which is again at row 1.

Merging (side by side)

We could also make a new data out of mapped output and unique author names by merging. To merge (side- by-side), we shall create a common variable named 'No of Wins'. To create 'no of wins', we need to know the total number of time each team has won. In case the data is too big, you need to make a pivot table, which will fetch you the sum/count, depending on your requirements. In this example, we will use count. You could download the pivot table from our blog. It has teams and number of time each team has won the cup.

```
In [65]: newp
Out[65]:
```

	Team
Team	
Australia	5
India	2
Pakistan	1
Srilanka	1
West Indies	2

Remember, we have our mapped output stored in tab and unique team names in **unq**.

```
In [130]: colvalues = [2, 2, 5, 1, 1]
```

Here we have defined a temporary container with 'no of wins'. However, the order of which the number was given is not according to the pivot tables. Instead, it is by unique team names, and you could display the same by typing unq and then press enter.

	Teams
0	West Indies
1	India
2	Australia
3	Pakistan
4	Srilanka

When we compare colvalues and unq data, we have at row 0, West Indies. According to the pivot table, West Indies have won twice, so we put 2 as corresponding value and so on. Since the data is very small, you could even count it manually and add the same. Here, we make use of pivot table to make you understand that it will be very much useful when you deal with similar exercises, especially when a large amount of data is being involved.

Now we shall create a column named 'No of Wins' and equate the values by the following code.

First, we shall add the column with values in unq data, which is the unique team name.

```
In [131]: unq['No of Wins'] = colvalues
```

```
In [132]: unq
Out[132]:
```

	Teams	No of Wins
0	West Indies	2
1	India	2
2	Australia	5
3	Pakistan	1
4	Srilanka	1

Similarly, let us add the same column with values in the mapped output, which is **tab**.

```
In [135]: tab['No of Wins'] = colvalues
```

```
In [136]: tab
Out[136]:
```

	Year of Win	No of Wins
0	[1975.0, 1979.0]	2
1	[1983.0, 2011.0]	2
2	[1987.0, 1999.0, 2003.0, 2007.0, 2015.0]	5
3	[1992.0]	1
4	[1996.0]	1

Now, we have added a common variable in both data sets. It is time to Merge and make a new data set. Well, in the output, we want Team names, followed by number of wins and year.

```
In [158]: merg = pd.merge(unq, tab, on = 'No of Wins', left_index = True, right_index = True)
```

Left side of the table   Right side of the table

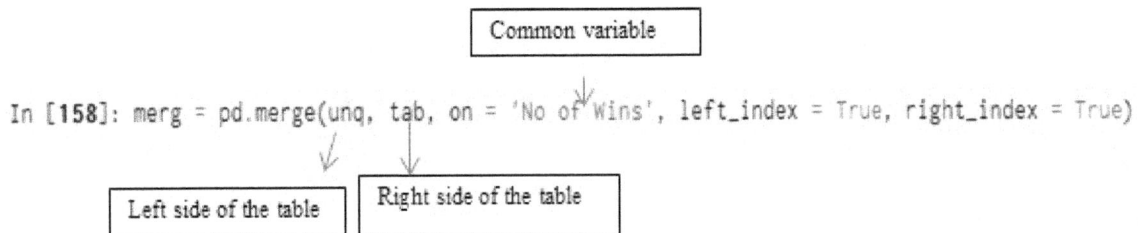

As explained, we have merged both data sets based on the column 'No. of Wins'. In code, left index and right index implies index of the 'unq' data and 'tab' respectively.

Let us view the output:

```
In [159]: merg
Out[159]:
```

	Teams	No of Wins	Year of Win
0	West Indies	2	[1975.0, 1979.0]
1	India	2	[1983.0, 2011.0]
2	Australia	5	[1987.0, 1999.0, 2003.0, 2007.0, 2015.0]
3	Pakistan	1	[1992.0]
4	Srilanka	1	[1996.0]

At this point, we have an entirely brand new data set. You could save it.

```
In [161]: merg.to_csv('D:/brandnewdata.csv')
```

Example 9.4

To proceed further, please load data **sports.xlsx**.

```
In [1]: import pandas as pd

In [2]: import numpy as np

In [3]: data = pd.read_excel('D:/sports.xlsx', 'Sheet1')
```

```
In [4]: data
Out[4]:
```

	Sports	Player
0	Cricket	Sachin Tendulkar
1	Soccer	Christiano Ronaldo
2	Cricket	Adam GilChrist
3	Tennis	Roger Federer
4	Soccer	Lionel Messi
5	Tennis	Maria Sharapova
6	Cricket	Ab Deviliers
7	Tennis	Sania Mirza

While you make a dictionary, please note that the columns with repetition of records/values/text, you should make it to the extreme right of the table. This is because, if it is on the left, and when you make a dictionary, it will check on data redundancy and you will lose the data. We shall illustrate the same here. In the data, we have column sports, which have cricket, soccer, and tennis, and it keeps repeating. Now let us make a dictionary and see the output.

In order to make a dictionary, first we have converted the data in to arrays.

```
In [5]: a = np.array(data)

In [7]: a
Out[7]:
array([[u'Cricket', u'Sachin Tendulkar'],
       [u'Soccer', u'Christiano Ronaldo'],
       [u'Cricket', u'Adam GilChrist'],
       [u'Tennis', u'Roger Federer'],
       [u'Soccer', u'Lionel Messi'],
       [u'Tennis', u'Maria Sharapova'],
       [u'Cricket', u'Ab Deviliers'],
       [u'Tennis', u'Sania Mirza']], dtype=object)

In [6]: dict(a)
Out[6]:
{u'Cricket': u'Ab Deviliers',
 u'Soccer': u'Lionel Messi',
 u'Tennis': u'Sania Mirza'}
```

You could verify the above result that, we have only 3 records and remaining records, which are being repeated irrespective of its values, have been omitted. To cater our need and preserve the entire data, we shall re-arrange our columns and then proceed for mapping.

```
In [8]: col = ['Player', 'Sports']

In [9]: newdata = data[col]
```

Let us view the re-arranged data.

```
In [10]: newdata
Out[10]:
```

	Player	Sports
0	Sachin Tendulkar	Cricket
1	Christiano Ronaldo	Soccer
2	Adam GilChrist	Cricket
3	Roger Federer	Tennis
4	Lionel Messi	Soccer
5	Maria Sharapova	Tennis
6	Ab Deviliers	Cricket
7	Sania Mirza	Tennis

Now we shall Convert new data to arrays.

```
In [11]: ara = np.array(newdata)

In [12]: ara
Out[12]:
array([[u'Sachin Tendulkar', u'Cricket'],
       [u'Christiano Ronaldo', u'Soccer'],
       [u'Adam GilChrist', u'Cricket'],
       [u'Roger Federer', u'Tennis'],
       [u'Lionel Messi', u'Soccer'],
       [u'Maria Sharapova', u'Tennis'],
       [u'Ab Deviliers', u'Cricket'],
       [u'Sania Mirza', u'Tennis']], dtype=object)
```

Now we shall make a dictionary.

```
In [14]: dct
Out[14]:
{u'Ab Deviliers': u'Cricket',
 u'Adam GilChrist': u'Cricket',
 u'Christiano Ronaldo': u'Soccer',
 u'Lionel Messi': u'Soccer',
 u'Maria Sharapova': u'Tennis',
 u'Roger Federer': u'Tennis',
 u'Sachin Tendulkar': u'Cricket',
 u'Sania Mirza': u'Tennis'}
```

Now you can notice that we have the entire data set; we shall make a new dictionary by grouping the repeating items.

```
In [15]: from collections import defaultdict

In [16]: newdct = defaultdict(list)

In [17]: for key, value in sorted(dct.iteritems()):newdct[value].append(key)

In [18]: newdct
Out[18]: defaultdict(<type 'list'>, {u'Cricket': [u'Ab [
u'Lionel Messi'], u'Tennis': [u'Maria Sharapova', u'Roge
```

A part of data has been shown above.

Let us get unique sports names.

```
In [19]: u = newdata.Sports.unique()

In [20]: u
Out[20]: array([u'Cricket', u'Soccer', u'Tennis'], dtype=object)
```

Let us convert arrays in to data frame.

```
In [21]: from pandas import DataFrame

In [21]: from pandas import DataFrame

In [22]: df = pd.DataFrame(u,columns = ['Sports'])
```

```
In [23]: df
Out[23]:
    Sports
0   Cricket
1   Soccer
2   Tennis
```

Now let us get the mapped output by mapping **df** and **newdict**.

```
In [24]: moutput = df.Sports.map(newdct)

In [25]: moutput
Out[25]:
0      [Ab Deviliers, Adam GilChrist, Sachin Tendulkar]
1                    [Christiano Ronaldo, Lionel Messi]
2          [Maria Sharapova, Roger Federer, Sania Mirza]
Name: Sports, dtype: object
```

Now we shall convert 'moutput' to a dataframe. Since we have already imported data frame, you need not import it again.

```
In [26]: noutput = pd.DataFrame(moutput, columns = ['Player Names'])

In [27]: noutput
Out[27]:
```

	Player Names
0	[Ab Deviliers, Adam GilChrist, Sachin Tendulkar]
1	[Christiano Ronaldo, Lionel Messi]
2	[Maria Sharapova, Roger Federer, Sania Mirza]

	Sports
0	Cricket
1	Soccer
2	Tennis

	Player Names
0	[Ab Deviliers, Adam GilChrist, Sachin Tendulkar]
1	[Christiano Ronaldo, Lionel Messi]
2	[Maria Sharapova, Roger Federer, Sania Mirza]

Exhibit 9.5 Mapped output

In the output, we have at row 1, Soccer in the Sports Column and corresponding values at row 1 in the mapped output is 'Christiano and Messi'. Similarly, at 0, you have Cricket and corresponding values/players at row 0 are 'Devilliers, Gilchrist, and Sachin'.

CHAPTER 10
Data Analysis

In this chapter, we demonstrate how to apply various data analysis tools using Python and generate the outputs. This session deals with both parametric and non-parametric tests. Python has emerged as an effective data analysis platform for meaningfully analyse data with high accuracy that we get from popular data analysis packages available in the market while enjoying the benefits of open source programming. Data analysis has become an integral part of the modern world with the introduction of data mining and text mining tools. Professionals in this field expect that Python with many of its advantages, including its open source nature, convenience and easy adaptability, is going to take a lead in the analytics world.

10.1

Pivot Tables:

Pivot table helps to get a better understanding of our data. To be more precise, pivot tables will allow us to summarize our data, which will, in turn, make analysis easy. This section will help you to make a pivot table in Python.

The following code will make a pivot table that explains number of students across each department. Use stud_clean.csv.

```
In [153]: pivot = data.pivot_table('Gender', rows = ['Dept'],cols = None, aggfunc = 'count', fill_value=0)
```

```
In [154]: pivot
Out[154]:
Dept
Arts         28
Commerce     48
Science      20
Name: Gender, dtype: int64
```

If you want to save the pivot table, and then do the following:

```
In [155]: pivot.to_csv('F:\pivot.csv')
```

Here, we want to make a pivot table of average semester marks for each department.

```
In [6]: pivot1 = data.pivot_table('Sem_marks', rows = ['Dept'],
    ...: cols = None, aggfunc ='mean', fill_value = 0)

In [161]: pivot1
Out[161]:
Dept
Arts        387.571429
Commerce    376.958333
Science     449.950000
Name: Sem_marks, dtype: float64
```

In the above code 'aggfunc', you can give any function depending on your need. Here we have given 'count' in the first case, and 'mean' in the second case. You could also give 'sum' or related functions depending on your needs.

10.2

Cross Tabulation

To be plain and simple, Cross tabulation is used to classify the data on various criteria in order to give meaningful insight from our data.

Cross tabulating 'Department' and 'Gender'.

```
In [175]: tab = pd.crosstab(data.Gender, data.Dept, margins = True)

In [176]: tab
Out[176]:
```

Dept	Arts	Commerce	Science	All
Gender				
Female	17	27	9	53
Male	11	21	11	43
All	28	48	20	96

To avoid margin total, you need to keep 'margins = False'. It is being demonstrated in the following:

```
In [49]: tab = pd.crosstab(data.Gender, data.Dept, margins = False)

In [50]: tab
Out[50]:
```

Dept	Arts	Commerce	Science
Gender			
Female	17	27	9
Male	11	21	11

10.3

This section deals with both parametric and Non-Parametric tests with the help of Python.

10.3.1

Linear Regression:

Fist we can treat semester marks as dependent variable and attendance as independent variable. Now we can proceed with the following codes. Please use **stud_clean.csv**.

```
In [246]: import scipy.stats as stats

In [247]: import statsmodels.api as sm

In [248]: import numpy as np

In [249]: import matplotlib.pyplot as plt

In [250]: x = data.Attendance

In [251]: y = data.Sem_marks

In [252]: X = sm.add_constant(x, prepend = True)

In [253]: results = sm.OLS(y, x).fit()
```

```
In [254]: print results.summary()
                          OLS Regression Results
==============================================================================
Dep. Variable:            Sem_marks    R-squared:                       0.872
Model:                          OLS    Adj. R-squared:                  0.870
Method:               Least Squares    F-statistic:                     645.0
Date:              Tue, 13 May 2014    Prob (F-statistic):           3.93e-44
Time:                      18:18:00    Log-Likelihood:                -615.27
No. Observations:                96    AIC:                             1233.
Df Residuals:                    95    BIC:                             1235.
Df Model:                         1
==============================================================================
                 coef    std err          t      P>|t|      [95.0% Conf. Int.]
------------------------------------------------------------------------------
Attendance     5.3309      0.210     25.397      0.000       4.914      5.748
==============================================================================
Omnibus:                      0.722    Durbin-Watson:                   1.785
Prob(Omnibus):                0.697    Jarque-Bera (JB):                0.800
Skew:                        -0.071    Prob(JB):                        0.670
Kurtosis:                     2.576    Cond. No.                        1.00
==============================================================================
```

Exhibit 10.1 Linear Regression

```
In [255]: intercept, slope = results.params
```

```
In [263]: intercept, slope
Out[263]: (397.3583685339525, -0.030137219989472774)
```

The above example doesn't show any significant relation among the predictor and predicted variables

10.3.2

Regression: another example

Open data wxyz_ca.xlsx and do the following:

```
In [6]: import scipy.stats as stats

In [7]: import statsmodels.api as sm

In [8]: import matplotlib.pyplot as plt

In [40]: from pandas.stats.api import ols

In [9]: x = data.Mkt_exp

In [10]: y=data.Sales


In [11]: X= sm.add_constant(x, prepend=True)

In [12]: results =  sm.OLS(y, X).fit()
```

```
In [13]: print results.summary()
                            OLS Regression Results
==============================================================================
Dep. Variable:                  Sales   R-squared:                       0.889
Model:                            OLS   Adj. R-squared:                  0.877
Method:                 Least Squares   F-statistic:                     72.04
Date:                Wed, 14 May 2014   Prob (F-statistic):           1.38e-05
Time:                        14:51:59   Log-Likelihood:                -126.79
No. Observations:                  11   AIC:                             257.6
Df Residuals:                       9   BIC:                             258.4
Df Model:                           1
==============================================================================
                 coef    std err          t      P>|t|      [95.0% Conf. Int.]
------------------------------------------------------------------------------
const        -1.664e+05   3.84e+04     -4.330      0.002   -2.53e+05  -7.95e+04
Mkt_exp        18.4188      2.170      8.488      0.000      13.510     23.328
==============================================================================
Omnibus:                        4.247   Durbin-Watson:                   0.452
Prob(Omnibus):                  0.120   Jarque-Bera (JB):                1.157
Skew:                           0.032   Prob(JB):                        0.561
Kurtosis:                       1.413   Cond. No.                     8.32e+04
==============================================================================
```

Exhibit 10.2 Linear Regression

Drawing the scatter plot and fitting the regression line:

Drawing the scatter plot

```
In [19]: plt.scatter(x, y)
```

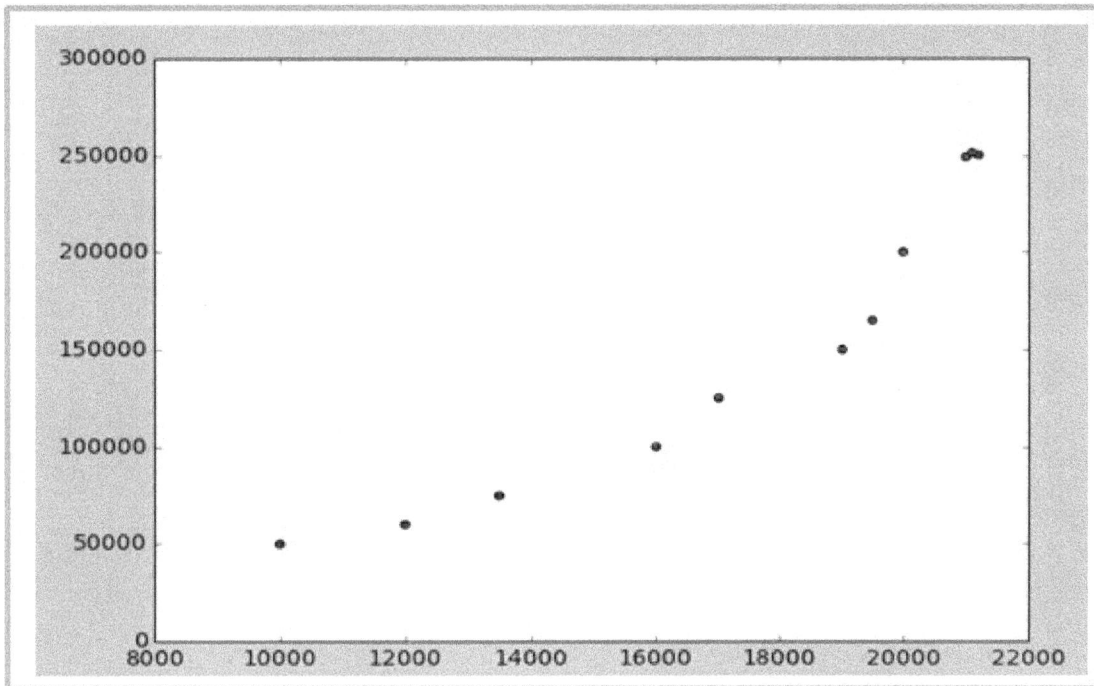

Exhibit 10.3 Scatter Plot

Fitting the regression line

```
In [14]: import numpy as np

In [15]: x = np.array([min(x), max(x)])

In [21]: y = intercept+slope*x

In [22]: plt.plot(x, y, 'r-')
```

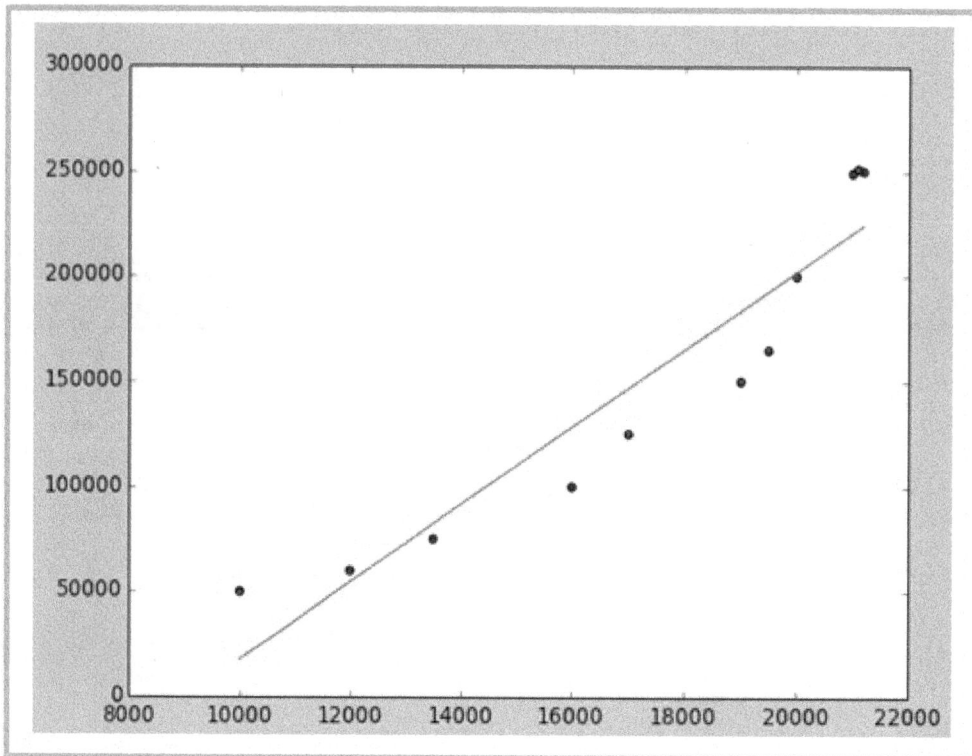

Exhibit 10.4 Scatter plot with regression line

Y predicted/Y hat

```
In [23]: x = (15000, 20000, 25000, 30000)

In [24]: X_h = sm.add_constant(x)

In [26]: y_hat = results.predict(X_h)

In [27]: y_hat
Out[27]:
array([ 109909.42899112,  202003.55569027,  294097.68238942,
        386191.80908858])
```

> While doing regression with Python, we add a constant to allow the calculation of Intercept. The value of the constant is 1. For that we enter a code 'X = sm.add_constant(x)'. This has no impact on the results.

```
In [28]: x = data.Mkt_exp

In [29]: X=sm.add_constant(x, prepend=True)

In [30]: X
Out[30]:
```

	const	Mkt_exp
0	1	10000
1	1	12000
2	1	13500
3	1	16000

10.3.3

Multiple Regression

Python codes are available to do multiple regression to predict a dependent variable out of a set of independent variables.

Data used for the purpose is **wxyz_ind**.

```
In [55]: data = pd.read_excel('F:\wxyz_ind.xlsx', 'Sheet1')

In [56]: data
Out[56]:
```

	Year	Sales	City	Mkt_exp
0	2000	75000	Banglore	5000
1	2001	100000	Trivandrum	10000
2	2002	150000	Chennai	12000

Here we have two predictor variables namely, 'Year' and 'Marketing Expense (Mkt_exp)' and one dependent variable called 'Sales'.

Multiple regression is most appropriate here.

Defining the variables

```
In [57]: x=data.Year

In [58]: z=data.Mkt_exp

In [59]: y=data.Sales
```

Add a column of ones to allow the calculation of the intercept

```
In [60]: X=sm.add_constant(zip(x, z), prepend=True)
```

Performing the multiple regression

```
In [61]: results = sm.OLS(y, X).fit()
```

Printing the result:

```
In [62]: print results.summary()
                            OLS Regression Results
==============================================================================
Dep. Variable:                  Sales   R-squared:                       0.961
Model:                            OLS   Adj. R-squared:                  0.952
Method:                 Least Squares   F-statistic:                     99.22
Date:                Thu, 30 Oct 2014   Prob (F-statistic):           2.25e-06
Time:                        10:31:01   Log-Likelihood:                -118.62
No. Observations:                  11   AIC:                             243.2
Df Residuals:                       8   BIC:                             244.4
Df Model:                           2
==============================================================================
                 coef    std err          t      P>|t|      [95.0% Conf. Int.]
------------------------------------------------------------------------------
const        -3.026e+07       6e+06     -5.043      0.001   -4.41e+07 -1.64e+07
x1            1.516e+04    3008.154      5.040      0.001    8223.198  2.21e+04
x2              2.8107       2.412      1.165      0.278      -2.752     8.373
==============================================================================
Omnibus:                        1.738   Durbin-Watson:                   2.080
Prob(Omnibus):                  0.419   Jarque-Bera (JB):                0.989
Skew:                           0.707   Prob(JB):                        0.610
Kurtosis:                       2.601   Cond. No.                     2.21e+07
==============================================================================
```

Exhibit 10.5 multiple regression

Note: x1 is Year and x2 is Mkt_Exp. If you change the order of x and z in the following code, the same will be followed in the output too.

Zip(x, z) in [60] refers to the Year and Mkt_exp in the data.

10.3.4

Logistic Regression

The following steps will guide you to perform logistic regression using Python:

Step 1: Importing necessary Python packages to perform logistic regression

```
In [1]: import pandas as pd

In [2]: import statsmodels.api as sm
```

Step 2: load the data 'Stud_clean.csv' from your respective location

```
In [5]: data = pd.read_csv('F:/stud_clean.csv')
```

Displaying a part of the data (first 5 records)

```
In [6]: data.head(5)
Out[6]:
```

	Stud_id	Gender	Dept	Attendance	Sem_marks	Name
0	M197	Female	Science	63	475	Ritu
1	M181	Male	Commerce	86	303	Victor
2	S137	Female	Commerce	79	587	Daven
3	M193	Male	Commerce	47	403	Fernado
4	C166	Female	Science	59	461	Rose

In this case, we want to predict gender using Attendance and Sem_marks. For that, we have to recode Gender as Female with 0 and Male with 1.

To do this; we will create a new column named 'Gen'.

```
In [7]: data.insert(2, 'Gen', ' ' , allow_duplicates=False)
```

	Stud_id	Gender	Gen	Dept	Attendance	Sem_marks	Name
0	M197	Female		Science	63	475	Ritu
1	M181	Male		Commerce	86	303	Victor

Now we perform recoding Gender using 'Replace' command

```
In [10]: rec = data.Gender.replace(['Female', 'Male'], [0, 1])
```

Here 'rec' is a temporary container to store the result of replacing female and male with 0 and 1 respectively.

Adding this result to the empty column 'Gen'

```
In [11]: data['Gen'] = rec
```

```
In [12]: data.head(2)
Out[12]:
```

	Stud_id	Gender	Gen	Dept	Attendance	Sem_marks	Name
0	M197	Female	0	Science	63	475	Ritu
1	M181	Male	1	Commerce	86	303	Victor

Now we will rank Attendance based on the following criteria

<=30 as 3 (Less or equal to 30)

>30 to <=60 as 2 (greater than 30 and less than or equal to 60)

Above 60 as 1

Here we make use of the 'IF' statement which has been discussed in the previous chapters.

First we create an empty column named 'Att_odr'

```
In [15]: data.insert(5, 'Att_odr', ' ', allow_duplicates=False)
```

```
In [16]: data.head(3)
Out[16]:
```

	Stud_id	Gender	Gen	Dept	Attendance	Att_odr	Sem_marks	Name
0	M197	Female	0	Science	63		475	Ritu
1	M181	Male	1	Commerce	86		303	Victor
2	S137	Female	0	Commerce	79		587	Daven

Now to do the ranking operation, we assign both 'Attendance' column and 'Att_odr' to temporary variables that would enable us to make the process easier.

```
In [17]: Att = data.Attendance
```

```
In [18]: odr = data.Att_odr
```

Now we write the IF code with assigning a Value for j as 0 because, in Python, rows start with zero.

```
In [22]: j = 0

In [23]: while j<96:
   ...:     i=Att.ix[j]
   ...:     if i <=30:
   ...:         odr.ix[j] = 3
   ...:     elif i >30 and i <=60:
   ...:         odr.ix[j]= 2
   ...:     else:
   ...:         odr.ix[j] = 3
   ...:     j = j+1
   ...: print 'jobe done'
   ...:
jobe done

In [24]: data.head(5)
Out[24]:
```

	Stud_id	Gender	Gen	Dept	Attendance	Att_odr	Sem_marks	Name
0	M197	Female	0	Science	63	3	475	Ritu
1	M181	Male	1	Commerce	86	3	303	Victor
2	S137	Female	0	Commerce	79	3	587	Daven
3	M193	Male	1	Commerce	47	2	403	Fernado
4	C166	Female	0	Science	59	2	461	Rose

At this point, save this data as **datanew.csv** which we will use it later. Please do not forget to remove the index column in the csv file, which is the Column A in Excel, without which it may not work in a right way once you load it back to Python.

Now we shall create dummy variables for Att_odr

```
In [25]: dummy = pd.get_dummies(data['Att_odr'],prefix = 'Attn')

In [26]: dummy.head(3)
Out[26]:
```

	Attn_2	Attn_3
0	0	1
1	0	1
2	0	1

Here, we select necessary columns from the data namely Gen and Sem_marks for analysis.

```
In [27]: cols = ['Gen', 'Sem_marks']
```

```
In [28]: cols
Out[28]: ['Gen', 'Sem_marks']
```

Now we create a new data frame by joining dummy with the selected variables/columns. So the new data name is given as, newdata.

```
In [29]: newdata = data[cols].join(dummy.ix[:, 'Attn_2':])
```

Here, this command implies that, dummy from Attn_2 on wards has to be added. In this case we have only two dummy variables namely Attn_2 and Attn_3

```
In [30]: newdata.head(3)
Out[30]:
```

	Gen	Sem_marks	Attn_2	Attn_3
0	0	475	0	1
1	1	303	0	1
2	0	587	0	1

For the convenience of performing the analysis, at this stage, it is advisable to save the newdata as 'datareg.csv'.

```
[31]: newdata.to_csv('F:\datareg.csv')
```

Now you can check the data in your respective folder, and delete the index column from the same.

	A	B	C	D	E	F
1		Gen	Sem_mark	Attn_2	Attn_3	
2	0	0	475	0	1	
3	1	1	303	0	1	
4	2	0	587	0	1	

After deleting index column A, it looks like the following

	A	B	C	D	E
1	Gen	Sem_marl	Attn_2	Attn_3	
2	0	475	0	1	
3	1	303	0	1	
4	0	587	0	1	

After this, you have to save the data in Excel. When you try to save and close the file, it will display the save option several times, and you keep on choose the save button/yes until it is saved and closed.

Once you have done this, load this data back to Python.

```
In [32]: regdata = pd.read_csv('F:\datareg.csv')
```

```
In [33]: regdata.head(5)
Out[33]:
```

	Gen	Sem_marks	Attn_2	Attn_3
0	0	475	0	1
1	1	303	0	1
2	0	587	0	1
3	1	403	1	0
4	0	461	1	0

Now we could proceed to perform logistic regression

Here we shall manually add a constant (1) to the data that will allow the calculation of intercept. Here we give the column name as 'intercept'.

```
In [36]: regdata['intercept'] = 1.0
```

```
In [37]: regdata.head(3)
Out[37]:
```

	Gen	Sem_marks	Attn_2	Attn_3	intercept
0	0	475	0	1	1
1	1	303	0	1	1
2	0	587	0	1	1

Here, Iv (Independent Variables) are Sem_marks, Att_2 and _3.

Dv (Dependent variable) is Gen

Selecting IV in the following code:

```
In [38]: iv = regdata.columns[1:]
```

```
In [39]: iv
Out[39]: Index([u'Sem_marks', u'Attn_2', u'Attn_3', u'intercept'], dtype=object)
```

In the above code, '1:' implies, columns from sem_marks on wards (which is column 1), as in Python columns starts with 0, which is Gen.

Performing logistic analysis

```
In [40]: logit = sm.Logit(regdata['Gen'], regdata[iv])
```

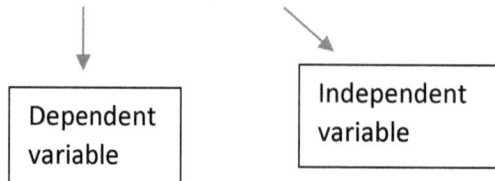

Dependent variable

Independent variable

Fitting the model

```
In [41]: results = logit.fit()
```

Printing the result

```
In [42]: print results.summary()
```

```
                        Logit Regression Results
========================================================================
Dep. Variable:             Gen    No. Observations:              96
Model:                   Logit    Df Residuals:                  93
Method:                    MLE    Df Model:                       2
Date:          Fri, 07 Nov 2014   Pseudo R-squ.:            0.007305
Time:                 13:05:36    Log-Likelihood:           -65.538
converged:               False    LL-Null:                  -66.020
                                  LLR p-value:               0.6174
========================================================================
                 coef    std err       z     P>|z|    [95.0% Conf. Int.]
------------------------------------------------------------------------
Sem_marks     -0.0004      0.002   -0.217    0.828    -0.004      0.003
Attn_2         0.9827        nan      nan      nan       nan        nan
Attn_3         0.5607        nan      nan      nan       nan        nan
intercept     -0.7540        nan      nan      nan       nan        nan
========================================================================
```

Exhibit 10.6 Logistic regression

10.3.5

Correlation

Correlation is the extent of the relation between two variables. It is one of the most popular statistical tools used by most of the researchers. This section will help you to do a Pearson Product Moment Correlation Spearman Correlation.

10.3.5a

Pearson's Product Moment Correlation

```
In [270]: from scipy.stats.stats import pearsonr

In [271]: x = data.Attendance

In [272]: y=data.Sem_marks

In [273]: result = pearsonr(x, y)

In [274]: result
Out[274]: (-0.0048731023972546457, 0.96241657161397298)
```

Finding covariance of attendance of attendance and marks

```
In [276]: data.Attendance.cov(data.Sem_marks)
Out[276]: -9.5530639794649446
```

10.3.5b

Spearman Correlation

Open the data, stud_clean

```
In [43]: data.head(5)
Out[43]:
```

	Stud_id	Gender	Gen	Dept	Attendance	Att_odr	Sem_marks	Name
0	M197	Female	0	Science	63	3	475	Ritu
1	M181	Male	1	Commerce	86	3	303	Victor
2	S137	Female	0	Commerce	79	3	587	Daven

Assigning x and y

```
In [44]: x = data.Att_odr
```

```
In [45]: y=data.Sem_marks
```

Importing spearman Python module

```
In [47]: from scipy.stats import spearmanr as smr
```

```
In [48]: smr(x, y)
Out[48]: (-0.088249285105169759, 0.39254780294273095)
```

10.3.6

t- test – 1 sample

We use t-test to test the significance of difference between two means.

Here we can see how to use one sample t-test with the help of Python. Follow the procedure given below:

Load datareg.csv in to Python as regdata

```
In [51]: regdata.head(3)
Out[51]:
```

	Gen	Sem_marks	Attn_2	Attn_3	intercept
0	0	475	0	1	1
1	1	303	0	1	1
2	0	587	0	1	1

Now we will take semester marks to compare the mean value of the sem_marks with the universal mean value of 420.

```
In [52]: x = regdata.Sem_marks
```

Importing necessary modules for both 1 sample and 2 sample t- tests.

```
from scipy.stats import ttest_1samp, ttest_ind
```

Performing 1 sample t- test

```
In [53]: t_statistic, p_value= ttest_1samp(x, 420)

In [58]: t_statistic, p_value
Out[58]: (array(-2.2014589784754546), 0.030125047612757715)
```

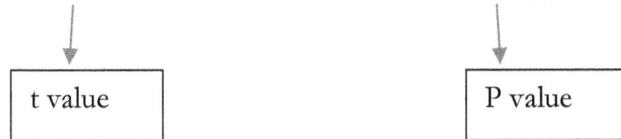

```
         ↓                                    ↓
    ┌──────────┐                        ┌──────────┐
    │ t value  │                        │ P value  │
    └──────────┘                        └──────────┘
```

10.3.7

t test with 2 sample

Here we use the **datanew.csv** which you have already saved while performing the logistic regression.

```
In [75]: data.head(3)
Out[75]:
```

	Stud_id	Gender	Gen	Dept	Attendance	Att_odr	Sem_marks	Name
0	M197	Female	0	Science	63	3	475	Ritu
1	M181	Male	1	Commerce	86	3	303	Victor
2	S137	Female	0	Commerce	79	3	587	Daven

```
In [70]: x= data.Att_odr

In [72]: y = data.Sem_marks

In [73]: t_statistic, p_value = ttest_ind(x, y)

In [74]: t_statistic, p_value
Out[74]: (array(-34.935666881392855), 1.2138989290638027e-84)
```

10.3.8

Paired t -test

Use datanew.csv for the analysis

```
In [4]: data.head(2)
Out[4]:
```

	Stud_id	Gender	Gen	Dept	Attendance	Att_odr	Sem_marks	Name
0	M197	Female	0	Science	63	3	475	Ritu
1	M181	Male	1	Commerce	86	3	303	Victor

First of all we have to select columns Attendance and Sem_marks and make a new data frame.

```
In [16]: cols = ['Attendance', 'Sem_marks']
```

```
In [17]: newdata = data[cols]
```

```
In [18]: newdata.head(3)
Out[18]:
```

	Attendance	Sem_marks
0	63	475
1	86	303
2	79	587

Convert this dataframe into an array format. (Use uppercase X); in order to do this, you have to import numpy. (Import numpy as np).

```
In [19]: X = np.array(newdata)
```

```
In [20]: X
Out[20]:
array([[  63.       ,   475.       ],
       [  86.       ,   303.       ],
       [  79.       ,   587.       ],
```

```
In [13]: from scipy.stats import ttest_1samp
```

Perform the analysis

```
In [30]: trial_1 = X[:,0]
```

```
In [31]: trial_2 = X[:,1]
```

```
In [33]: t_statistic, p_value = ttest_1samp(trial_1 - trial_2, 0)
```

```
In [34]: t_statistic, p_value
Out[34]: (array(-28.584304168288195), 1.8880131387991314e-48)
```

t value   P value

10.3.9

Paired Wilcoxon test using the same steps above (paired t-test) except the following steps

```
In [25]: from scipy.stats import wilcoxon

In [35]: z_statistic, p_value = wilcoxon(trial_1 - trial_2)

In [36]: z_statistic, p_value
Out[36]: (0.0, 1.780203752559748e-17)
```

Z score   P value

10.3.10

Wilcoxon test – 1 sample

Here we want to take semester marks to compare the mean value of the 'sem_ marks' with the universal mean value of, say, '420' (you can use any values based on your research).

```
In [105]: from scipy.stats import wilcoxon
```

```
In [106]: regdata.head(3)
Out[106]:
```

	Gen	Sem_marks	Attn_2	Attn_3	intercept
0	0	475	0	1	1
1	1	303	0	1	1
2	0	587	0	1	1

```
In [107]: x = regdata.Sem_marks
```

Here sem_ marks is in the column format. It is very important to make it to arrays.

```
In [110]: x
Out[110]:
0    475
1    303
```

For the following operations, we will import **numpy**.

```
In [117]: import numpy as np
```

Converting in to arrays (here we use capital X to store the converted array format of small x)

```
In [113]: X = np.array(x)
```

```
In [115]: X
Out[115]:
array([475, 303, 587, 403, 461,
       282, 206, 450, 201, 291,
```

Performing Wilcoxon 1 sample test

```
In [114]: z_statistic, p_value = wilcoxon(X - 420)
```

```
In [116]: z_statistic, p_value
Out[116]: (1741.5, 0.045621412536666905)
```

Z value	P value

10.3.11

Two sample Wilcoxon Test /Mann Whitney U test

Same code is used to run both 2s sample Wilcoxon and Mann Whitney U test.

```
In [75]: data.head(3)
Out[75]:
```

	Stud_id	Gender	Gen	Dept	Attendance	Att_odr	Sem_marks	Name
0	M197	Female	0	Science	63	3	475	Ritu
1	M181	Male	1	Commerce	86	3	303	Victor
2	S137	Female	0	Commerce	79	3	587	Daven

```
In [70]: x= data.Att_odr
```

```
In [119]: y = data.Sem_marks
```

Performing the analysis

```
In [120]: from scipy.stats import mannwhitneyu

In [122]: u, p_value = mannwhitneyu(x,y)

In [123]: u, p_value
Out[123]: (0.0, 1.2622234850802662e-34)
```

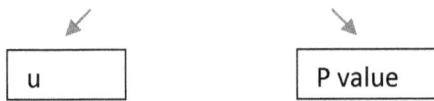

u   P value

10.3.12

ANOVA

ANOVA is used to test the significance of difference among more than two variables. This section will guide you to perform ANOVA successfully.

Use datanew.csv for the analysis

```
In [38]: from statsmodels.stats.anova import anova_lm

In [39]: from statsmodels.formula.api  import ols

In [51]: data.head(3)
Out[51]:
```

	Stud_id	Gender	Gen	Dept	Attendance	Att_odr	Sem_marks	Name
0	M197	Female	0	Science	63	3	475	Ritu
1	M181	Male	1	Commerce	86	3	303	Victor
2	S137	Female	0	Commerce	79	3	587	Daven

```
In [48]: anova = ols('Attendance ~ Sem_marks', data).fit()

In [49]: result = anova_lm(anova)
```

```
In [50]: result
Out[50]:
```

	df	sum_sq	mean_sq	F	PR(>F)
Sem_marks	1	0.715112	0.715112	0.002232	0.962417
Residual	94	30112.914425	320.350153	NaN	NaN

Exhibit 10.7 Anova

```
In [52]: anova.params
Out[52]:
Intercept      69.924770
Sem_marks      -0.000788
dtype: float64
```

If there are more than two variables, then use the following code:

```
In [53]: anova = ols('Attendance ~ Sem_marks + Dept', data).fit()

In [54]: result = anova_lm(anova)

In [55]: result
Out[55]:
```

	df	sum_sq	mean_sq	F	PR(>F)
Dept	2	358.553260	179.276630	0.554578	0.576222
Sem_marks	1	14.556207	14.556207	0.045029	0.832421
Residual	92	29740.520070	323.266522	NaN	NaN

```
In [56]: anova.params
Out[56]:
Intercept          69.817174
Dept[T.Commerce]   -1.016690
Dept[T.Science]    -5.522491
Sem_marks           0.003681
dtype: float64
```

10.3.13

Chi Square – Goodness of Fit

Open datanew.csv for the analysis

```
In [124]: data.head(3)
Out[124]:
```

	Stud_id	Gender	Gen	Dept	Attendance	Att_odr	Sem_marks	Name
0	M197	Female	0	Science	63	3	475	Ritu
1	M181	Male	1	Commerce	86	3	303	Victor
2	S137	Female	0	Commerce	79	3	587	Daven

```
[125]: import numpy as np

[126]: from scipy.stats import chisquare as csq

[127]: x = data.Attendance
```

Converting Attendance column in to arrays

```
[128]: obs = np.array(x)
```

```
[129]: csq(obs, f_exp=None, ddof=0, axis=0)
[129]: (432.58431816325526, 1.4923639807722953e-44)
```

Chi square

P value

10.3.14

Fishers R or Fishers Exact Test

Here we want to make a 2 * 2 table, for doing this test. We can use cross tabulation for this purpose.

Use **datanew.csv** for the analysis

```
In [51]: from scipy.stats import fisher_exact as fisherR
```

```
In [53]: data.head(3)
Out[53]:
```

	Stud_id	Gender	Gen	Dept	Attendance	Att_odr	Sem_marks	Name
0	M197	Female	0	Science	63	3	475	Ritu
1	M181	Male	1	Commerce	86	3	303	Victor
2	S137	Female	0	Commerce	79	3	587	Daven

Selecting required columns, namely Gen and Att_odr

```
In [63]: cols=['Gen', 'Att_odr']
```

```
In [64]: newdata = data[cols]
```

```
In [65]: newdata.head(2)
Out[65]:
```

	Gen	Att_odr
0	0	3
1	1	3

Cross tabulating the data

```
In [66]: cdata = pd.crosstab(newdata.Gen, newdata.Att_odr, margins=False)
```

```
In [67]: cdata
Out[67]:
```

Att_odr	2	3
Gen		
0	16	37
1	17	26

Performing Fisher R

```
In [70]: oddsratio, pvalue = fisherR(cdata)
```

```
In [71]: oddsratio, pvalue
Out[71]: (0.66136724960254367, 0.39082534912491351)
```

10.3.15

Chi- square test for independence or Pearson's chi -squared statistic

```
In [72]: from scipy.stats import chi2_contingency as chi
```

Use the same data as used to do Fishers R – (cdata)

Note: If you are loading the data from Excel to perform the test, then you should select the required columns, and then cross-tabulate the same and use for the analysis. For further clarification, follow the steps as it is from Fishers R analysis.

```
In [77]: chi2, p, dof, ex = chi(cdata, correction = False)
```

```
In [78]: chi2, p, dof, ex
Out[78]:
(0.91924573890348349,
 0.33767309455711081,
 1,
 array([[ 18.21875,  34.78125],
        [ 14.78125,  28.21875]]))
```

```
In [79]: chi2
Out[79]: 0.91924573890348349
```

Here, you can make 'correction = False or True' according to the situation.

10.3.16

G test or Log Likelihood Ratio

Use the same data as used above (cdata)

```
In [72]: from scipy.stats import chi2_contingency as chi
```

Note: if you have already imported '**chi2_contingency**', you need not import it again. However, if you are doing this analysis or any operations that need some packages to be imported for the first time, then you have to import the same.

Performing G test

```
In [82]: g, p, dof, expct= chi(cdata, lambda_ = 'log-likelihood')
In [83]: g, p
Out[83]: (0.55047640490567007, 0.45812310067842255)
```

10.3.17

Cressie-Read Power Divergence Statistic and Goodness of fit

Use datanew.csv

```
In [85]: data.head(3)
Out[85]:
```

	Stud_id	Gender	Gen	Dept	Attendance	Att_odr	Sem_marks	Name
0	M197	Female	0	Science	63	3	475	Ritu
1	M181	Male	1	Commerce	86	3	303	Victor
2	S137	Female	0	Commerce	79	3	587	Daven

```
In [88]: from scipy.stats import power_divergence as pd
```

Selecting 'Sem_marks'

```
In [96]: obs = data.Sem_marks
```

The following code converts 'obs' in to an array and storing back to the variable 'obs' itself

```
In [98]: obs = np.array(obs)
```

Performing the analysis

```
In [99]: pd(obs, lambda_='log-likelihood')
Out[99]: (2983.5203300088715, 0.0)
```

You can also give expected observations while doing the analysis.

The example is given below:

```
In [100]:     obs = [15, 20, 25, 30, 35]
```

```
In [101]:     exp = [20, 20, 20, 20, 20]
```

```
In [102]: pd(obs, exp, lambda_='log-likelihood')
Out[102]: (66.027727034126514, 1.5628496973159145e-13)
```

If you have both expected and observed values in a table, such as Excel or other CSV files, you have to assign the columns to the temporary containers namely 'obs' and 'exp.' Please refer the section on coding for details.

10.3.18

Kolmogorov – Smirnov Test for goodness of fit or K test

Use datanew.csv

```
In [3]: data.head(3)
Out[3]:
```

	Stud_id	Gender	Gen	Dept	Attendance	Att_odr	Sem_marks	Name
0	M197	Female	0	Science	63	3	475	Ritu
1	M181	Male	1	Commerce	86	3	303	Victor
2	S137	Female	0	Commerce	79	3	587	Daven

```
In [4]: from scipy.stats import kstest as k
```

```
In [5]: k(data['Sem_marks'], 'norm')
Out[5]: (1.0, 0.0)
```

Test value		P value

CHAPTER 11
Practise Exercises

Use wxyz_ca.xlsx

1. Open data wxyz_ca.xlsx.

2. Display summary statistics.

3. Make a Bar chart on variable Sales.

4. Calculate percentage change in Sales and display the same.

5. Create bar chart on Percentage change in Sales.

Answers

    1.   Loading data wxyz_ca.xlsx

```
In [17]: data
Out[17]:
```

	Year	Sales	City	Mkt_exp
0	2000	50000	Dryden	10000
1	2001	60000	Mississauga	12000

    2.   Displaying the summary statistics:

```
In [18]: data.describe()
```

```
Out[18]:
```

	Year	Sales	Mkt_exp
count	11.000000	11.000000	11.000000
mean	2005.000000	152272.727273	17300.000000
std	3.316625	77149.323923	3949.177129
min	2000.000000	50000.000000	10000.000000
25%	2002.500000	87500.000000	14750.000000
50%	2005.000000	150000.000000	19000.000000
75%	2007.500000	224500.000000	20500.000000
max	2010.000000	251000.000000	21200.000000

3. Bar chart on variable Sales:

```
In [19]: sales = data.Sales
```

```
In [37]: data.plot(x ='Year', y='Sales', kind = 'bar')
Out[37]: <matplotlib.axes.AxesSubplot at 0xa987c70>
```

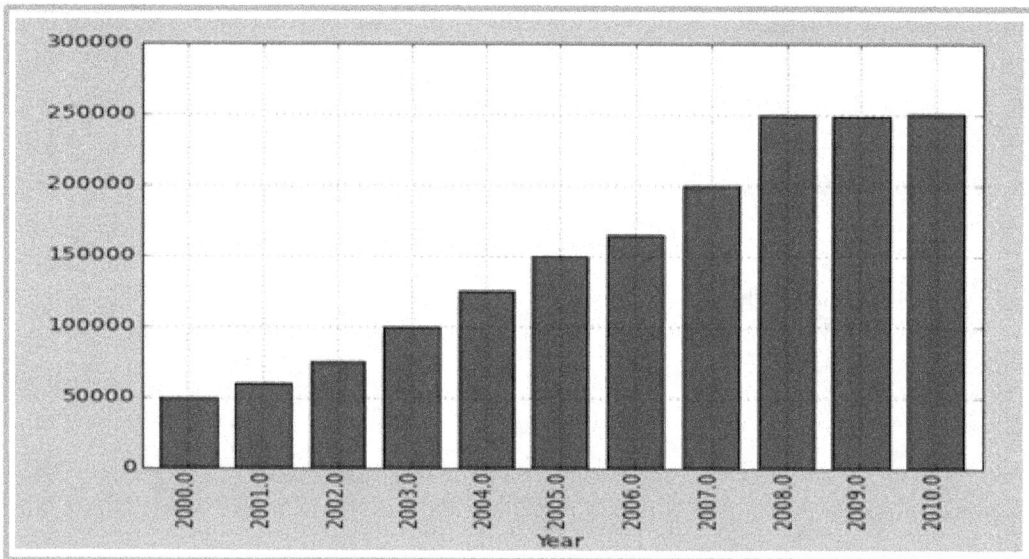

Exhibit 11.1 bar plot of sales data

4. Calculating Percentage Change in Sales using **pct_change()**.

```
In [21]: result = sales.pct_change()
```

```
In [22]: result
Out[22]:
0           NaN
1      0.200000
2      0.250000
3      0.333333
4      0.250000
5      0.200000
6      0.100000
7      0.212121
8      0.250000
9     -0.004000
10     0.008032
```

First year, that is '0', it is shown as NaN because this is the starting year.

5. Bar chart on percentage change in Sales:

```
In [23]:        result.plot(kind='Barh', rot=0)
```

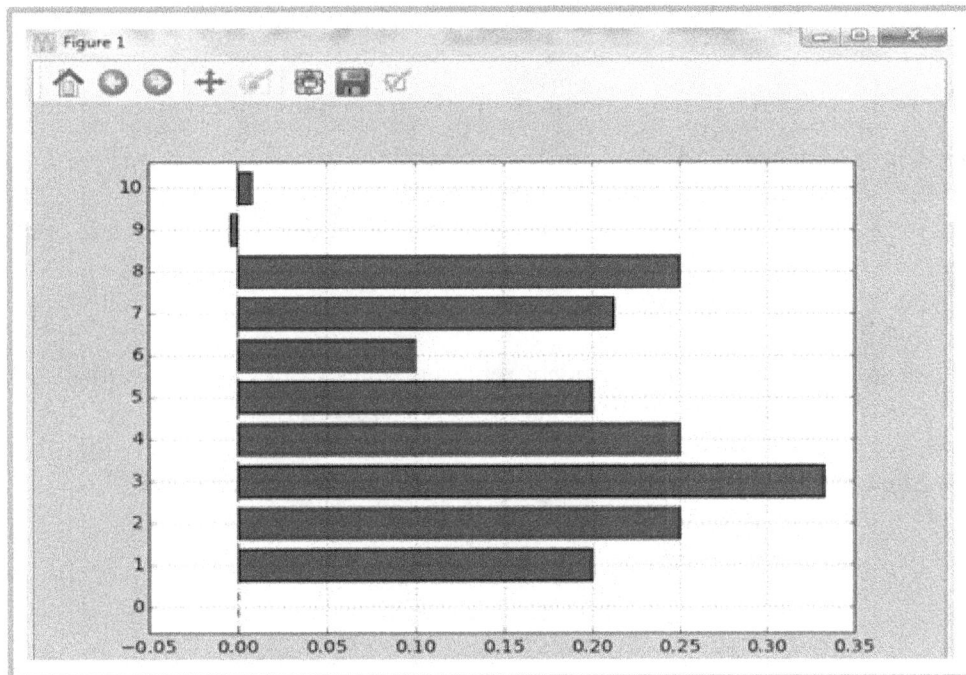

Exhibit 11.2 bar chart on percentage change in sales

CHAPTER 12
Practice Makes Perfect

In this chapter, we give yet another exercise for you to work out. We urge you to try it yourself, before referring to the answers. You should be able to answer these questions, based on your learning from Chapters 1 (section 1.5 coding in Python, an easy process), 2, 3 and 4. The main objective of this chapter is to make you more and more familiar with coding in Python. Once you learned these basic coding and related operation/functions, you should feel more comfortable using Python, which will, in turn, helps you to do data analysis with much ease and convenience. The more you practice, the better you will be with Python. The real learning comes, when you put your knowledge into practice. Therefore, you could always, get your data, and follow this book to carry out necessary coding and related computations.

Exercise 12.1

1. Open Stud_clean1.xlsx in Python and view first 10 records.
2. View the list of female students in Science stream.
3. View the list of Male students in Commerce stream and also compute the total number of male students in commerce stream.
4. View the list of students (both Male and Female) in Arts stream and find out how many students are studying Arts.
5. The College is planning to select student representatives from various streams, such as Arts, Science, and Commerce (2 from each stream) based on few criteria:

    Semester wise attendance should be 85% or above. If there are too many students with 85% or above, then the next criteria is with highest semester marks among them.
6. Identify the topper (student with highest mark) in all three streams.

Answers:

1. Opening stud_clean1.xlsx in Python

```
In [79]: import pandas as pd

In [80]: data = pd.read_excel('D:/stud_clean1.xlsx', 'stud_clean')
```

Excel sheet name

Viewing first 10 records:

```
In [81]: data.head(10)
Out[81]:
```

	Stud_id	Gender	Dept	Attendance	Sem_marks	Name
0	M197	Female	Science	63.000000	475	Ritu
1	M181	Male	Commerce	86.000000	303	Victor
2	S137	Female	Commerce	79.000000	587	Daven
3	M193	Male	Commerce	47.000000	403	Fernado
4	C166	Female	Science	59.000000	461	Rose
5	S138	Male	Commerce	88.000000	452	Vijay
6	A102	Female	Arts	97.000000	589	Honey
7	A124	Male	Commerce	97.000000	355	Randy
8	C173	Female	Arts	97.000000	473	Jannet
9	C155	Male	Science	69.343634	411	Pillai

2. List of Female students in Science Stream.

```
In [83]: gen = data[data['Gender']=='Female']
```

The above code will filter 'female' students from the entire college. In this case, it is from Arts, Science, and Commerce.

```
In [84]: gen.head(2)
Out[84]:
```

	Stud_id	Gender	Dept	Attendance	Sem_marks	Name
0	M197	Female	Science	63	475	Ritu
2	S137	Female	Commerce	79	587	Daven

Now we will filter 'Female' students from Science department.

```
In [85]: ans = gen[gen['Dept'] =='Science']
```

View a part of the data:

```
In [86]: ans.head(5)
Out[86]:
```

	Stud_id	Gender	Dept	Attendance	Sem_marks	Name
0	M197	Female	Science	63	475	Ritu
4	C166	Female	Science	59	461	Rose
15	C158	Female	Science	97	450	Ancy
26	C161	Female	Science	92	571	Nicemary
41	M192	Female	Science	52	544	Isha

3. List of Male students in Commerce stream

Same step as above. First we will filter all the 'Male' students from all departments.

```
In [87]: mgen=data[data['Gender']=='Male']
```

```
In [89]: mgen.head(5)
Out[89]:
```

	Stud_id	Gender	Dept	Attendance	Sem_marks	Name
1	M181	Male	Commerce	86.000000	303	Victor
3	M193	Male	Commerce	47.000000	403	Fernado
5	S138	Male	Commerce	88.000000	452	Vijay
7	A124	Male	Commerce	97.000000	355	Randy
9	C155	Male	Science	69.343634	411	Pillai

Now we will filter out Male students from Commerce stream.

```
In [90]: ans = mgen[mgen['Dept']=='Commerce']
```

```
In [91]: ans.head(5)
Out[91]:
```

	Stud_id	Gender	Dept	Attendance	Sem_marks	Name
1	M181	Male	Commerce	86	303	Victor
3	M193	Male	Commerce	47	403	Fernado
5	S138	Male	Commerce	88	452	Vijay
7	A124	Male	Commerce	97	355	Randy
10	M184	Male	Commerce	49	279	Morris

Now computing the total number of male students in commerce stream using **len** function.

```
In [92]: len(mgen)
Out[92]: 43
```

There are 43 Male students in Commerce stream.

4. Filtering out all students from Arts stream

```
In [93]: answer = data[data['Dept']=='Arts']
```

```
In [94]: answer.head(5)
Out[94]:
```

	Stud_id	Gender	Dept	Attendance	Sem_marks	Name
6	A102	Female	Arts	97	589	Honey
8	C173	Female	Arts	97	473	Jannet
11	M178	Male	Arts	52	508	Dharel
17	A113	Male	Arts	97	291	Michael
19	A106	Female	Arts	45	306	Peter

Now, using 'Len' function, we will compute total number of students in Arts section.

```
In [97]: len(answer)
Out[97]: 28
```

There are 28 students in Arts stream.

5. Stream/department wise selection
Arts

```
In [98]: art = data[data['Dept'] =='Arts']

In [99]: art.head(3)
Out[99]:
```

	Stud_id	Gender	Dept	Attendance	Sem_marks	Name
6	A102	Female	Arts	97	589	Honey
8	C173	Female	Arts	97	473	Jannet
11	M178	Male	Arts	52	508	Dharel

Now we will follow the criteria to select 2 students from Arts stream.

a. List of students with attendance 85% or above

```
In [100]: att = art[art['Attendance']>=85]

In [101]: att
Out[101]:
```

	Stud_id	Gender	Dept	Attendance	Sem_marks	Name
6	A102	Female	Arts	97	589	Honey
8	C173	Female	Arts	97	473	Jannet
17	A113	Male	Arts	97	291	Michael
25	A118	Male	Arts	89	443	Anuja
37	C169	Female	Arts	99	411	Joe
48	M177	Female	Arts	99	257	Fernado
91	C168	Female	Arts	86	430	B

```
In [102]: len(att)
Out[102]: 7
```

We have 7 students with 85 or greater than 85% attendance in Arts stream. We need only two students. Therefore, we will apply criteria two which is of 'highest marks'.

b. Identifying students with highest marks among the list of seven students

```
In [106]: h = max(att.Sem_marks)

In [107]: stud = att[att['Sem_marks']==h]

In [108]: stud
Out[108]:
```

	Stud_id	Gender	Dept	Attendance	Sem_marks	Name
6	A102	Female	Arts	97	589	Honey

In the above codes, we used 'max' function to find the highest marks in the group of seven students. That operation is being stored in a temporary variable named 'h'. Now, 'h' is the criteria, with maximum marks. In 'stud', another temporary variable, we have done the coding to filter out 'sem_marks', with the criteria 'h', which in turn implies, maximum/highest semester marks among seven students

You could do the same in another way; the following code will demonstrate the same:

```
In [119]: stud2= att[att['Sem_marks'] >450]

In [120]: stud2
Out[120]:
```

	Stud_id	Gender	Dept	Attendance	Sem_marks	Name
6	A102	Female	Arts	97	589	Honey
8	C173	Female	Arts	97	473	Jannet

Here, you have to give a certain cut-off value, in this case, it is 'above 450', and here we can see that two students having marks above the cut-off point. Suppose in the list, there are ten students, you could manually identify the student records, but if it is a huge list, you could first identify the highest marks using max function. Once you have identified the maximum value, it would be easier for you to give a cut-off value and then identify the second highest number/value for your analysis as follows:

```
In [121]: max(att.Sem_marks)
Out[121]: 589.0
```

Now you know, the highest mark is 589, so you could think of any value that could serve as a cut-off value, say 450 or 500 depending on your needs.

Here in Arts we have now two students, both with 97% attendance and with first and second highest marks.

Commerce stream

```
In [139]: com = data[data['Dept'] == 'Commerce']
```

```
In [140]: com.head(4)
Out[140]:
```

	Stud_id	Gender	Dept	Attendance	Sem_marks	Name
1	M181	Male	Commerce	86	303	Victor
2	S137	Female	Commerce	79	587	Daven
3	M193	Male	Commerce	47	403	Fernado
5	S138	Male	Commerce	88	452	Vijay

Now identifying students according to our criteria

```
In [141]: catt=com[com['Attendance'] >=85]
```

```
In [142]: catt.head(3)
Out[142]:
```

	Stud_id	Gender	Dept	Attendance	Sem_marks	Name
1	M181	Male	Commerce	86	303	Victor
5	S138	Male	Commerce	88	452	Vijay
7	A124	Male	Commerce	97	355	Randy

```
In [143]: len(catt)
Out[143]: 13
```

We have 13 students with 85 or more percentage in attendance.

Now we will select 2 students out 13, based on marks.

```
In [144]: max(catt.Sem_marks)
Out[144]: 593.0
```

This is the highest mark. So possibly we could think of a cut- off value, say 500.

```
In [147]: cstud2 = catt[catt['Sem_marks'] >=500]
```

```
In [148]: cstud2
Out[148]:
```

	Stud_id	Gender	Dept	Attendance	Sem_marks	Name
20	S133	Male	Commerce	90	593	David
81	M194	Female	Commerce	91	549	B

So we have found 2 students from Commerce stream.

Now we will perform similar steps to find out 2 students from Science stream

Science Stream.

```
In [149]: sc = data[data['Dept']== 'Science']
```

```
In [150]: sc.head(2)
Out[150]:
```

	Stud_id	Gender	Dept	Attendance	Sem_marks	Name
0	M197	Female	Science	63	475	Ritu
4	C166	Female	Science	59	461	Rose

Applying the criteria:

```
In [151]: ssc = sc[sc['Attendance']>=85]
```

```
In [153]: len(ssc)
Out[153]: 4
```

Here we have only 4 students with attendance equal to or above 85% attendance.

```
In [154]: ssc
Out[154]:
```

	Stud_id	Gender	Dept	Attendance	Sem_marks	Name
15	C158	Female	Science	97	450	Ancy
26	C161	Female	Science	92	571	Nicemary
78	M189	Female	Science	99	298	A
84	A119	Male	Science	91	562	A

Remember, if you want to view the entire data, you just need to type the data name, here in this example, we have stored students with >=85% attendance in science stream in a temporary variable 'ssc'. If you want to view only a part of the data, then type **data.head(number).**

Here you could manually select two students with higher marks. But in order to get more practice and to get familiar with Python, we advise you to perform the following codes for further computations:

```
In [159]: max(ssc.Sem_marks)
Out[159]: 571.0
```

571 is the highest marks

```
In [155]: len(ssc)
Out[155]: 4

In [156]: sstuds = ssc[ssc['Sem_marks']>=500]

In [157]: sstuds
Out[157]:
```

	Stud_id	Gender	Dept	Attendance	Sem_marks	Name
26	C161	Female	Science	92	571	Nicemary
84	A119	Male	Science	91	562	A

We have found 2 students from science stream too.

Job done!!!

6. Identifying the toppers

   a. Identifying the Topper in Arts department

```
In [160]: art = data[data['Dept']== 'Arts']

In [161]: art.head(3)
Out[161]:
```

	Stud_id	Gender	Dept	Attendance	Sem_marks	Name
6	A102	Female	Arts	97	589	Honey
8	C173	Female	Arts	97	473	Jannet
11	M178	Male	Arts	52	508	Dharel

```
In [162]: high = max(art.Sem_marks)

In [163]: topper = art[art['Sem_marks']== high]

In [164]: topper
Out[164]:
```

	Stud_id	Gender	Dept	Attendance	Sem_marks	Name
6	A102	Female	Arts	97	589	Honey

Student Honey is the topper in Arts department.

While giving conditions such as data[data['Dept'] = ='Arts'] , for the condition 'Arts', we have used single inverted commas whereas in the above example we haven't used inverted commas for high; topper = art[art['Sem_marks'] = = high] because, high is not a plain text, as it carries a function max(art.Sem_marks). Except such occasions, plain texts are entered in single inverted commas. Numbers are also entered without inverted commas.

    a.   Identifying the Topper in Commerce department

```
In [165]: com = data[data['Dept']== 'Commerce']

In [166]: com.head(3)
Out[166]:
```

	Stud_id	Gender	Dept	Attendance	Sem_marks	Name
1	M181	Male	Commerce	86	303	Victor
2	S137	Female	Commerce	79	587	Daven
3	M193	Male	Commerce	47	403	Fernado

```
In [167]: top = max(com.Sem_marks)

In [168]: topper = com[com['Sem_marks']== top]

In [169]: topper
Out[169]:
```

	Stud_id	Gender	Dept	Attendance	Sem_marks	Name
20	S133	Male	Commerce	90	593	David

a. Identifying the Topper in Science department

```
In [170]: sc = data[data['Dept'] == 'Science']

In [171]: sc.head(3)
Out[171]:
```

	Stud_id	Gender	Dept	Attendance	Sem_marks	Name
0	M197	Female	Science	63.000000	475	Ritu
4	C166	Female	Science	59.000000	461	Rose
9	C155	Male	Science	69.343634	411	Pillai

```
In [172]: topper = max(sc.Sem_marks)
```

If you want to view the result then follow the code

```
In [173]: topper
Out[173]: 594.0
```

This show the maximum/highest marks in the science department
Viewing the final results – identifying the topper.

```
In [174]: the_topper = sc[sc['Sem_marks'] == topper]

In [175]: the_topper
Out[175]:
```

	Stud_id	Gender	Dept	Attendance	Sem_marks	Name
71	S141	Female	Science	82	594	B

Exercise 12.2

Toronto Library Fairy-tale Story book section

Here we have data of books based on Fairy-tale stories available in a library. To proceed further, please import **torlib.xlsx**.

1. Import excel data in to a temporary variable named 'info' and view the library database
   In order to load excel data, we will first import pandas via an alias 'pd'

   ```
   In [39]: import pandas as pd

   In [40]: info = pd.read_excel('D:/torlib.xlsx', 'Sheet1')
   ```

   Now viewing the data:

```
In [46]: info
Out[46]:
```

	Bcode	Book Name	Author	Publisher	Year
0	B101	Alice in Wonderland	Lewis Carrol	Macmillan	1865
1	B102	Beauty and the Beast	Jeanne	Buki Editions	1740
2	B103	Cinderella	Anne Anderson	Domain Books	2004
3	B104	Winter (The Lunar Chronicles)	Marissa Meyer	Feiwel and Friends	2015
4	B105	The Game of Logic	Lewis Carrol	Macmillan	1886
5	B106	Sapphire Blue (Precious stone trilogy)	Kerstin Gier	Henry Holt	2012
6	B105	Lion Heart	A.C.Gaughen	Bloomsburry	2015
7	B108	Shades of Earth	Beth Revis	Razorbill	2013
8	B109	The Fractured Light	Ammie Kaufman	Disney	2015
9	B110	Scarlett	Marissa Meyer	Feiwel and Friends	2013

2. A library member wants to know the details of the book 'The Game of Logic. Write the codes for the same.

```
In [48]: info[info['Book Name']=='The Game of Logic']
Out[48]:
```

	Bcode	Book Name	Author	Publisher	Year
4	B105	The Game of Logic	Lewis Carrol	Macmillan	1886

Note: **info['Book Name']** implies the Column name Book name. Here we are trying to match a book name with in the data with the column name book name. That's why we have info[info['Book Name']=='The Game of Logic'].

3. Write the Codes to display the books of the author 'Marissa Meyer'

```
In [49]: info[info['Author']=='Marissa Meyer']
Out[49]:
```

	Bcode	Book Name	Author	Publisher	Year
3	B104	Winter (The Lunar Chronicles)	Marissa Meyer	Feiwel and Friends	2015
9	B110	Scarlett	Marissa Meyer	Feiwel and Friends	2013

4. One of the library members is searching for the books published by Macmillan. Please help him by displaying the list of Macmillan books

```
In [50]: info[info['Publisher']=='Macmillan']
Out[50]:
```

	Bcode	Book Name	Author	Publisher	Year
0	B101	Alice in Wonderland	Lewis Carrol	Macmillan	1865
4	B105	The Game of Logic	Lewis Carrol	Macmillan	1886

5. List the books by Marissa Meyer, published in 2013
In order to do this, first, we will group year 2013 via following code:

```
In [63]: gyear = info[info['Year']==2013]
```

If you want to view the data grouped based on year 2013, then do the following:

```
In [64]: gyear
Out[64]:
```

	Bcode	Book Name	Author	Publisher	Year
7	B108	Shades of Earth	Beth Revis	Razorbill	2013
9	B110	Scarlett	Marissa Meyer	Feiwel and Friends	2013

Now we want by Marissa Meyer which is published in the year 2013.

```
In [65]: gyear[gyear['Author']=='Marissa Meyer']
Out[65]:
```

	Bcode	Book Name	Author	Publisher	Year
9	B110	Scarlett	Marissa Meyer	Feiwel and Friends	2013

If you want to use the aforementioned result, then you have to store the result in a temporary container. Say result = gyear[gyear['Author']=='Marissa Meyer'].

Now you could type result and press enter, you will be able to see the output.
The following will explain the same:

```
In [66]: result = gyear[gyear['Author']=='Marissa Meyer']

In [67]: result
Out[67]:
```

	Bcode	Book Name	Author	Publisher	Year
9	B110	Scarlett	Marissa Meyer	Feiwel and Friends	2013

6. Write a code to view first 5 records of the data set

```
In [68]: info.head(5)
Out[68]:
```

	Bcode	Book Name	Author	Publisher	Year
0	B101	Alice in Wonderland	Lewis Carrol	Macmillan	1865
1	B102	Beauty and the Beast	Jeanne	Buki Editions	1740
2	B103	Cinderella	Anne Anderson	Domain Books	2004
3	B104	Winter (The Lunar Chronicles)	Marissa Meyer	Feiwel and Friends	2015
4	B105	The Game of Logic	Lewis Carrol	Macmillan	1886

7. Write a code to view last 5 records of the data set

```
In [70]: info.tail(5)
Out[70]:
```

	Bcode	Book Name	Author	Publisher	Year
5	B106	Sapphire Blue (Precious stone trilogy)	Kerstin Gier	Henry Holt	2012
6	B105	Lion Heart	A.C.Gaughen	Bloomsburry	2015
7	B108	Shades of Earth	Beth Revis	Razorbill	2013
8	B109	The Fractured Light	Ammie Kaufman	Disney	2015
9	B110	Scarlett	Marissa Meyer	Feiwel and Friends	2013

8. View last 2 records

```
In [71]: info.tail(2)
Out[71]:
```

	Bcode	Book Name	Author	Publisher	Year
8	B109	The Fractured Light	Ammie Kaufman	Disney	2015
9	B110	Scarlett	Marissa Meyer	Feiwel and Friends	2013

Here, in order to view first few records, we use '.head (number)' and to view last few records, we use '.tail (number)'.

Exercise 12.3

Sorting

This section will give you more practice on Sorting. In order to do the exercise, use data **torlib.xlsx**.

Sorting based on Book Name, Ascending Order

We will load data torlib.xlsx, to do that, first we have to import Pandas.

```
In [1]: import pandas as pd

In [2]: book = pd.read_excel('D:/torlib.xlsx', 'Sheet1')
```

Here we have loaded data in to a temporary container named book. Now we will display first few records of the loaded data.

```
In [3]: book.head(4)
Out[3]:
```

	Bcode	Book Name	Author	Publisher	Year
0	B101	Alice in Wonderland	Lewis Carrol	Macmillan	1865
1	B102	Beauty and the Beast	Jeanne	Buki Editions	1740
2	B103	Cinderella	Anne Anderson	Domain Books	2004
3	B104	Winter (The Lunar Chronicles)	Marissa Meyer	Feiwel and Friends	2015

The following code will sort the data based on ascending order:

```
In [4]: book.sort_index(by='Book Name')
Out[4]:
```

	Bcode	Book Name	Author	Publisher	Year
0	B101	Alice in Wonderland	Lewis Carrol	Macmillan	1865
1	B102	Beauty and the Beast	Jeanne	Buki Editions	1740
2	B103	Cinderella	Anne Anderson	Domain Books	2004
6	B105	Lion Heart	A.C.Gaughen	Bloomsburry	2015
5	B106	Sapphire Blue (Precious stone trilogy)	Kerstin Gier	Henry Holt	2012
9	B110	Scarlett	Marissa Meyer	Feiwel and Friends	2013
7	B108	Shades of Earth	Beth Revis	Razorbill	2013
8	B109	The Fractured Light	Ammie Kaufman	Disney	2015
4	B105	The Game of Logic	Lewis Carrol	Macmillan	1886
3	B104	Winter (The Lunar Chronicles)	Marissa Meyer	Feiwel and Friends	2015

In the code we haven't specified whether the sorting is of ascending or descending order based on book name; however, we got the output in ascending order. Do you remember the reason?
Well it is because, Python, by default, will do sorting in ascending order.

Sorting based on Book Name: Descending order

Here we will sort the data in descending order and the variable on which the data has to be sorted is Book Name.

The following code will illustrate the same:

```
In [5]: book.sort_index(by='Book Name', ascending = False)
```

To sort in descending order, in the aforementioned code, we have to specify as ascending = False.

After typing the code, press enter, you will get the output.

.

Out[5]:

	Bcode	Book Name	Author	Publisher	Year
3	B104	Winter (The Lunar Chronicles)	Marissa Meyer	Feiwel and Friends	2015
4	B105	The Game of Logic	Lewis Carrol	Macmillan	1886
8	B109	The Fractured Light	Ammie Kaufman	Disney	2015
7	B108	Shades of Earth	Beth Revis	Razorbill	2013
9	B110	Scarlett	Marissa Meyer	Feiwel and Friends	2013
5	B106	Sapphire Blue (Precious stone trilogy)	Kerstin Gier	Henry Holt	2012
6	B105	Lion Heart	A.C.Gaughen	Bloomsburry	2015
2	B103	Cinderella	Anne Anderson	Domain Books	2004
1	B102	Beauty and the Beast	Jeanne	Buki Editions	1740
0	B101	Alice in Wonderland	Lewis Carrol	Macmillan	1865

Similarly you can sort the data based on Author or publisher too.

Sorting based on Author

In [6]: book.sort_index(by='Author')
Out[6]:

	Bcode	Book Name	Author	Publisher	Year
6	B105	Lion Heart	A.C.Gaughen	Bloomsburry	2015
8	B109	The Fractured Light	Ammie Kaufman	Disney	2015
2	B103	Cinderella	Anne Anderson	Domain Books	2004
7	B108	Shades of Earth	Beth Revis	Razorbill	2013
1	B102	Beauty and the Beast	Jeanne	Buki Editions	1740
5	B106	Sapphire Blue (Precious stone trilogy)	Kerstin Gier	Henry Holt	2012
0	B101	Alice in Wonderland	Lewis Carrol	Macmillan	1865
4	B105	The Game of Logic	Lewis Carrol	Macmillan	1886
9	B110	Scarlett	Marissa Meyer	Feiwel and Friends	2013
3	B104	Winter (The Lunar Chronicles)	Marissa Meyer	Feiwel and Friends	2015

By default, it is in ascending order.

Sorting the book data based on Year: Ascending order

```
In [7]: book.sort_index(by='Year')
Out[7]:
```

	Bcode	Book Name	Author	Publisher	Year
1	B102	Beauty and the Beast	Jeanne	Buki Editions	1740
0	B101	Alice in Wonderland	Lewis Carrol	Macmillan	1865
4	B105	The Game of Logic	Lewis Carrol	Macmillan	1886
2	B103	Cinderella	Anne Anderson	Domain Books	2004
5	B106	Sapphire Blue (Precious stone trilogy)	Kerstin Gier	Henry Holt	2012
7	B108	Shades of Earth	Beth Revis	Razorbill	2013
9	B110	Scarlett	Marissa Meyer	Feiwel and Friends	2013
3	B104	Winter (The Lunar Chronicles)	Marissa Meyer	Feiwel and Friends	2015
6	B105	Lion Heart	A.C.Gaughen	Bloomsburry	2015
8	B109	The Fractured Light	Ammie Kaufman	Disney	2015

Sorting on Year, Descending order

Here we will sort the data based on Year, descending order. The following code will perform the same:

```
In [8]: book.sort_index(by='Year', ascending = False)
Out[8]:
```

	Bcode	Book Name	Author	Publisher	Year
8	B109	The Fractured Light	Ammie Kaufman	Disney	2015
6	B105	Lion Heart	A.C.Gaughen	Bloomsburry	2015
3	B104	Winter (The Lunar Chronicles)	Marissa Meyer	Feiwel and Friends	2015
9	B110	Scarlett	Marissa Meyer	Feiwel and Friends	2013
7	B108	Shades of Earth	Beth Revis	Razorbill	2013
5	B106	Sapphire Blue (Precious stone trilogy)	Kerstin Gier	Henry Holt	2012
2	B103	Cinderella	Anne Anderson	Domain Books	2004
4	B105	The Game of Logic	Lewis Carrol	Macmillan	1886
0	B101	Alice in Wonderland	Lewis Carrol	Macmillan	1865
1	B102	Beauty and the Beast	Jeanne	Buki Editions	1740

You could follow similar coding for your own data. Suppose you want to save the result of our sorted data, do the following:

We will use sorting by year, descending and save the data in Excel.

This is very simple. You need to perform sorting and assign it in a temporary container and then save the data.

The following code will execute the same:

```
In [11]: dsorted = book.sort_index(by='Year', ascending = False)
```

Here we have performed sorting and assigned to a temporary variable named 'dsorted'.

Now we will view the result, and for a change, we will view last 2 records of the sorted data and remember it is being sorted on descending order.

```
In [12]: dsorted.tail(2)
Out[12]:
```

	Bcode	Book Name	Author	Publisher	Year
0	B101	Alice in Wonderland	Lewis Carrol	Macmillan	1865
1	B102	Beauty and the Beast	Jeanne	Buki Editions	1740

Now we will save the data.

```
In [13]: dsorted.to_csv('D:/dsorted.csv')
```

Sorted data is saved.

Similarly, you could save all your results, such as edited data, filtered and sorted data, or anything for that matter, which will make it convenient for you to do your analysis. If you want to access the saved data back in Python, then you should know what to do right.

Import pandas and load the data and view it. Can you try now?

```
In [14]: d=pd.read_csv('D:/dsorted.csv')
```

Now we load back the saved data.

```
In [15]: d.head(3)
Out[15]:
```

	Unnamed: 0	Bcode	Book Name	Author	Publisher	Year
0	8	B109	The Fractured Light	Ammie Kaufman	Disney	2015
1	6	B105	Lion Heart	A.C.Gaughen	Bloomsburry	2015
2	3	B104	Winter (The Lunar Chronicles)	Marissa Meyer	Feiwel and Friends	2015

CHAPTER 13
Describing Data – Visual & Numeric

This chapter is a combination of Descriptive Statistics and Data visualization, and specifically aimed to give you more practice with visualization and descriptive statistics based on the chapters which you have already covered. Numerical data do not make much sense unless we describe it. When we describe the data, it will give meaningful insights. Perhaps it will breathe life to the data. As we all know, we could define and describe a data by using descriptive statistics and by using appropriate data visualization tools. Here, we specifically deal with three sets of numeric data, with which, you could relate to any real-time data, which could be a part of your studies/research.

Exercise 13.1

To proceed further, please import data **stat.xlsx**.

```
In [87]: dat = pd.read_excel('D:/stat.xlsx', 'Sheet1')
```

```
In [88]: dat.head(3)
Out[88]:
```

	Set One	Set Two	Set Three
0	5	3	5
1	6	4	6
2	7	5	6

First let us have a study on 'Set One'.

To do this, first, we will assign column Set One to a temporary container s1.

```
In [89]: s1=dat['Set One']
```

No we shall view a part of the data.

```
In [90]: s1.head(4)
Out[90]:
0    5
1    6
2    7
3    7
```

Well, now what?

Now let us view the data visually. The best tool to have a better visual representation of data is a Histogram. However, the visualization tool changes with the type of data and our requirements.

In order to draw a histogram, you need to import the following:

```
In [91]: import numpy as np
```

```
In [92]: import matplotlib.mlab as mlab
```

```
In [94]: import matplotlib.pyplot as plt
```

Now we shall directly assign column 'Set one' to 'x'.

```
In [96]: x = dat['Set One']
```

Now we shall draw a Histogram

```
In [101]: n, bins, patches = plt.hist(x, bins=7, normed =1, facecolor = 'green', alpha=0.5)
```

Normed = 1, or you could give Normed = True.

Here we have bins as 7 because we have only 7 numbers from 5 to 11 (including 5) and each bin has the frequency / number of times each corresponding value is repeated. For example 7 is repeated three times and so on.

Let us view the data:

```
In [102]: s1
Out[102]:
0       5
1       6
2       7
3       7
4       7
5       8
6       8
7       8
8       8
9       8
10      8
11      9
12      9
13      9
14      10
15      10
```

We have 15 numbers in total this is because few numbers are being repeated.

Now let us view the Histogram

```
In [101]: n, bins, patches = plt.hist(x, bins=7, normed =1, facecolor = 'green', alpha=0.5)
```

Now press enter.

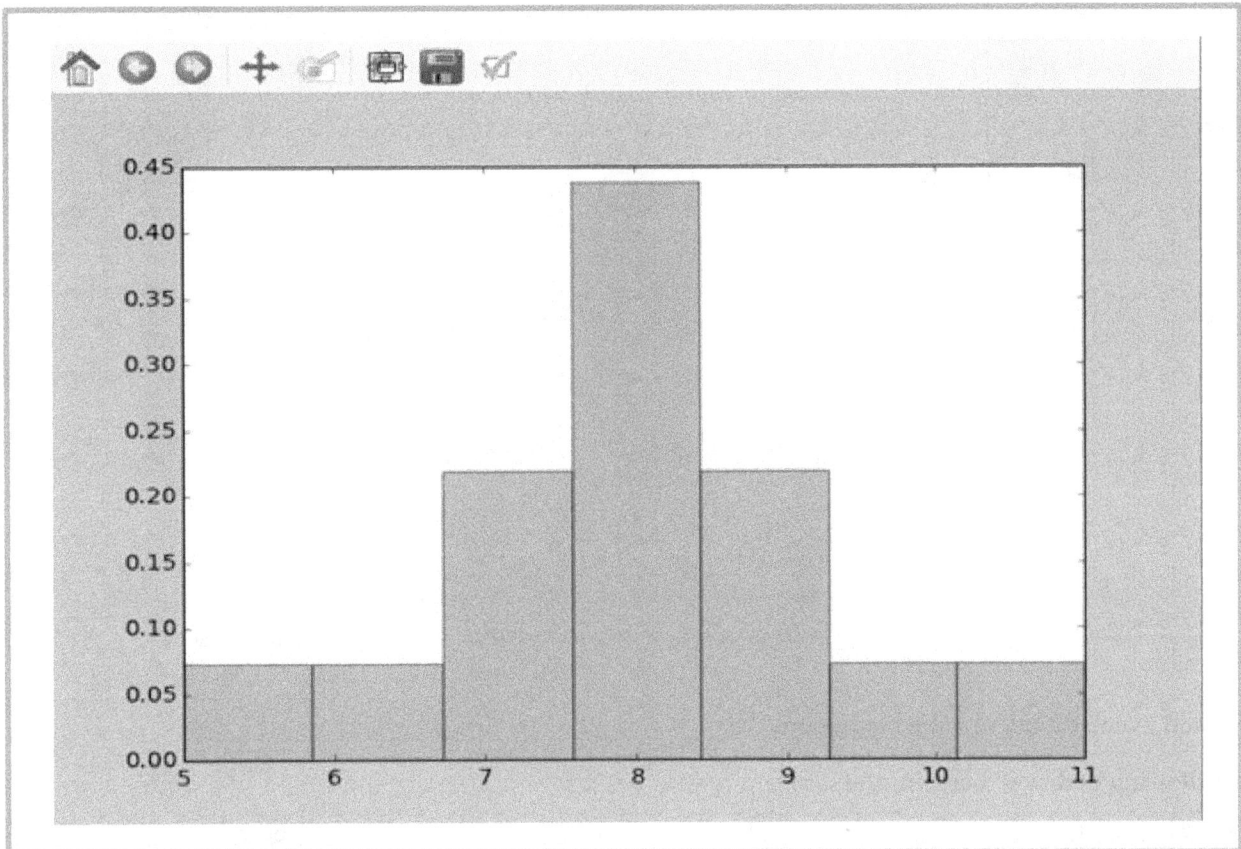

Exhibit 13.1 Histogram

You have the save option at the top of the figure.

In case you want, you can add a goodness of fit.

```
In [124]: mu = mean(x)

In [125]: sigma = std(x)

In [126]: y = normpdf(bins, mu, sigma)
```

And view the histogram with goodness of fit.

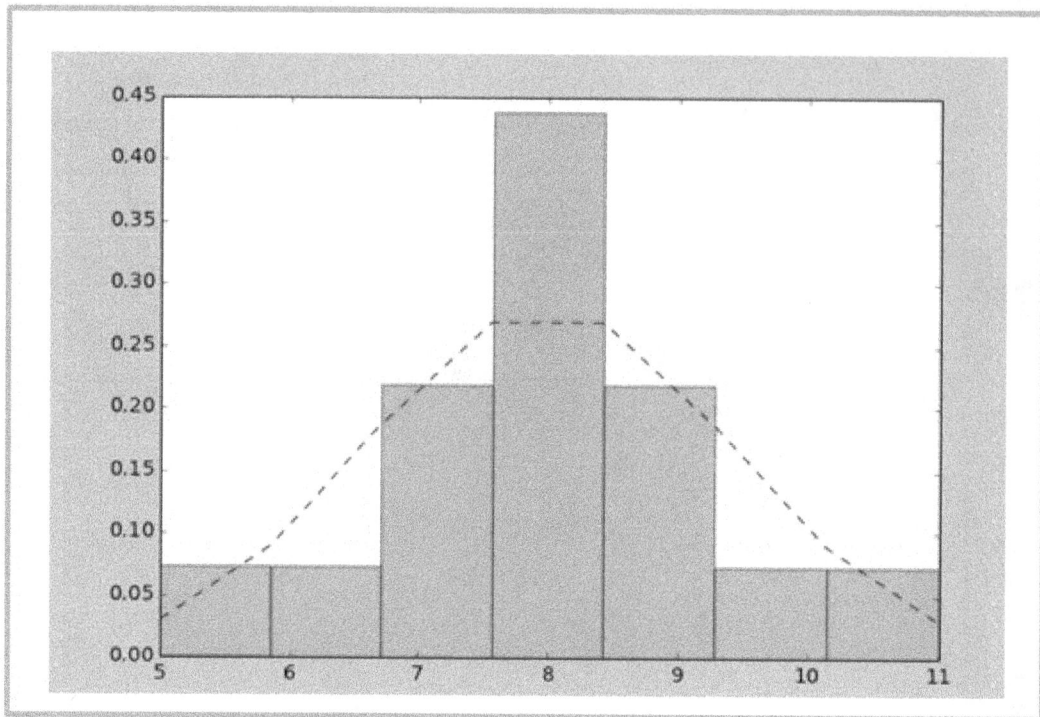

Exhibit 13.2 Histogram with goodness of fit – normal distribution

We could even add title for the histogram.

The following code will perform the same.

```
In [130]: plt.title('Histogram for Set One: $\mu = 8.0$, $\sigma = 1.41$', color = 'blue')
Out[130]: <matplotlib.text.Text at 0x8282e90>
```

For better clarity, we are giving the code in two sections.

```
In [130]: plt.title('Histogram for Set One: $\mu = 8.0$,
Out[130]: <matplotlib.text.Text at 0x8282e90>

 $\sigma = 1.41$', color = 'blue')
```

After typing the code, press enter, you will get the following output

.

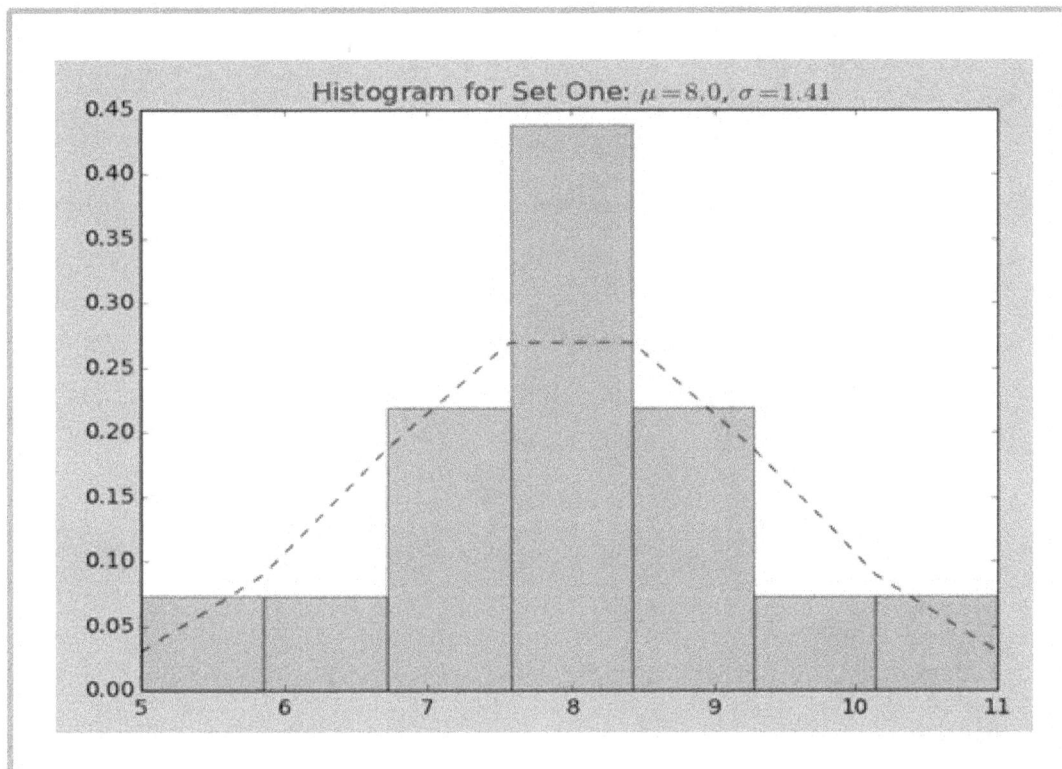

Exhibit 13.3 output with labels

Well, this is the visual representation of data set one. The histogram shows a symmetrical distribution of the data 'Set one'. Therefore, the skew is zero.

Describing data numerically

Compute Mean, Median and Mode for the data

```
In [185]: mean(x)
Out[185]: 8.0

In [186]: median(x)
Out[186]: 8.0
```

Well, we have computed mean and median using functions. In order to compute Mode, we have to import by using the following code

```
In [187]: from scipy.stats import mode

In [188]: mode(x)
Out[188]: (array([ 8.]), array([ 6.]))
```

Here we have mode as 8 which repeated 6 times.

As you have already known, for a symmetrical distribution, the mean, median and mode will be the same.

Simultaneously you could do the following:

```
In [225]: s1 = dat['Set One']

In [226]: s1.describe()
Out[226]:
count    16.000000
mean      8.000000
std       1.460593
min       5.000000
25%       7.000000
50%       8.000000
75%       9.000000
max      11.000000
```

How about the Skewness?

```
In [189]: x.skew()
Out[189]: 0.0
```

Skew will be a zero as well.

Exercise 13.2

Import data **stat1.xlsx**

Load and view the data

```
In [228]: data = pd.read_excel('D:/stat1.xlsx', 'Sheet1')
```

```
In [229]: data
Out[229]:
```

	Num
0	5
1	6
2	7
3	7
4	7
5	8
6	8
7	8
8	8
9	9

Here we have set of numbers. Now let's make a histogram for the same.

Please do not forget to import necessary modules/libraries, such as matplotlib.mlab and matplotlib.pyplot and numpy .

We will equate 'column Num' to 'x'.

```
In [230]: x=data.Num
```

Now we will plot and view the histogram:

```
In [232]: n, bins, patches = plt.hist(x, bins=5, normed =True, facecolor = 'purple')
```

Now press enter, you will get the following output:

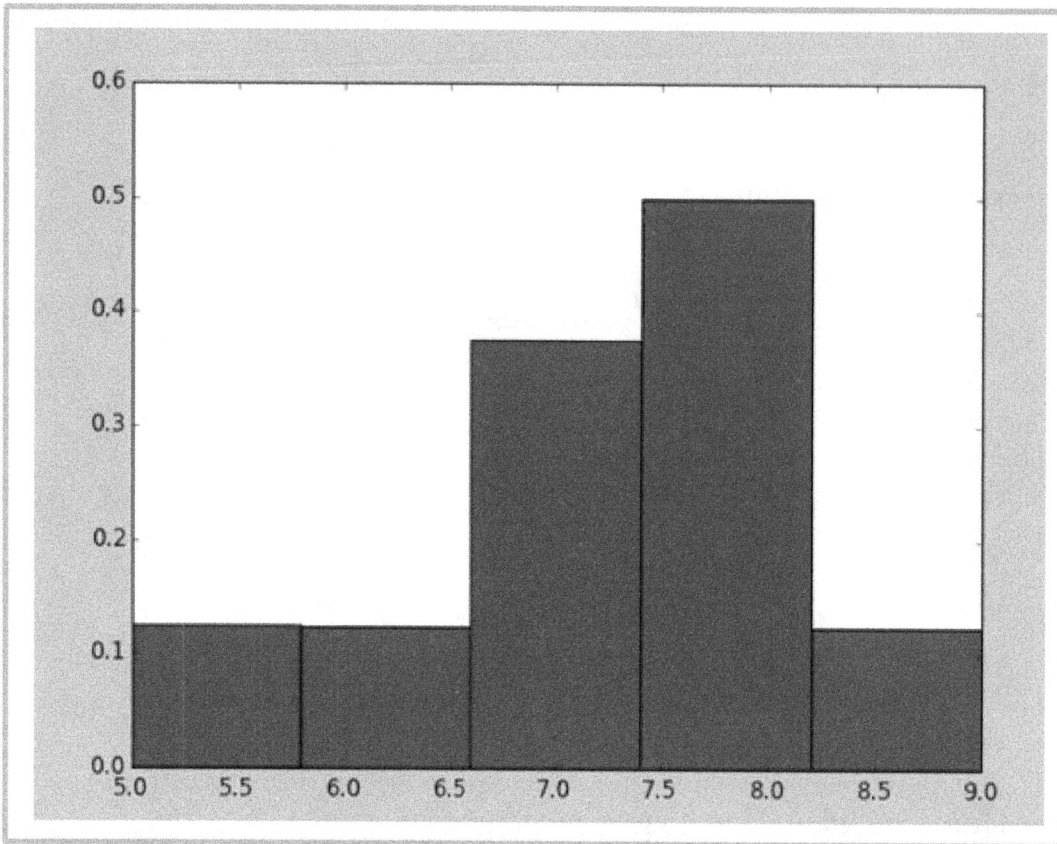

Exhibit 13.4 Histogram-Visual representation of data stat1.xlsx

Now we shall plot titles for the graph by the following code:

```
In [242]: plt.title('Histogram:$\mu:7.2$, $\sigma=1.1$', color = 'yellow')
Out[242]: <matplotlib.text.Text at 0xaa4eed0>
```

Now, press enter, you will get the following output:

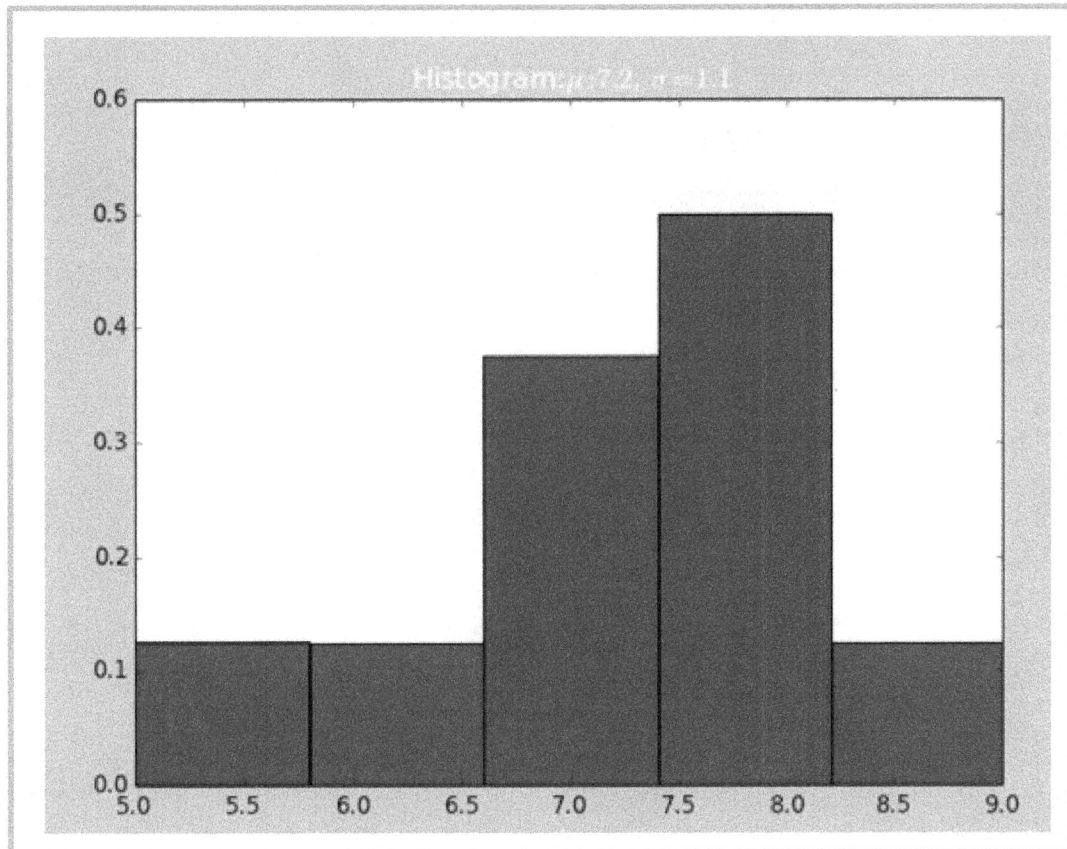

Exhibit 13.5 Histogram with chart title

Now we shall compute the summary statistics.

```
In [244]: x.describe()
Out[244]:
count    10.000000
mean      7.300000
std       1.159502
min       5.000000
25%       7.000000
50%       7.500000
75%       8.000000
max       9.000000
dtype: float64
```

Here we said **x.describe**, because, we have assigned column Num to x. Now we shall compute the mode

```
In [245]: mode(x)
Out[245]: (array([ 8.]), array([ 4.]))
```

Please do not for forget to import mode, or else you will get an error.

From this Histogram we know that, the data is skewed to the left. Now let us have a check on Skewness.

```
In [246]: x.skew()
Out[246]: -0.72701499925736401
```

The result says, it is negatively skewed, or skewed to the left.

Exercise 13.3

Load data **stat2.xlsx.**

```
In [258]: data = pd.read_excel('D:/stat2.xlsx', 'Sheet1')
```

Viewing a part of the data:

```
In [255]: data
Out[255]:
```

	Numbers
0	5
1	6
2	6
3	6
4	7
5	7
6	7
7	8
8	9

Assigning column Numbers to x and plotting the histogram:

```
In [260]: n, bins, patches = plt.hist(x, bins=5, normed =1, facecolor = 'violet')
```

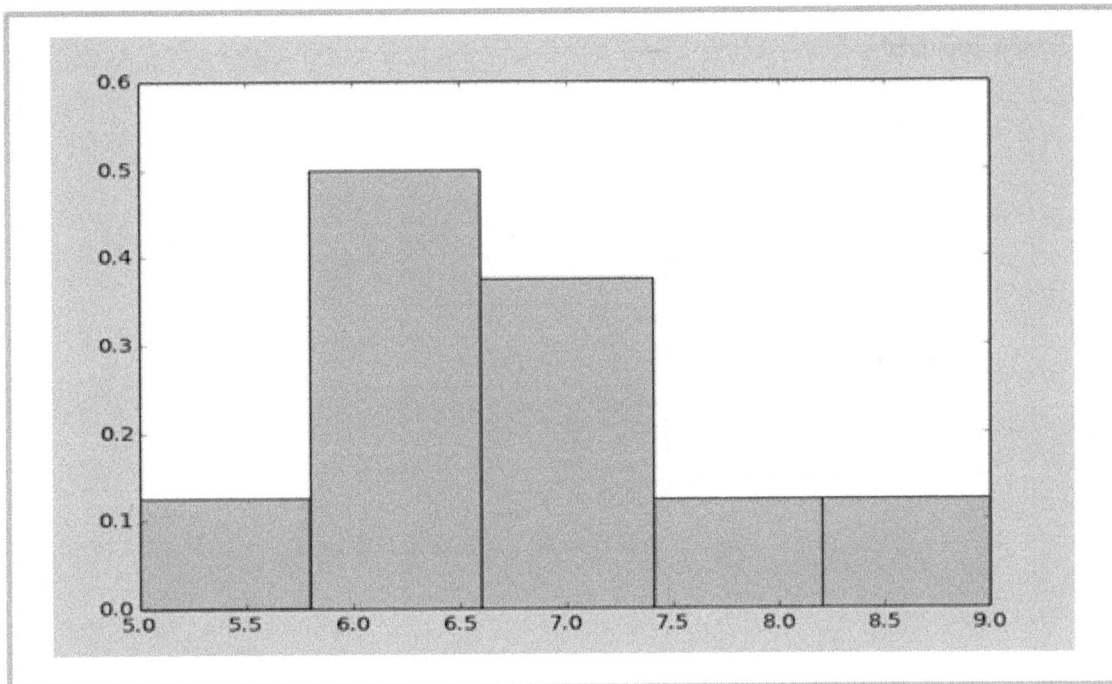

Exhibit 13.6 Histogram stat2.xlsx

In this case, it is skewed to the right.

```
In [261]: x.skew()
Out[261]: 0.72701499925727542
```

You could also do a summary statistic.

```
In [262]: x.describe()
Out[262]:
count    10.000000
mean      6.700000
std       1.159502
min       5.000000
25%       6.000000
50%       6.500000
75%       7.000000
max       9.000000
dtype: float64
```

Exercise 13.4

Load data **stat1.xlsx**.

```
In [250]: data = pd.read_excel('D:/stat1.xlsx', 'Sheet1')
```

Now we shall view the data'.

```
In [251]: data
Out[251]:
```

	Num
0	5
1	6
2	7
3	7
4	7
5	8
6	8
7	8
8	8
9	9

13.4.1

Compute Inter Quartile Range

First we have to find Q1, Q2 and Q3. The following code will help us finding the same.

```
In [252]: data.describe()
```

	Num
count	10.000000
mean	7.300000
std	1.159502
min	5.000000
25%	7.000000
50%	7.500000
75%	8.000000
max	9.000000

Here we have Q1 (25%) as 7.

Q2, the median 7.5.

Q3 (75%) as 8.0

IQR = Q3-Q1

   = 8.0- 7.0

```
In [253]: 8.0-7.0
Out[253]: 1.0
```

Therefore, IQR is 1.

13.5

Calculate Range, Kurtosis, Standard deviation and variance for data 'stat1.xlsx'.

First, load the data.

```
In [263]: data = pd.read_excel('D:/stat1.xlsx', 'Sheet1')
```

View the part of a data:

```
In [264]: data.head(3)
Out[264]:
```

	Num
0	5
1	6
2	7

Before we compute, first let us assign the column 'Num' to a temporary variable 'col'.

```
In [265]: col = data.Num
```

Now we shall compute Range.

```
In [266]: high = max(col)
```

Viewing the result stored in high.

```
In [267]: high
Out[267]: 9.0
```

```
In [268]: low = min(col)
```

```
In [269]: low
Out[269]: 5.0
```

Range = high − low

```
In [270]: high - low
Out[270]: 4.0
```

Kurtosis

We make use of **.kurt ()** function to calculate kurtosis.

```
In [272]: col.kurt()
Out[272]: 0.51196737147238636
```

Standard deviation and Variance

Standard deviation:

```
In [274]: std(col)
Out[274]: 1.100000000000001
```


We have already assigned the column 'Num' from the data 'stat1.xlsx' to a temporary container col at the beginning of exercise 12.5. If you haven't assigned it, you have to load the data stat1.xlsx and assign the column Num to the variable col. Then proceed with the calculation of standard deviation. You have to follow the same in order to compute Variance.

Variance

```
In [275]: var(col)
Out[275]: 1.2100000000000022
```

13.6

Normalization

Data transformation is one of the concerns of the data analysts when they find the data is not normally distributed or when the researcher finds the levels of IVs are not homogeneous, a criterion proposed by statistical theories for ensuring the suitability of data for parametric tests. We apply data transformation techniques with an intention to make the distribution normal or close to that and to make the difference in the variances of the levels of IVs minimum. For this what we do is to apply the same mathematical formula to each of the values of the variable. However, it is not fair to apply different transformations to arrive at a statistical significance. For the purpose of data transformation, we often square the data, often use x^a or 10^x reciprocals, roots, logarithms, etc.(Clark-Carter,2004).

Researchers are often concerned with the symmetry of the distribution when they need to conduct the parametric test. Here the terms Skewness and Kurtosis comes to the scenario, which addresses the symmetry and peakedness of a distribution. If the distribution is not symmetrical and its tail extending to the right is called positively skewed distribution. An asymmetrical distribution with a tail extending to the left is called negatively skewed distribution. For a perfectly normal distribution, the Skewness would be zero.

On the other hand, Kurtosis is the measure of peakedness of the distribution. For a perfectly normal distribution (Gaussian curve) Kurtosis would be zero, a more peaked distribution is said to have positive kurtosis and less peaked (than the normal) distribution has negative kurtosis. We can use data transformation techniques to make the distribution more symmetrical in order to meet the requirements of being eligible for certain statistical tests.

In the previous examples, especially in this chapter, we have seen three sets of data, with symmetrical distribution, negative skew and positive skew respectively. In the case of Skewness, mostly researchers tend to reduce it by normalizing the data for their analysis.

Here we consider 'stat1.xlsx'.

First and foremost import pandas and load the data in to a temporary variable named dat. You could give any name for the temporary variable.

```
In [367]: dat = pd.read_excel('D:/stat1.xlsx', 'Sheet1')
```

Now we shall view the data by the following code:

```
In [368]: dat
Out[368]:
```

	Num
0	5
1	6
2	7
3	7
4	7
5	8
6	8
7	8
8	8
9	9

Now we shall make a histogram of the data.

```
In [369]: import numpy as np
```

```
In [370]: import matplotlib.mlab as mlab
```

```
In [371]: import matplotlib.pyplot as plt
```

```
In [372]: x = dat.Num
```

Now we shall plot the histogram and view the chart.

```
In [373]: n, bins, patches = plt.hist(x, bins = 5, normed = True, color ='orange', alpha=0.5)
```

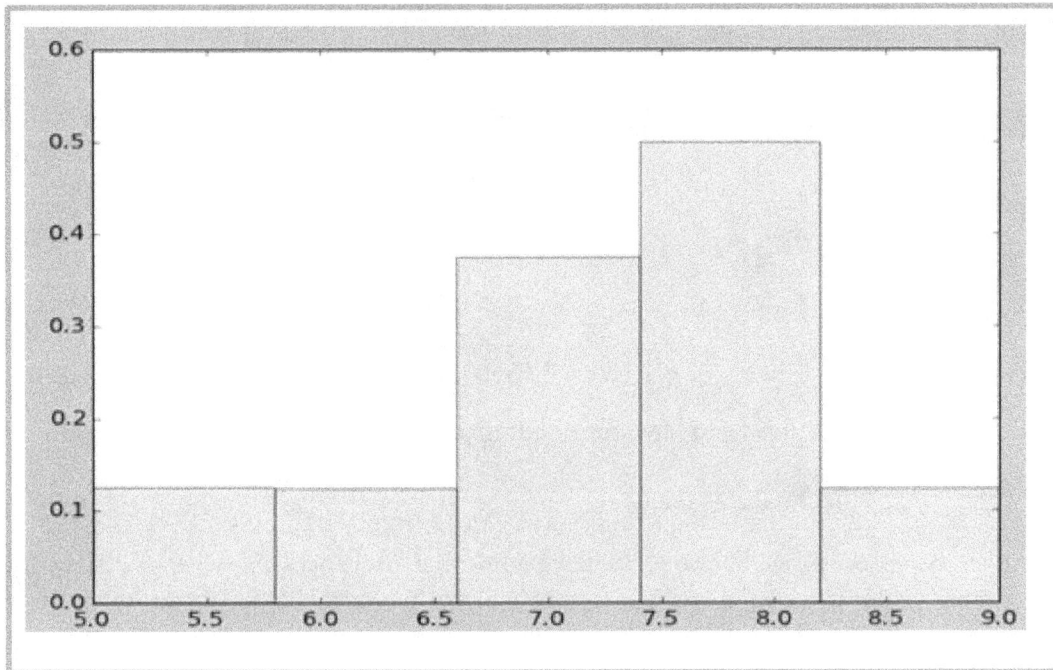

Exhibit 13.7 Histogram of data stat1.xlsx — negatively skewed/skewed to the left side

Here we have a negative skew or it is skewed to the left. To confirm, we could follow the following code:

```
In [374]: x.skew()
Out[374]: -0.72701499925736401
```

Hence it is not a normal distribution. Now we shall normalize the data.

In order to perform normalization using Python, you need to import necessary modules.

```
In [375]: from sklearn import preprocessing as pps
```

Here we are importing module '**pre-processing**' into a temporary variable named 'pps'. You could give any name. For example, you could give as, from sklearn import pre-processing as 'pp' or any name of your choice. While you name a temporary container, you should try to give something short and simple to re -use it again and again.

Once you are done with importing the module preprocessing, the next step is to convert your data/column into a 2D array.

The following codes will illustrate the same:

```
In [377]: twod = np.array([x])
```

Here we have converted the column 'Num' in to a 2D array and have the new format stored in variable named 'twod'.

Now you could view the data.

```
In [378]: twod
Out[378]: array([[ 5.,  6.,  7.,  7.,  7.,  8.,  8.,  8.,  8.,  9.]])
```

Here you might notice that, '5' is being displayed as '**5.**', which in turn implies 5.0, 6.0 and so on.

Now we shall perform normalization and have the result in a temporary container named norm.

```
In [379]: norm = pps.normalize(twod)
```

Here 'pps' implies pre-processing, because, we have imported preprocessing as 'pps'. Suppose, for your analysis; you import pre-processing as 'prs', the code will be 'prs.normalize'. If you import it as 'p', then 'p.normalize'. Twod is the 2d array, which we have computed.

Now we shall view the result of normalization process.

Type norm and press enter; you will get the following output:

```
In [380]: norm
Out[380]:
array([[ 0.21417647,  0.25701176,  0.29984706,  0.29984706,  0.29984706,
         0.34268235,  0.34268235,  0.34268235,  0.34268235,  0.38551764]])
```

Here your data/column has been normalized. You could either use this result as it is for further analysis. You could use it as 'norm'. Simultaneously, you could also round the decimals up to three.

The following code will round the decimals.

```
In [387]: deci = np.around(norm, decimals = 3)
```

Here we made use of 'np.around'. np implies numpy, because, we have imported 'numpy' as 'np'. If you import 'numpy' as 'yo', you should use 'yo.around'.

Simultaneously you could use 'np.round' for the same purpose.

```
In [389]: np.round(norm, decimals = 4)
Out[389]:
array([[ 0.2142,  0.257 ,  0.2998,  0.2998,  0.2998,  0.3427,  0.3427,
         0.3427,  0.3427,  0.3855]])
```

But if you want to save it back to your original data, as a different column, then you need to convert it back to a Data frame and then append to your data. Here we make use of 'deci', where we have rounded decimals to three places.

In order to convert it to a 'Data Frame', first you have to import pandas data frame.

```
In [390]: from pandas import DataFrame
```

```
In [391]: normdata = pd.DataFrame(deci)
```

Now we shall view the converted data:

```
In [392]: normdata
Out[392]:
```

	0	1	2	3	4	5	6	7	8	9
0	0.214	0.257	0.3	0.3	0.3	0.343	0.343	0.343	0.343	0.386

You could the same for further analysis too. In case you want to append it with the original data, then we shall do the following:

First we will transpose the 'normdata', to change the shape.

```
In [393]: tdata = DataFrame.transpose(normdata)
```

View the result:

```
In [394]: tdata
Out[394]:
```

	0
0	0.214
1	0.257
2	0.300
3	0.300
4	0.300
5	0.343
6	0.343
7	0.343
8	0.343
9	0.386

Now we shall append it to the original data. Before that, viewing the original data:

```
In [395]: dat.head(2)
Out[395]:
```

	Num
0	5
1	6

Now we shall append 'tdata' to the new data and will give column name as 'normalised'.

```
In [403]: dat['Normal'] = tdata
```

Here we define the column name and equate the values of 'tdata', which will, in turn, append the same to the original data.

Now let us view the data:

```
In [404]: dat
Out[404]:
```

	Num	Normal
0	5	0.214
1	6	0.257
2	7	0.300
3	7	0.300
4	7	0.300
5	8	0.343
6	8	0.343
7	8	0.343
8	8	0.343
9	9	0.386

We could now make a histogram for the normalised data.

If you haven't already imported the necessary modules and libraries for histogram, please import it now and then follow the codes:

```
In [405]: x = data.Normal
```

```
In [406]: x
Out[406]:
0    0.214
1    0.257
2    0.300
```

We defined 'x' and viewed few of the values. Now making the histogram and viewing the same.

```
In [407]: n, bins, patches = plt.hist(x, bins = 5, normed = True, color ='orange', alpha=0.5)
```

After typing the above code and press enter, you will get the histogram in a different window. You have to minimize the same, in case you want to add chart title or any other arrangements. We can now plot the title for the graph.

```
In [408]: plt.title('Histogram of Normalized data', color = 'purple')
Out[408]: <matplotlib.text.Text at 0xa98aa50>
```

After typing enter, open the chart window, you will see the following output:

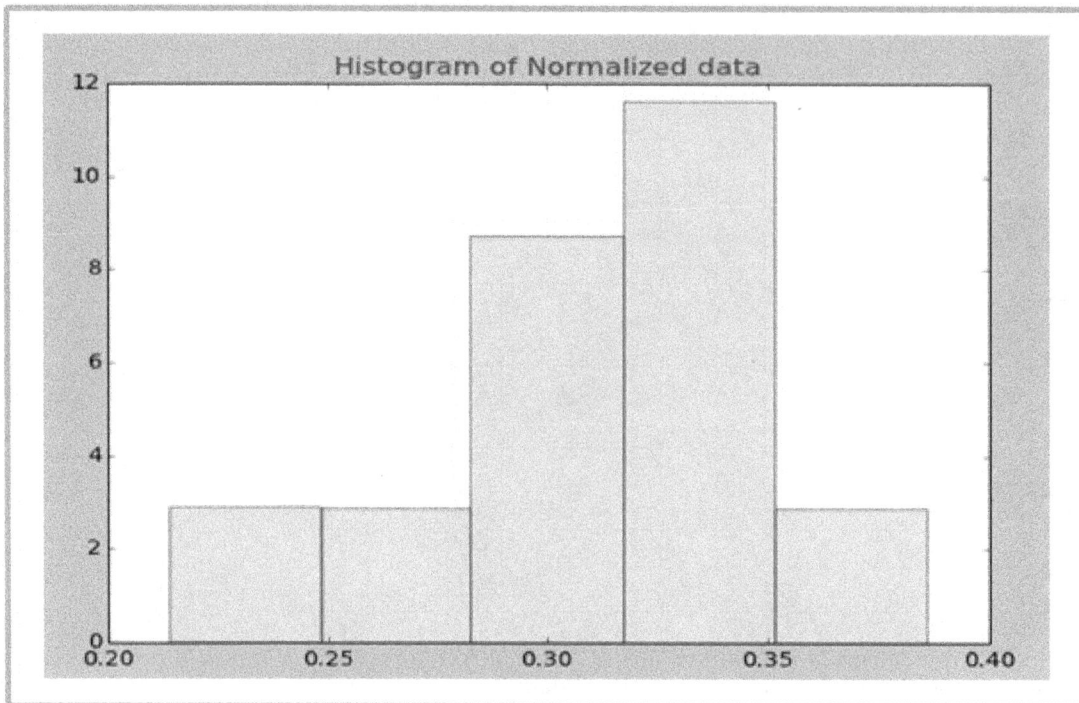

Exhibit 13.8 Histogram of normalized data

Here you might notice that the histogram is slightly skewed to the left. However, a perfect normality is only a statistical assumption. Also, we have rounded off the normalized values, which might have an impact on the output.

13.6.1

Now let us consider data 'stat2.xlsx'.

```
In [409]: data = pd.read_excel('D:/stat2.xlsx', 'Sheet1')
```

```
In [410]: data
Out[410]:
```

	Numbers
0	5
1	6
2	6

We have opened the data and view a part of it. In order to view a part, you need to give 'data.head(number)'.

```
In [411]: data.head(3)
Out[411]:
```

	Numbers
0	5
1	6
2	6

Please do not forget to import pandas before loading the data.

Now let us once again view the histogram of the data.

```
In [412]: x = data.Numbers
```

Here we have assigned column numbers to temporary variable 'x'.

Now we shall plot the histogram.

```
In [413]: n, bins, patches = plt.hist(x, bins = 5, normed = True, color ='orange', alpha=0.5)
```

When you press enter, you will get the histogram on a different window and minimize the same.

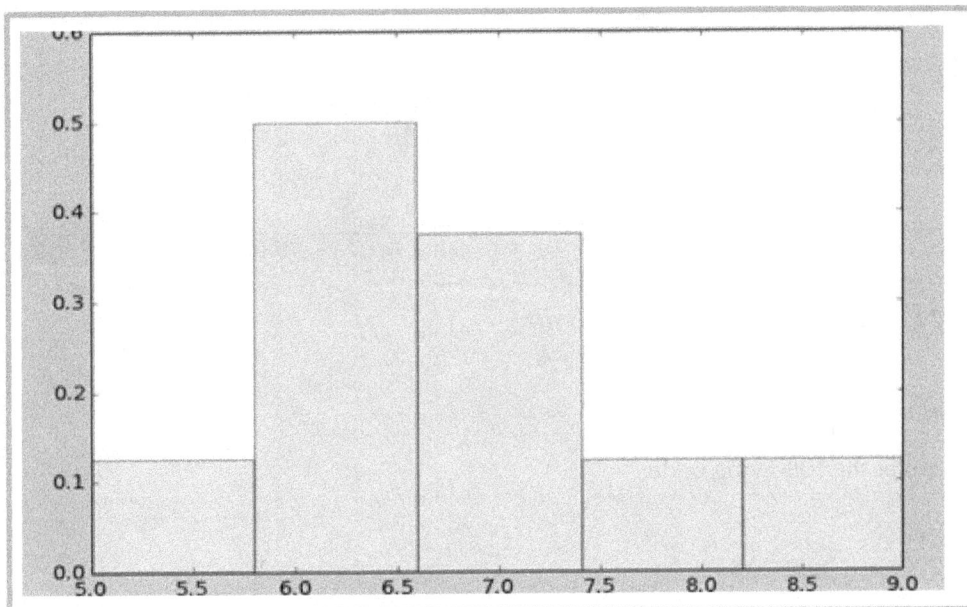

Exhibit 13.9 Histogram of stat2.xlsx – positively skewed / skewed to the right side

Now let's name the histogram.

```
In [415]: plt.title('Histogram: Origial data', color = 'purple')
Out[415]: <matplotlib.text.Text at 0xa906370>
```

Now maximise the window to view the histogram with title.

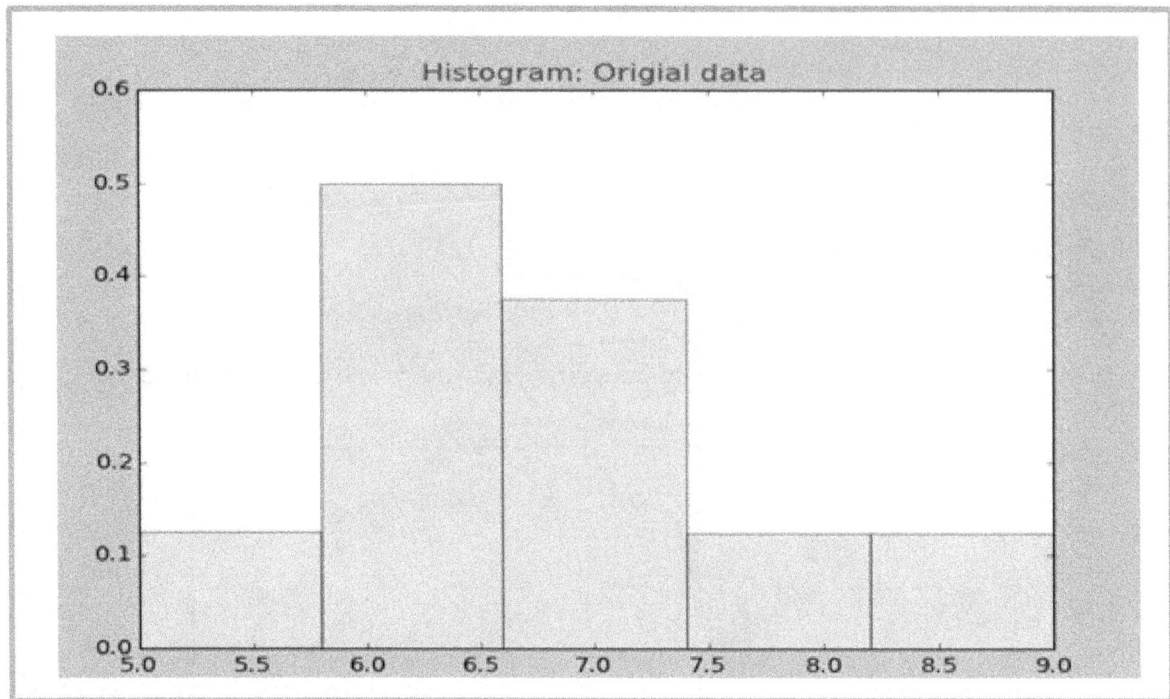

Exhibit 13.10 Histogram of stat2.xlsx with chart title

Here we the data is skewed to the right.

Let us re confirm it via the following code:

```
In [416]: x.skew()
Out[416]: 0.72701499925727542
```

Now we shall perform the steps for normalising the data.

First and foremost, we shall import necessary modules. However, if you have, then, no need to import it again.

```
In [417]: from sklearn import preprocessing as p
```

Now we shall convert our data to a 2d array.

You must be wondering, why we need to convert data into a 2d array. (An array is the collection of information in linear order.)This is because, if we directly normalize the data, it will make each and every value within the data/column to 1. This is because; Python data frame automatically rounds off the decimal value.

The following code will convert data in to 2d array:

```
In [421]: twod = np.array([x])
```

Please import numpy, before writing the aforementioned code, in case you haven't.

As you know, we have performed conversion of data into 2d array into a temporary container named twod. Now we shall type twod and press enter, and will get the following output:

```
In [422]: twod
Out[422]: array([[ 5.,   6.,   6.,   6.,   6.,   7.,   7.,   7.,   8.,   9.]])
```

Now we shall normalize the 2d array.

```
In [423]: twodnorm = p.normalize(twod)
```

Here we said, 'p.normalize', this is because, we have imported pre-processing as 'p', where as in the previous example, we have imported preprocessing as 'pps'. As we said earlier, you could give any name for the temporary container as per your choice. However, please give the names, that could be easily relate with the main function/analysis/module, this is because, when you have multiple temporary containers, it would be easy for you to recognise which one belongs to what, or else you will be confused and lost and might have to do everything from the beginning.

Now let us view the result. Remember we have normalised 2d array data twod and stored in to another temporary variable named 'twodnorm'.

```
In [424]: twodnorm
Out[424]:
array([[ 0.23287322,  0.27944786,  0.27944786,  0.27944786,  0.27944786,
         0.3260225 ,  0.3260225 ,  0.3260225 ,  0.37259715,  0.41917179]])
```

Here we have the normalized output. You could use this data for further use. You could also round off the decimals to three places.

We have rounded it off to three decimals.

Now viewing the results:

```
In [512]: r = np.around(twodnorm, decimals = 3)
```

In variable 'r', we have stored the results and now will view the same:

```
In [513]: r
Out[513]:
array([[ 0.233,  0.279,  0.279,  0.279,  0.279,  0.326,  0.326,  0.326,
         0.373,  0.419]])
```

If you want to append the results back to the original data, first you need to convert 2d array in to data frame via following code:

```
In [514]: d = pd.DataFrame(r)
```

```
In [515]: d
Out[515]:
```

	0	1	2	3	4	5	6	7	8	9
0	0.233	0.279	0.279	0.279	0.279	0.326	0.326	0.326	0.373	0.419

Now if you want to append the results to the original data, first you should transpose the data.

```
In [516]: td = DataFrame.transpose(d)
```

Here we are transposing/changing the shape of the data.

```
In [517]: td
Out[517]:
```

	0
0	0.233
1	0.279
2	0.279
3	0.279
4	0.279
5	0.326
6	0.326
7	0.326
8	0.373
9	0.419

Now we shall append back to the original data.

```
In [436]: tnormdata
Out[436]:
```

	0
0	0.214
1	0.257
2	0.300
3	0.300
4	0.300
5	0.343
6	0.343
7	0.343
8	0.343
9	0.386

Now we shall append to the original data.

Before that let's have a look on the original data.

```
In [437]: data
Out[437]:
```

	Numbers
0	5
1	6
2	6
3	6
4	6
5	7
6	7
7	7
8	8
9	9

Now we will append the normalised data.

```
In [518]: data['Normed'] = td
```

We have created a new column 'Normed' and at the same time transferred the values from 'td' to the column normed.

```
In [519]: data
Out[519]:
```

	Numbers	Normed
0	5	0.233
1	6	0.279
2	6	0.279
3	6	0.279
4	6	0.279
5	7	0.326
6	7	0.326
7	7	0.326
8	8	0.373
9	9	0.419

It is not necessary to append the normalised data, unless required.

Now we shall make a histogram with the normalised data.

```
In [520]: x=data.Normed
```

Let us view x:

```
In [523]: x
Out[523]:
0     0.233
1     0.279
2     0.279
3     0.279
4     0.279
5     0.326
6     0.326
7     0.326
8     0.373
9     0.419
Name: Normed, 
```

Now let's make a histogram:

```
In [525]: n, bins, patches = plt.hist(x, bins = 5, normed = True, color = 'blue', alpha = 0.5)
```

```
In [527]: plt.title('Histogram of Normalised data', color = 'red')
Out[527]: <matplotlib.text.Text at 0xa89a990>
```

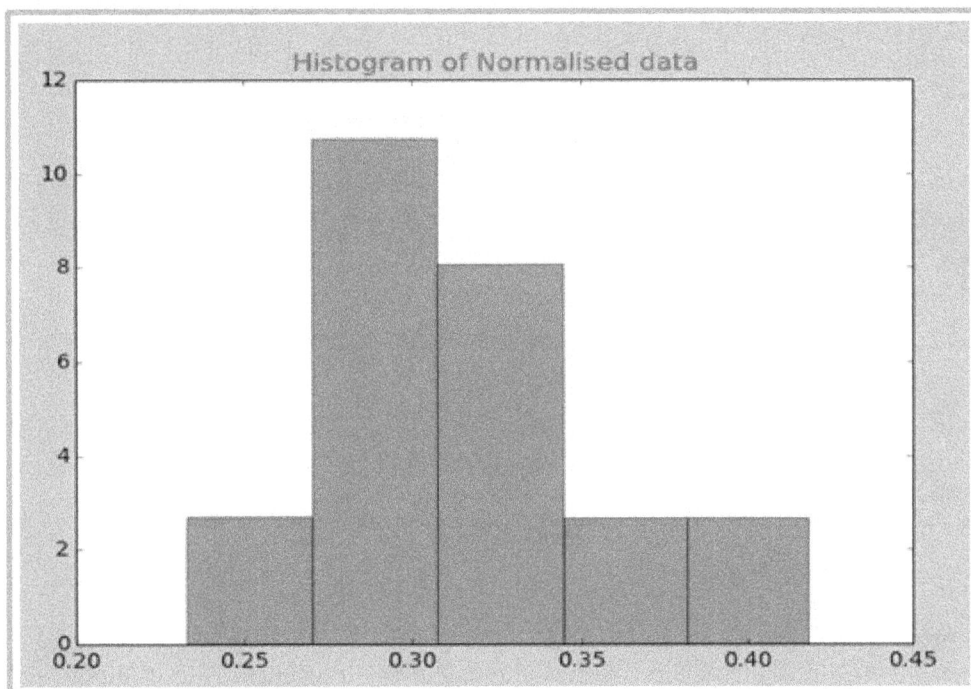

Exhibit 13.11 Histogram of normalised stat2.xlsx data

As we have explained in the previous example, perfect normality is only a statistical assumption. Here, the data is slightly skewed to the right. However, we have rounded off the normalized values, which could have some impact on the output.

If you are not fine with slight Skewness, you need not round off the decimals; use the normalized data as it is.

Exercise 13.7

Converting data to Binary values

This section illustrates how to convert data to binary values.

For this exercise please import **bn.xlsx**.

The following code will illustrate the same:

```
In [77]: import pandas as pd
```

```
In [78]: data = pd.read_excel('D:/bn.xlsx', 'Sheet1')
```

Display the data:

	Bn
0	1
1	0
2	2
3	1
4	-1
5	0
6	2
7	-2
8	0
9	0
10	1
11	0
12	-2
13	1

Now we shall import 'preprocessing' as 'p'.

```
In [80]: from sklearn import preprocessing as p
```

Performing the process in a temporary container 'b'

```
In [81]: b = pp.Binarizer().fit(data.Bn)
```

Now we shall transform the data and view the result:

```
In [82]: b.transform(data.Bn)
Out[82]: array([ 1.,  0.,  1.,  1.,  0.,  0.,  1.,  0.,  0.,  0.,  1.,  0.,  0.,  1.])
```

Now we shall view the data:

```
In [87]: data
Out[87]:
```

	Bn
0	1
1	0
2	1
3	1
4	0
5	0
6	1
7	0
8	0
9	0
10	1
11	0
12	0
13	1

Exercise 13.8

Pivot Tables

Another powerful tool to view the data is pivot table. Under certain circumstances we need to tweak the visual of the data so that it is more meaningful, depending on your requirement.

13.8.1

In order to proceed further, please import data **worldcup.xlsx**.

Here, we have the list of teams who have won cricket world cup from 1975. The information to make the data is from www.totalsportek.com.

```
In [48]: import pandas as pd

In [50]: data
Out[50]:
```

	Year	Team
0	1975	West Indies
1	1979	West Indies
2	1983	India
3	1987	Australia
4	1992	Pakistan
5	1996	Srilanka
6	1999	Australia
7	2003	Australia
8	2007	Australia
9	2011	India
10	2015	Australia

Here we have the list of team who have won cricket world cup.

Suppose, you are asked to help a sports analyst to make a TV presentation on world cup cricket matches. In the data, we have teams who won the cup along with the year. Now the analyst wants a different view of the data, where, you have teams those who won the world cup along with the number of times each team won.

In order to help him, we shall make a pivot table and assign/define it in a temporary container named 'pt'.

```
In [59]: pt =data.pivot_table('Team', rows=['Team'], cols = None, aggfunc = 'count', fill_value = 0)
```

Now, type 'pt' and press enter.

You will get the following output:

```
In [60]: pt
Out[60]:
Team
Australia        5
India            2
Pakistan         1
Srilanka         1
West Indies      2
Name: Team, dtype: int64
```

Chapter 13 : Describing Data - Visual & Numeric

Please note that, in the above code, which is used to create a pivot table, we gave 'Team' within the code. This is not a temporary container. Most of the time we assign the column to a temporary container and make use of that in the analysis. Here we give the column directly.

If you want to save, please use the following code:

```
In [62]: pt.to_csv('D:/cricket.csv')
```

If you want to view pivot in a table format, then do the following:

```
In [63]: from pandas import DataFrame
```

In case you haven't imported pandas, then first please import pandas and then follow the aforementioned code.

Converting 'pt' to a data frame.

```
In [64]: newp = pd.DataFrame(pt)
```

Viewing the result:

```
In [65]: newp
Out[65]:
```

	Team
Team	
Australia	5
India	2
Pakistan	1
Srilanka	1
West Indies	2

Well, for now, let us use pivot which we stored in temporary variable 'pt'.

Viewing pt:

```
In [100]: pt
Out[100]:
Team
Australia        5
India            2
Pakistan         1
Srilanka         1
West Indies      2
Name: Team, dtype: int64
```

Make a Bar chart with titles and labels

```
In [101]: pt.plot(kind = 'bar', rot = 0, color  = 'brown')
Out[101]: <matplotlib.axes.AxesSubplot at 0xa155f70>
```

When you press enter, after typing the above code, you will get the following output, and you have to minimize for further arrangements.

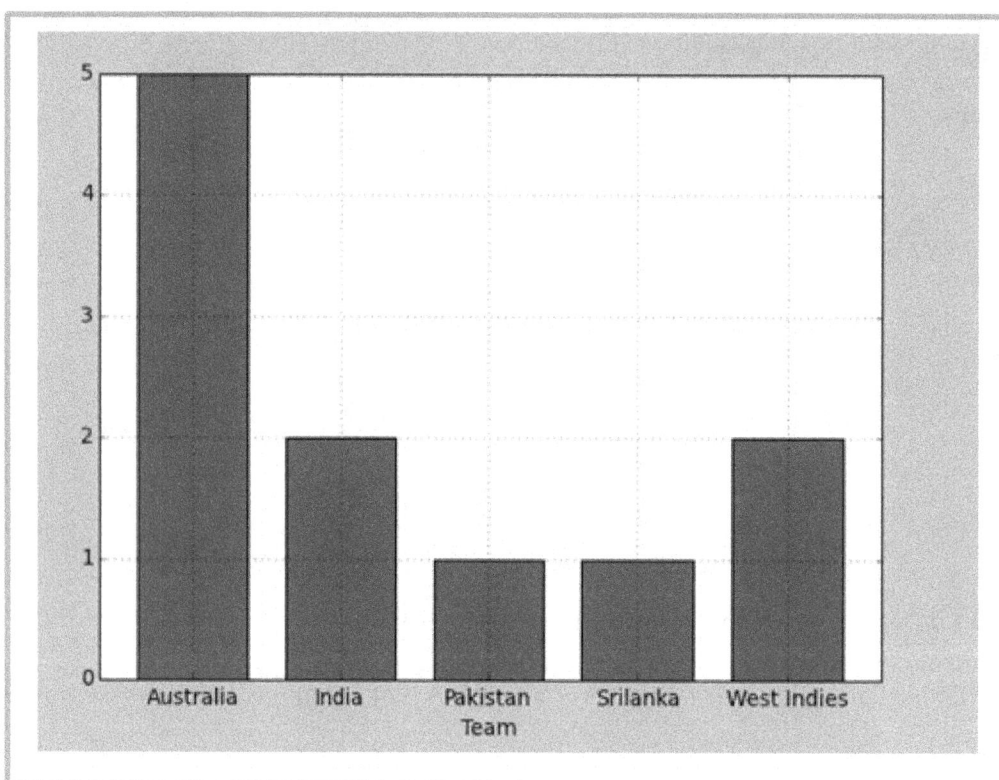

Exhibit 13.12 Bar chart of Cricket world cup winning teams

In the chart, we have given label for x axis. However, now lets us change the color of the x label.

```
In [106]: plt.xlabel('Team', color = 'red')
Out[106]: <matplotlib.text.Text at 0xa23de30>
```

Well, though we have already had x label, still we have to mention the name to get the color changed.

At this point you could maximize the chart window and check if the color has changed or not.

Now we shall plot Y axis.

```
In [108]: plt.ylabel('Numbers of Wins', color = 'red')
Out[108]: <matplotlib.text.Text at 0xa4a65d0>
```

If you maximize the chart window, you could see the label names.

Now we shall add the title.

```
In [110]: plt.title('Cricket World cup;1975 -2016 : Teams with number of wins', color = 'red')
Out[110]: <matplotlib.text.Text at 0xa4bd0b0>
```

When you maximize the window, you could see the following output:

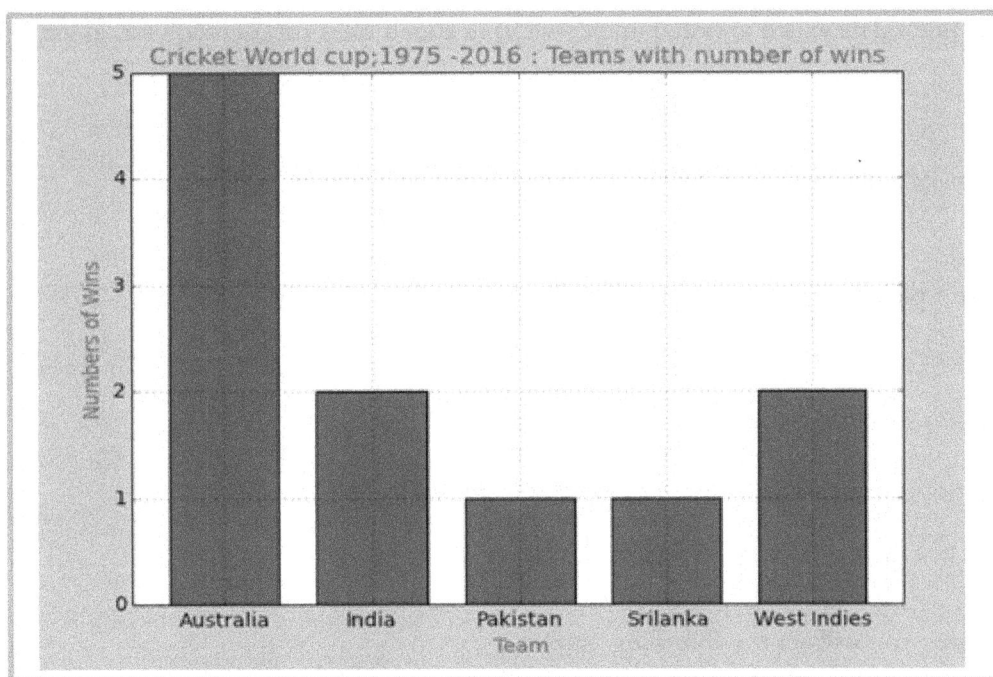

Exhibit 13.13 Bar chart with chart title and labels

Simultaneously, we could make a pie-chart for the same.

Have you saved 'pt' as **cricket.csv**, if not first you save it as 'cricket.csv'.

Then you should open it as 'piedata'.

```
In [145]: piedata = pd.read_csv('D:/cricket.csv')
```

```
In [146]: piedata
Out[146]:
```

	Team	No of Wins
0	Australia	5
1	India	2
2	Pakistan	1
3	Srilanka	1
4	West Indies	2

After saving the pivot data which is stored in 'pt', we have added titles for each column in excel and saved the file.

Now we could make a pie chart.

In order to make a pie chart, first we shall assign the following:

```
In [161]: labels = piedata['Team']
```

```
In [162]: x = piedata['No of Wins']
```

Now we shall plot the pie-chart.

```
In [163]: plt.pie(x, labels = labels)
Out[163]:
```

When you hit enter, you will get the following output:

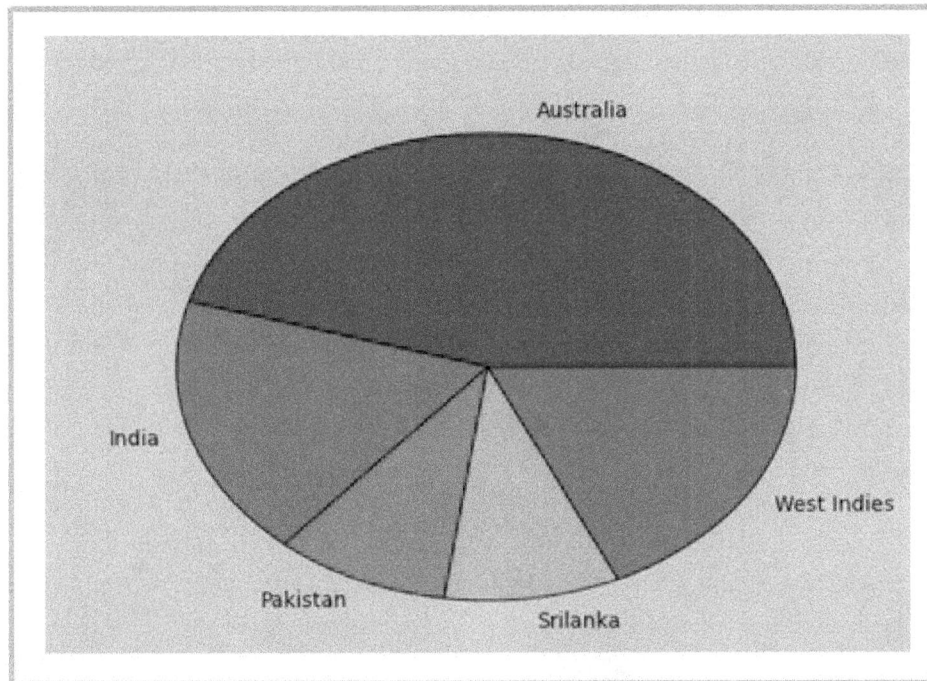

Exhibit 13.14 Pie chart on data cricket.csv

Customization of Pie-Chart

Here we can give a chart title, change the colors to our choice and maybe we could add percentages. You could save previous pie-chart and close the window.

First we will create a customized pie chart.

```
In [174]: plt.pie(x, labels = labels, autopct = '%1.1f%%', colors = ('r', 'y', 'g', 'c', 'm'), shadow = True, startangle=0)
```

For clarity we shall give a different view of the code.

```
In [174]: plt.pie(x, labels = labels, autopct = '%1.1f%%',

colors = ('r', 'y', 'g', 'c', 'm'), shadow = True, startangle=0)
```

When you press enter, you will get the following output:

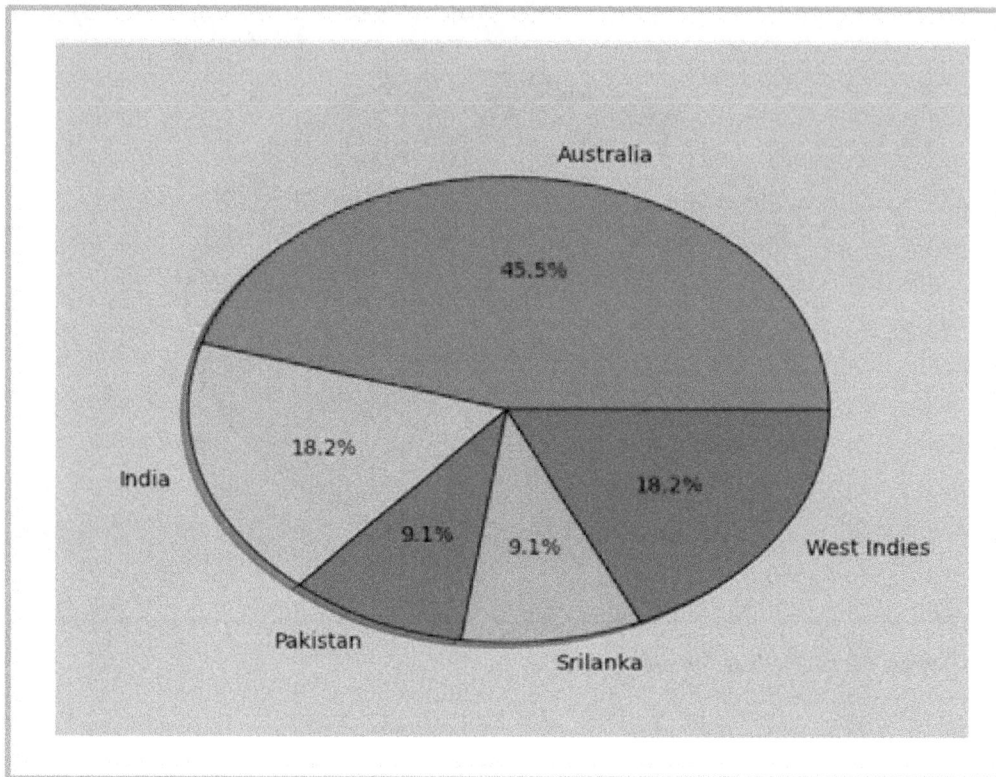

Exhibit 13.15 Customized output of Pie chart

Now we shall add the chart title.

```
In [178]: plt.title('Pie Chart: World Cup Winning Teams with Percentage of Wins;1975-2015', color = 'purple')
Out[178]: <matplotlib.text.Text at 0xdbcbc50>
```

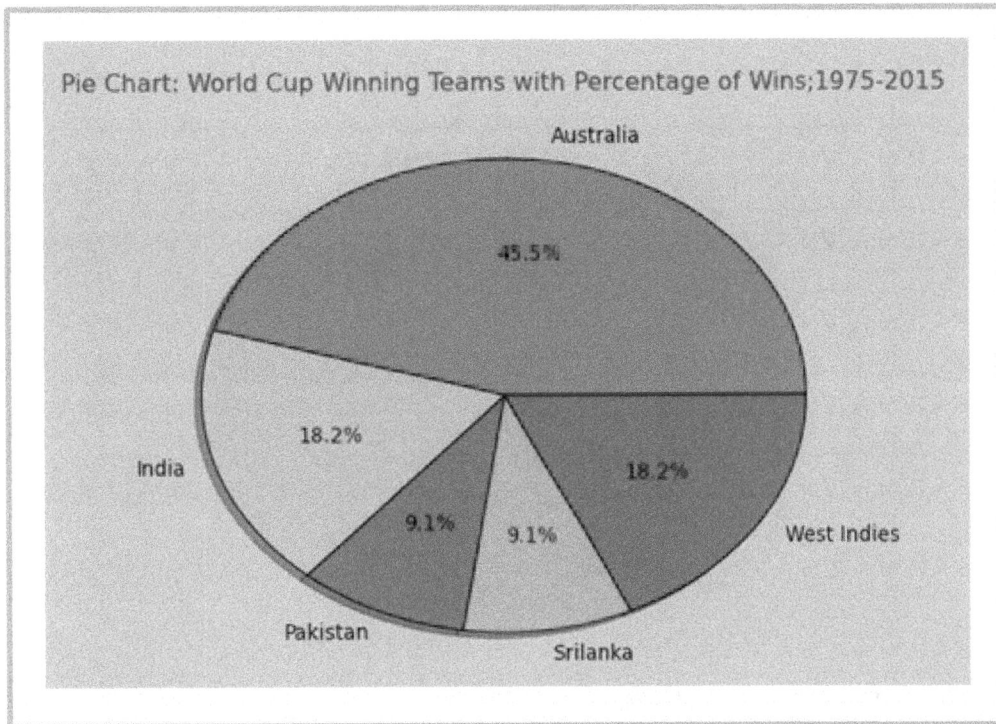

Exhibit 13.16 Pie chart with title

Suppose if you want to highlight anything specific, then you need to use the **explode** features.

The following will illustrate the same:

```
In [51]: explode = (0, 0.2, 0, 0, 0)
```

Here the numbering starts from Australia, then India and so on. Therefore first '0' implies Australia second '0' implies India and the rest follows. In order to explode, we could make it as 0.2 the maximum and for a slight explode 0.1.

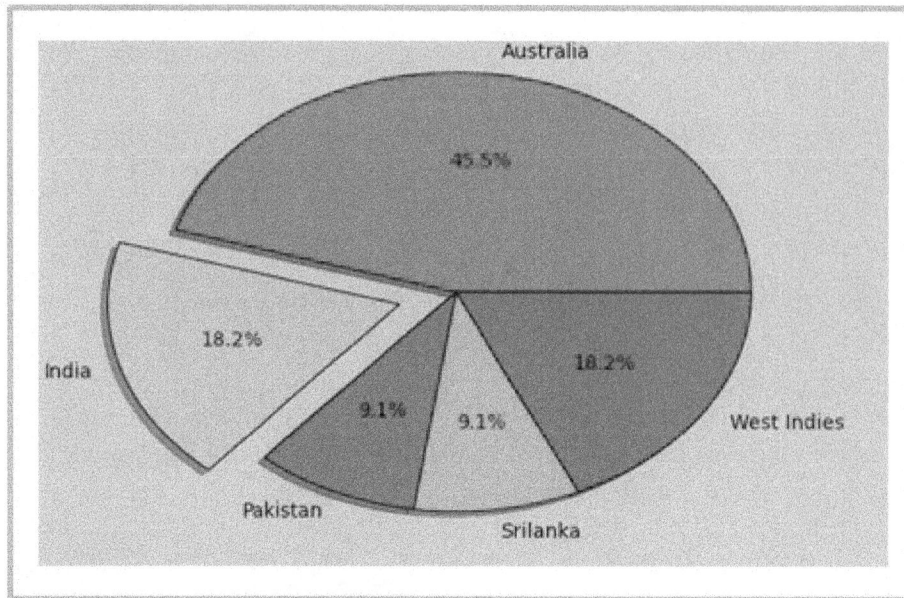

Exhibit 13.17 Pie chart with feature 'explode'

Now we will see another example.

```
In [55]: explode = (0, 0, 0, 0, 0.1)
```

Now let us view the output:

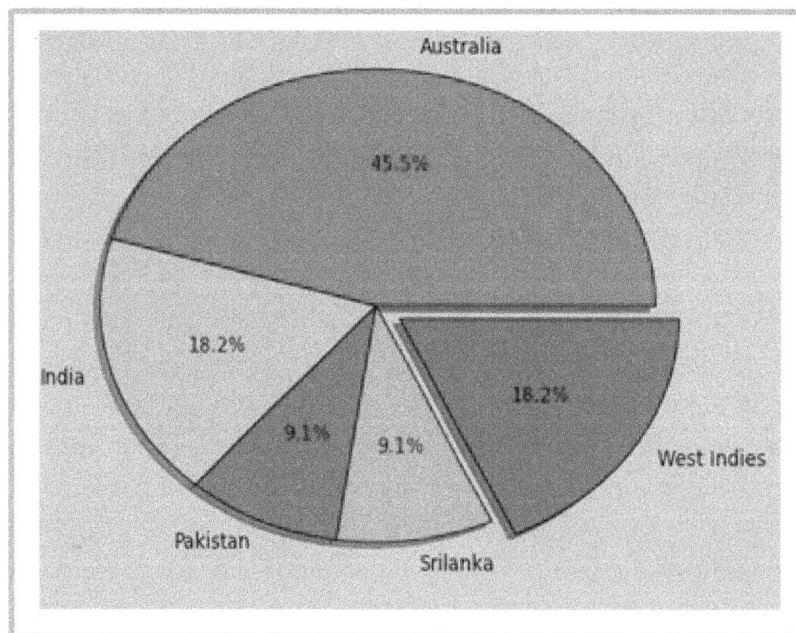

Exhibit 13.18 Pie chart with feature 'explode'

Simultaneously, you could have multiple explode based on the requirements.

For example, highlight two nations with second most win percentage. From the Pie chart, we know that it is India and West Indies.

You could give colors to a temporary variable and could make use of that in the code; the following will illustrate the same:

```
In [56]: explode = (0, 0.1, 0, 0, 0.1)
```

Second location in the chart from left   Fifth location in the chart from left side.

```
In [18]: colors = ('c', 'g', 'y', 'b', 'm')

In [19]: plt.pie(x, explode = explode, labels = labels, colors = colors, autopct = '%1.1f%%', shadow = True, startangle = 01)
Out[19]:
```

Adding title

```
In [28]: plt.title('Teams with Cricket Worldcup Wins;1975 - 2015', color = 'green')
Out[28]: <matplotlib.text.Text at 0x7ccdbf0>
```

Now we shall view the output as follows:

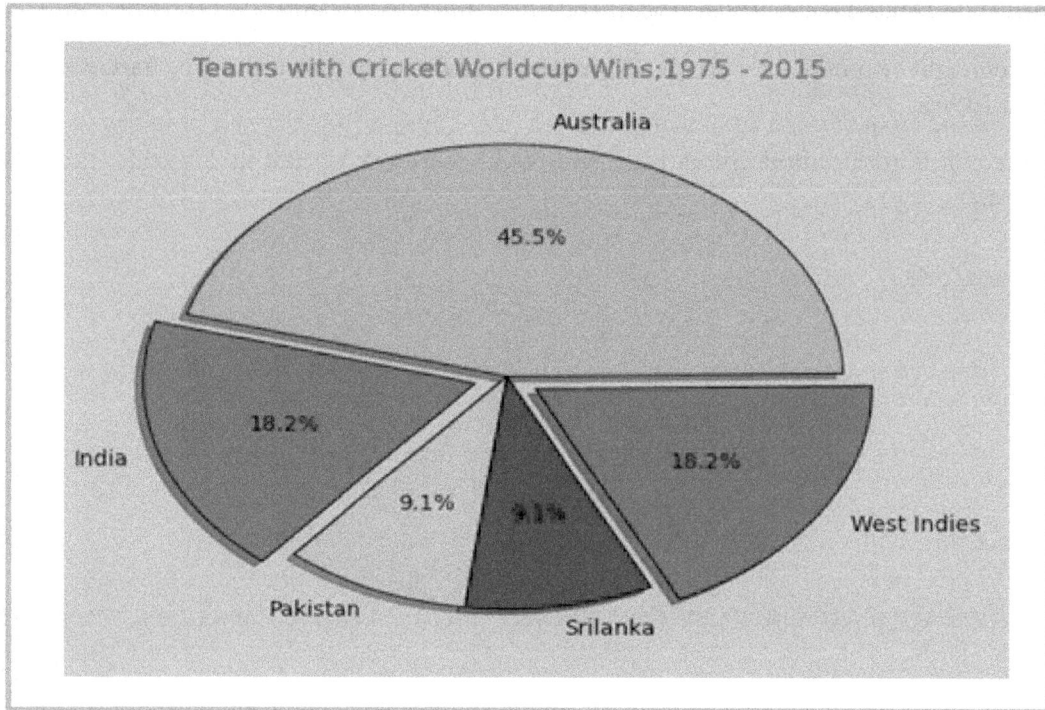

Exhibit 13.19 Pie chart with feature 'explode'

Let us have an alteration in the start angle by making it to 90.

```
In [15]: plt.pie(data['No of Wins'], labels = data.Team, autopct ='%1.1f%%', startangle = 90)
```

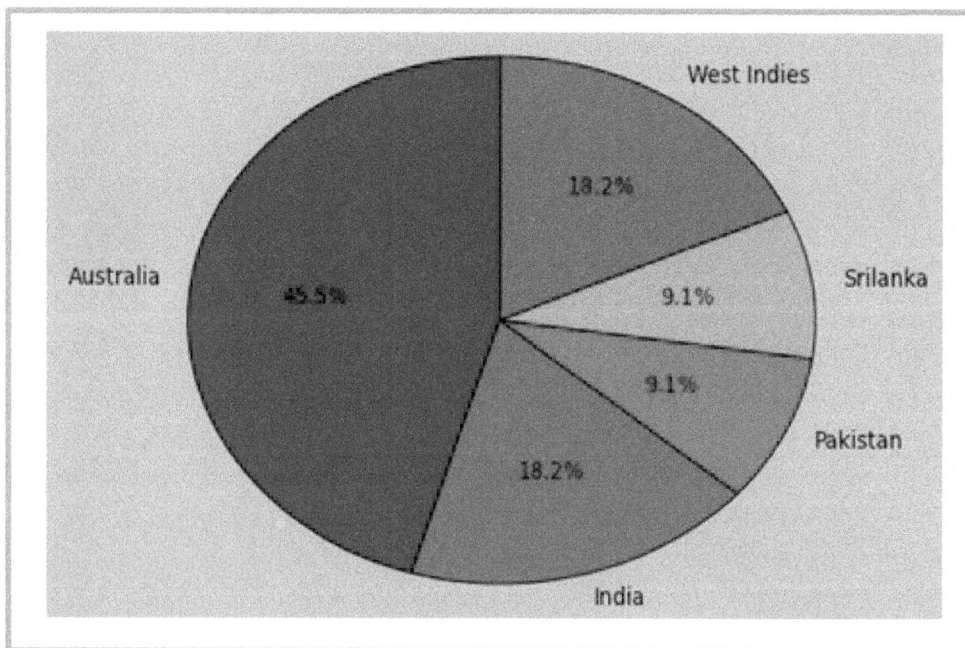

Exhibit 13.20 Pie chart with angle 90

References

1. McKinney, W. (2013). *Python for Data Analysis*. US: O'Reilly.

2. Retrieved June 4, 2014 from http://matplotlib.org/users/screenshots.html#simple-plot
   http://matplotlib.org/index.html

3. Retrieved, June 4, 2014 from http://markthegraph.blogspot.com/2015/05/using-Python-statsmodels-for-ols-linear.html
   Linear Regression

4. Retrieved , June 4, 2014 from http://stackoverflow.com/questions/3949226/calculating-pearson-correlation-and-significance-in-Python
   Correlation - Pearson Product Moment Correlation

5. Retrieved, June 10, 2014 from http://www.scipy-lectures.org/packages/statistics/index.html#multiple-regression-including-multiple-factors
   Multiple Regression

6. Retrieved, June 10, 2014 from http://blog.yhat.com/posts/logistic-regression-and-Python.html
   Logistic regression

7. Retrieved, Sep 12, 2014 from http:/l/docs.scipy.org/doc/scipy-0.14.0/reference/generated/scipy.stats.spearmanr.html http://scipy.org/

8. Retrieved, Sep 15, 2014 from https://gist.github.com/mblondel/1761714

9. Retrieved, Sep 27, 2014   from
   http://nbviewer.jupyter.org/github/herrfz/dataanalysis/blob/master/week5/anova_with_multiple_factors.ipynb

10. Retrieved, Oct 5, 2014   from
    http://docs.scipy.org/doc/scipy/reference/generated/scipy.stats.chisquare.html

11. Retrieved, Oct 7, 2014 from http://docs.scipy.org/doc/scipy-0.14.0/reference/generated/scipy.stats.fisher_exact.html

12. Retrieved, Oct 7, 2014 from http://docs.scipy.org/doc/scipy-0.16.0/reference/generated/scipy.stats.power_divergence.html

13. Retrieved ,Oct 8, 2014 from http://docs.scipy.org/doc/scipy-0.14.0/reference/generated/scipy.stats.chi2_contingency.html

14. Retrieved ,Jan 6,2015 from http://scikit-learn.org/stable/modules/preprocessing.html

15. Garrett, H. E. (1958). *Statistics in Psychology and Education*. Bombay: Vakils, Feffer, and Simons, Pvt. Ltd.

16. Morrison, D. F. (1967). *Multivariate Statistical Methods*. New York: Mc Graw Hill Book Company.

17. Cohen, J. W. (1988). *Statistical Power Analysis for the Behavioural Sciences* (2nd ed.). Hillsdale, N.J. : Larence Erlbaum Associates

18. Clark-Carter(2004). Quantitative Psychological Research: A Student's Handbook. NY:Psychology Press

Index

APPENDIX - I
A Few Things to Know

This section is all about few things you need to take care of while coding in Python. It reminds you about few important steps and facts which you should never forget while coding in Python, especially when you want to deal with your data. It also talks about few common errors that might occur while you write and execute codes and also teaches you few other things that are useful to you while writing codes in Python.

Loading External data

In order to import external data such as Excel, first and foremost you have to **import Pandas** and specify the path name of your file. It is advised not to keep the Excel data in a folder; instead you could save in a particular drive itself so that you could easily type the path. For example, **'D: /sstat1.xlsx', 'sheet1'**which will make things simpler.

However, if you have all your data is being saved within a folder, you could use the following code to open the Excel data from that folder in Python.

In this example, data **bn.xlsx** is being saved in a folder named 'Mydata' in D drive. We shall access the same.

```
In [134]: import pandas as pd
In [135]: data = pd.read_excel('D:/Mydata/bn.xlsx', 'Sheet1')
```

```
In [136]: data
Out[136]:
```

	Bn
0	1
1	0
2	2
3	1
4	-1
5	0
6	2
7	-2
8	0
9	0
10	1

In such cases, you have to specify the drive name, folder name, then the filename with extension and sheet name in case of Excel.xlsx files.

Import necessary modules/packages

In order to perform certain data manipulations and analyses, please do not forget to import necessary packages/modules, otherwise you will get an error message. For example, to open external data in Python, it is imperative to import **Pandas**. Similarly, to make various visualizations, we need to import 'matplotlib.mlab' and 'matplotlib.pyplot'. Also you need to import necessary packages, when and where ever necessary, without which you will get an error message.

Saving your edited data

Though we could save our data/file with any name, in some systems while saving, filenames starting with 'a', 'b', 'n', 'r', 't', or 'v' will give you an error. If it happens, please use file names starting with letters than these. It is not so common, but such kind of errors could occur even though it is rare; this could be due to a system error, not of Python. In order to save your edited data, use 'data.to_csv', where, data is a temporary variable, where you stored the original data. Suppose, if you want to store/assign your data in 'rec', then to save it, you need to use 'rec.to_csv'.

Indentation

Proper indentation is required and is a must when you deal with 'While' and 'IF' statements. Alternatively, you will get an indentation error and program will not run successfully. You will find the details about indentation in chapter 2.

Drawing/plotting Figures/Charts

When you give the code for drawing a chart, for example, a bar chart, the chart will open in a new window.

For instance, we shall load **stat2.xlsx** and draw a bar chart.

```
In [115]: data= pd.read_excel('D:/stat2.xlsx', 'Sheet1')

In [116]: data
Out[116]:
```

	Numbers
0	5
1	6
2	6
3	6
4	6
5	7
6	7
7	7
8	8
9	9

Now we write the following code:

```
In [124]: x.plot(kind = 'bar', rot = 0)
Out[124]: <matplotlib.axes.AxesSubplot at 0x7f4a250>
```

When you press enter, you will get a new window with the

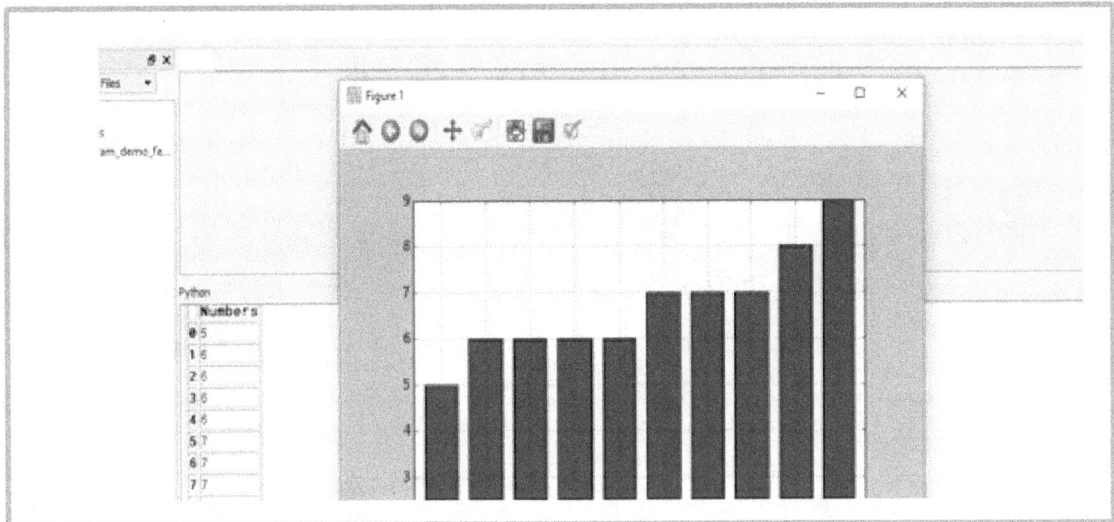

Exhibit A1 on plotting figures

If you want to do further operations on the chart, you have to minimize the window.'
For example, you want to add chart labels and chart title, then minimize the bar chart window and do the following:

```
In [125]: plt.xlabel('X axis')
Out[125]: <matplotlib.text.Text at 0x7f03f10>

In [126]: plt.xlabel('X axis', color = 'red')
Out[126]: <matplotlib.text.Text at 0x7f03f10>

In [127]: plt.ylabel('Y axis', color='red')
Out[127]: <matplotlib.text.Text at 0x82dc3b0>

In [128]: plt.title('Simple bar chart', color='red')
Out[128]: <matplotlib.text.Text at 0x82f6270>
```

While you run each code, i.e., when you press enter after typing the code, you will get 'output'. For example:

```
In [125]: plt.xlabel('X axis')
```

Now when you press enter, you will get the following

```
Out[125]: <matplotlib.text.Text at 0x7f03f10>
```

Then you can maximize the chart window and check if you got the desired result on the chart. Once you did all the necessary operations, you can maximize the window and you save it.

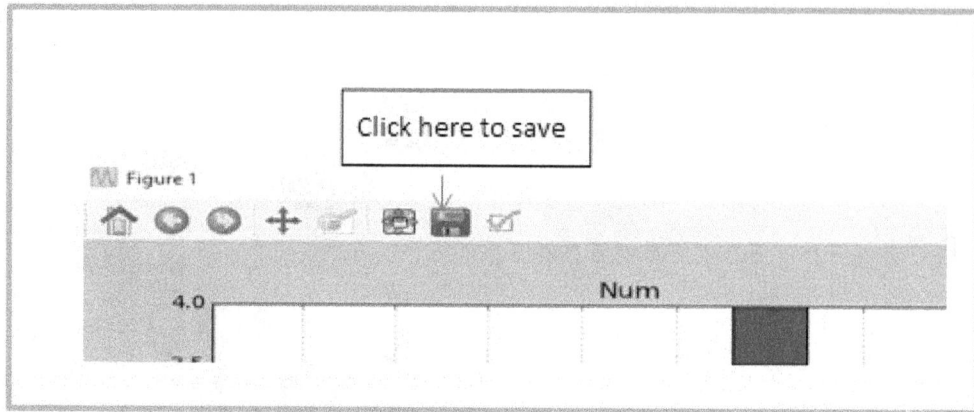

Exhibit A2 on customizing a chart

14.6

Saving diagrams/charts

You might have noticed that figures/charts are being opened in a different window. Above the window, you will have options to save the figures. The following illustrates the same, here we will display the top portion of the diagram window:

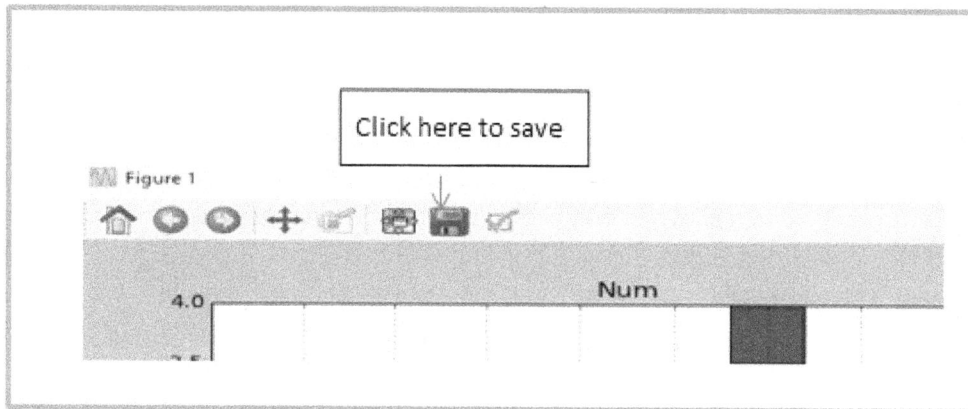

Exhibit A.3 on saving a chart

In order to save the figure, you need to click on the 'save' icon on the top of the chart window. Once you click, you will get the following options:

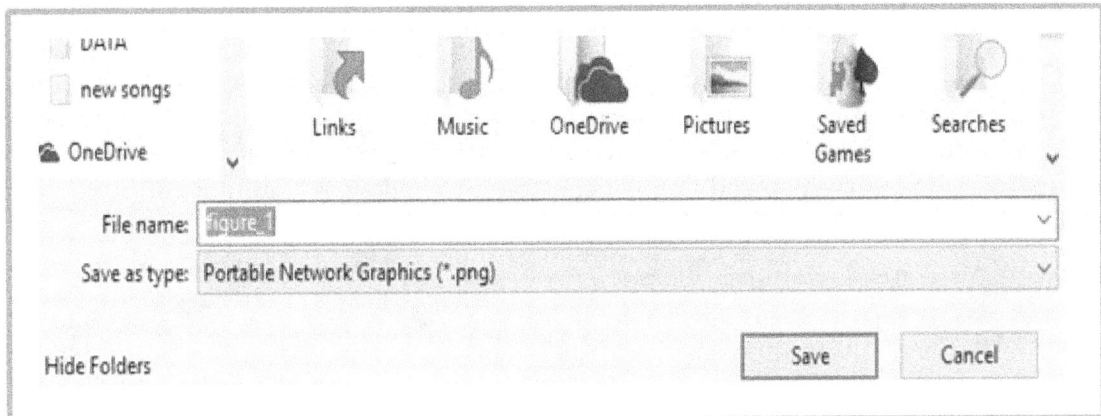

Exhibit 1A4 on saving a chart

Here you can change file name and you can save it us in any format.

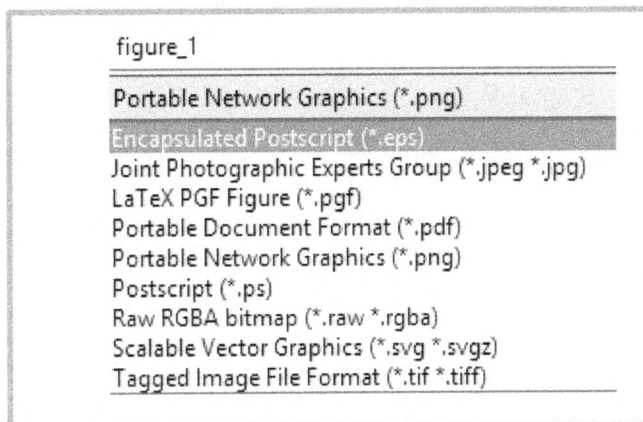

Exhibit A5 on saving a chart

Once you choose the extension, you can click 'save'. In order to open, please go to the location and double click; you will get the saved output.

14.7

Accessing previously executed codes

Once you finished executing the code, and if you want to go back to the previous code, simply press up arrow on your keyboard. Once you press 'up arrow, you will get the previously typed code. If you keep on pressing, you can access all previously typed codes, and you can edit the same. However, if you scroll up and find the code on the window, you cannot edit it, you can only see it. The following will illustrate the same:

```
In [9]: import pandas as pd

In [10]:
```

This is the code we have executed. Now we have pandas imported as 'pd'. But we want to make some changes to the code and import it as 'gr'. We could either retype the whole thing, which we do not want to do because it takes lot of time to do so. Instead, you press the up arrow. The following screen shows, you can see the edited code, which is a result of pressing the up arrow of the keyboard.

```
In [9]: import pandas as pd

In [10]: import pandas as pd
```

When we pressed the up arrow, we could access the previous code in an editable format as you could see the cursor next to pd, we can make the necessary changes now and execute the code.

```
In [9]: import pandas as pd

In [10]: import pandas as gr
```

Well, once you have executed any code, try pressing up arrow you could easily access the previous codes in an editable format. If you keep pressing the up arrow, you will get all the codes that were executed previously, and you could edit and re-execute again. Similarly press down arrow to move to the next code in a downward position.

Types of Errors

Its time to explain some of the most common errors that might occur while writing and executing codes, they are;

1. Syntax Error
2. Indentation Error
3. Name Error
4. IO Error
5. Import Error
6. Attribute Error
7. Logical Error
8. Type Error

Let us learn each, in detail.

1. **Syntax error:**
   As the name suggests, it is the error in the syntax of a particular code sequence. It could be a character, or symbol or a sign that must be part of any code sequence depending on the programming language.
   If such an error happens, the program will not execute successfully, as it is interrupted. An example is given below:

```
In [27]: a=3

In [28]: if a=3:  ──────→  [ Syntax Error ]
    ...:       print a
    ...:  else:
    ...:       print 'hellow'
    ....
  File "<ipython-input-28-dedb306ff0f3>", line 1
    if a=3:
         ^
SyntaxError: invalid syntax
```

Here we have an error in the syntax. It should have been 'if a= =3', instead of a=3. We have to use two equal signs.

1. Indentation error

You can read in detail about Indentation in Chapter 2, section 2.5. Such errors could occur while you deal with Loops statements such as 'While' and conditional statements 'IF'. A slight change in the indentation could give you such an error. The following illustrates the same:

```
In [25]: if a==3:
    ...:        print a
    ...:    else:
    ...:          print '2'
    ...:
File "<ipython-input-25-c075bb0a92a6>", line 3
    else:
        ^
```

`IndentationError: unindent does not match any outer indentation level`

Here the problem is with 'else'. It is not properly indented. A slight change in the indentation will give you an error. 'Else:' should have been typed exactly in line with 'if'.

2. Name Error:

Name error occurs if you enter any variable/temporary containers, or any text that is not inbuilt within Python or any other programming language. Temporary containers are defined by the user, whereas we do have functions, which are inbuilt. For e.g. we have mean (), which is a function in Python. So any text we enter, which is not known to Python will create an error and it is called 'Name Error'.

```
In [29]: k
```

Here we haven't defined 'k' (such as k= 8 or k ='Yellow') and therefore, we get the following error message:

`NameError: name 'k' is not defined`

Since K is not defined, Python do not understand what that is all about. Not only in Python, in any programming language, it will be treated as an error.

2. **IO Error:**

   While loading Excel data in Python (not only for Excel, but for any external data in Python), you must give correct file name and location such as 'C', 'F' or any other drive name you choose; otherwise, you will get an error. IO error occurs, when the program is not able to read the specified file on a specified location. This is because either the file name is not correct, or the location is wrong. The following will explain this:

   ```
   In [30]: import pandas as pd
   In [32]: data = pd.read_csv('D:/stud_cl.csv')
   ──→ IOError: File D:/stud_cl.csv does not exist
   ```

   Here we got an IO error, because, file name stud) c1.csv do not exist in location 'D' drive.

3. **Import Error**

   Yet another most common error that could occur in Python is Import error. An import error could occur while you try to import specific modules or libraries in Python. The main reason on why such an error could occur is that either it is not spelled correctly, or that module is not found or not being installed properly.

   For example:

   ```
   In [1]: import panda
   ImportError: No module named panda
   ```

   Here, there is no module named panda in Python, it is **pandas** (don't forget s); therefore, we got an import error.

   ```
   In [10]: import num
   ImportError: No module named num
   ```

   We have library named 'numpy', which is Numerical Python, and Python do not have any module named as num.
   Import error will give the error message as soon as it occurs; without importing necessary modules, we will not be able to do certain analysis and computations.

4. **Attribute Error**

An attribute error is found when we specify wrong attributes of the language. Such types of error will interrupt the program while executing it and will give an error message. Here, **read_csv** is an attribute, and we wrongly spelled as read_cs and therefore that error occurred. The following example will explain the same:

```
In [3]: pd.read_cs('D:/stud_clean.cscv')
```

This is true not only to 'read_csv', but to all other attributes, such as 'read_excel' and so on.

```
AttributeError: 'module' object has no attribute 'read_cs'
```

Another example on attribute error in Python

```
In [7]: j.to_excel('D:/jj.csv')
```

```
AttributeError: 'int' object has no attribute 'to_excel'
```

Here, Python has no attribute such as 'to_ excel'.

5. **Logical Error**

The logical error is a special case of error, because irrespective of the error, the program will run. However, we might not get the desired output. In other words, such errors never interrupts the program and give an error message as in the case of IO error, syntax error, or others. Here, the program executes smoothly as usual, but you will not get the desired output, and that is what might be confusing for you. you may not know, what went wrong or where is the mistake. Such types of mistakes are due to the Logic used. The following code will explain it further:

```
In [4]: j=0

In [6]: while j>4:
   ...:     print j
   ...:     j=j+1
   ...: print 'end'
   ...:
end
```

Here you can see that the program executed successfully, but did not come out with the desired output. We assign '0' to' j', so it should print '0' first. Then it will take '0+1' as 'j=j+1' and again print 'j'. That did not happen right? Well, that's due to the logical error. Also we did not get any error messages either!!

Well, here is the explanation. The error is in the logic. Let us review the following code:

```
In [6]: while j>4:
```

This is the logic here, as it is also the opening statement of this loop. We gave j as '0'. And in the code we gave 'j>4'. This means, while 'j' is greater than '4', print j, and 'j=j+1'. But in our case, j is zero and not greater than 4 and that is the Logic error. The correct code to get desired result is as follows

```
In [8]: j=0

In [9]: while j<=4:
   ...:     print j
   ...:     j=j+1
   ...: print 'end'
   ...:
0
1
2
3
4
end
```

This is the correct logic, where j should be less than or equal to 4, print j, and j=j+1 and program repeats, until j is 4.

6. **Type Error**

   Such type of errors tends to occur only with codes that require more than one argument. The following will explain the same:

   ```
   In [12]: d= pd.read_excel('D:/stud_cealn1.xlsx')
   ```

   Here, we are trying to import an Excel file in Python using above mentioned code.

```
TypeError: read_excel() takes at least 2 arguments (1 given)
```

Here, a Type error has occurred because this particular code takes two arguments such as 'filename' and 'sheet name', whereas, here we have given only filename and therefore, we got the error message.

The following will help you to understand this:

```
In [15]: d= pd.read_excel('D:/stud_clean1.xlsx', 'stud_clean')
```

```
In [16]: d.head(2)
Out[16]:
```

	Stud_id	Gender	Dept	Attendance	Sem_marks	Name
0	M197	Female	Science	63	475	Ritu
1	M181	Male	Commerce	86	303	Victor

Here we have entered both the arguments, such as File name and Sheet name and got the output.

About the Authors

Manoj Morais, is the Managing Director and CEO at Aspire Analytic Solutions New York, US. He is also a Marketing Research Professional and Data Scientist with deep knowledge in data analysis, programming and machine learning and proficient in adapting new generation tools in research. He has Masters in Economics and Business Management and has Post graduation in Marketing Research & Analytics from Centennial College, Canada. In addition to that he has done a certificate course on Statistical Thinking for Data Science and Analytics from Columbia University, Columbiax. He is proficient in Computer programming especially open source programming and has developed programs part of his educational projects and has proved proficiency in SAS, Python, Excel, SQL, SPSS, Foxpro and VB.His machine learning skills and interest has taken him to a next level. Currently, he is researching on Text mining, analytics. His research also includes Text classifiers, such as naïve Bayes classifier and Decision tree classifier, and much more.

He was working as a Department Manager at an MNC in Canada. Prior to that he worked for LMG Global Canada and also worked as a Business consultant back in India. He was also involved in variety of marketing and social science research projects.

Apart from data science, he has advanced knowlege in western music and have composed many albums and still working on a few musical projects.

Sreekumar Radhakrishna Pillai, PhD is a Researcher and Registered Psychotherapist in Toronto, Canada. He has over ten years' experience in academic and community based research, and has worked in three countries. He received doctorate degree in Psychology; completed Bridge Training Programme for Internationally Trained Psychologists and Allied Mental Health Professionals in Canada; Masters in Applied Psychology; and two bachelor degrees with majors in Psychology and Education. In addition, he has Graduate Certificate in Marketing Research and Analytics.

He taught Research Methodology and Project Management at Master's program in Educational Leadership and Management at Haramaya University, Ethiopia during his tenure as an Assistant Professor; he was also a Major Advisor for graduate level dissertation, and a Member of Examining Board of The Thesis defence .He taught Research Methodology at Master of Philosophy (M.Phil) Program at Dept. of Psychology, Sree Sankaracharya University, India. Moreover, he has worked with a few community based research Projects as Research Analyst, Research Officer and Investigator. He has advanced knowledge in Research Methodology (both quantitative and qualitative), Statistics, Psychometrics and Marketing Research Analytics; and proficient in using various Software and Packages, including Python, for Data Processing and Analysis. He is a member of College of Registered Psychotherapist of Ontario; and Ontario College of Teachers. He has published studies in academic journals.